THEORIES AND METHODS
FOR PRACTICE OF
CLINICAL PSYCHOLOGY

THEORIES AND METHODS
FOR PRACTICE OF
CLINICAL PSYCHOLOGY

MALCOLM HIGGINS ROBERTSON
AND
ROBERT HENLEY WOODY

INTERNATIONAL UNIVERSITIES PRESS, INC.
Madison   Connecticut

Library of Congress Cataloging-in-Publication Data

Robertson, Malcolm.
    Theories and methods for practice of clinical psychology /
Malcolm Higgins Robertson and Robert Henley Woody.
        p.   cm.
    Includes bibliographical references and indexes.
    ISBN 0-8236-6518-6
    1. Clinical psychology.   I. Woody, Robert Henley.   II. Title.
RC467.R55   1996
616.89—DC20   96-25085
                                                                CIP

Manufactured in the United States of America

Dedication

We recognize that our careers and this book have been facilitated by the support and love of our families. We dedicate this book to our spouses, Joan M. Robertson and Jane Divita Woody, and to our children, Tim, Suzanne, Greg, Chris, and Michelle Robertson, and Jennifer, Robert, and Matthew Woody.

Contents

Introduction

The fiscal, social, and political conservatism that followed in the wake of the 1994 U.S. Congressional elections has compelled the science and profession of psychology to re-examine the traditional alignment with, and support for, Democratic party principles and priorities. As a consequence, public relations programs have been mounted to educate the new Congress about psychology's contribution to the betterment of society through health care practice, scientific progress, education reform, and public-interest commitments. The goals and priorities of each of the four areas are being challenged and their implementation slowed; regrettably, those of the public-interest area (e.g., early childhood intervention, crime reduction and rehabilitation of youthful offenders, prevention of violence in the home and workplace, and aid to the poor and the homeless) are clearly the most vulnerable to a major setback.

Against this backdrop of conservative developments, clinical psychology, like all the health care disciplines, is faced with the prospect of unprecedented changes. Buffeted from one side by the behavioral scientists insisting on improved quality assurance, and from the other side by managed health care systems and government regulatory bodies mandating stricter utilization review and more efficient use of services, the profession is striving to respond constructively to external pressures, and at the same time to maintain a strong fiduciary relation with both the consumer and society at large.

There are, of course, pundits who would argue that having to respond to multiple pressures from within and outside the profession is both a mark and price of success. A more positive mark of success, we believe, is that since the authors' (1988) publication, *Becoming a Clinical Psychologist*, the profession has further penetrated the health care marketplace in applying its knowledge base and skill bank to the antecedent life-style factors associated with a variety of health conditions, as well as helping to prevent or ameliorate the cognitive and emotional sequelae of many medical illnesses and disorders. Furthermore, another health psychology subspecialty, occupational health, has been added to the existing subspecialties of behavioral medicine, pediatric psychology, clinical geropsychology, and psychopharmacology.

Moreover, since our 1988 publication professional psychology's most widely known and highly regarded diploma board, the American Board of Professional Psychology (ABPP), has added four more specialty fields to its thorough and stringent determination of superior competence. The new specialties are health psychology, behavioral psychology, family psychology, and group psychology, to go with the already existing diplomate status in clinical psychology, counseling psychology, school psychology, clinical neuropsychology, forensic psychology, and industrial–organizational psychology.

Other tangible evidence of progress achieved in this decade are the steady gains in obtaining hospital privileges and in securing a foothold in education and training for limited prescription privileges. Relatedly, the profession has strengthened its presence in the judicial system, which is also reflected in the additional graduate programs that offer a joint Ph.D./J.D. degree. In the judicial context, mention must also be made of the fact that with the strong tradition of scientific study of memory, psychology has become a natural arbiter in the swirling controversy over the issues of recovered memories and child testimony.

Finally, not to be overlooked are the efforts spearheaded by both the science and practice of psychology to address the wide spectrum of addictive behaviors, the growing epidemic of violence, and the many manifestations of victimization in our society. With candid acknowledgment of the problems, barriers, and pitfalls facing the profession, we seek to articulate an optimistic perspective: Here clinical psychology emerges with a bright potential because the nature of clinical psychology training makes acceptance of changing social priorities and the fashioning of new roles and services readily attainable. We believe that clinical psychology does, in fact, have a highly positive potential, which will benefit society and clients, and provide the clinical psychologist with personal and professional enrichment.

Having said that, a brief overview of *Theories and Methods for Practice of Clinical Psychology* is in order. The first chapter is guided by the assumption that to understand, predict, and ameliorate abnormal behavior, a clinical psychologist is expected to have firm knowledge of what constitutes both normal and abnormal behavior. To wit, an accurate assessment and diagnosis of psychopathology and formulation of treatment goals presupposes an informed understanding of the range of normal psychological functioning, not only within our society's majority culture, but within the various minority cultures as well. The next two chapters examine first, the critical issues of assessment as applied to normal and abnormal conditions; and second, diagnostic principles and the process of arriving at a psychodiagnosis. Following are two chapters on psychotherapy; the first covers current models of psychotherapy and various psychotherapeutic strategies; the second addresses current literature on outcome effectiveness, alternative modalities of group and marital–family therapies, various forms of time-limited psychotherapy, and then outlines emerging trends, challenges, and new directions. The concluding chapter delineates five trends that are expected to have long-lasting impact on the application of clinical psychology's theories and methods.

The book, and the companion volume, *A Career in Clinical Psychology: From Training to Employment* (1996), are intended for advanced undergraduate students tentatively considering clinical psychology as a graduate major, and graduate students in the professional psychology fields of clinical, counseling, and school psychology who are seeking a basic familiarity with clinical services and practice settings. The reader will note that the terms *clinical psychologist* and *professional psychologist* are used interchangeably with the acknowledgment that counseling and school psychology are subsumed under the term *professional psychology*. The term *professional psychology* affirms the American Psychological Association's (APA) principle that besides specialty training, a trainee must acquire a generic core of basic and applied knowledge of psychology. The volume should also be useful as a reference and/or professional development source for new and established practitioners who desire to update their knowledge and career planning. In short, both volumes offer a reality-based perspective of what is required to enter and succeed in the field of clinical psychology.

Chapter 1

Normality and Abnormality: Critical Issues in Assessment and Treatment

To understand, predict, and ameliorate abnormal behavior, a clinical psychologist is expected to have a firm knowledge of what constitutes normal behavior, especially the organismic and environmental variables that mediate the development and stability of normal behavior. Ironically, many clinical psychologists understand a great deal more about the absence than the presence of mental health, and are strongly inclined to define normality as a symptom-free condition. Nevertheless, in theory if not in practice, clinical psychologists assume that accurate diagnosis of psychopathology and formulation of treatment goals presuppose an informed understanding of the range of normal psychological functioning, not only within the majority culture, but within various minority cultures in the United States.

NORMALITY

The terms *normality*, *mental* or *psychological health*, *psychological maturity*, *adjustment*, *psychological competence* are often used interchangeably, and all lack a solid operational definition. Basically, there is considerable variation among the terms in what they denote and connote.

White (1969) points out that the meaning of a term such as *mental adjustment* derives from the study of abnormal behavior and stresses the absence of what is negative; whereas a term such as *psychological maturity* is preferable because it is usually based on studies of persons who have been found to cope successfully with life. However, one limitation of the term *psychological maturity* is that it has an adult reference point and is ordinarily a measure of developmental outcome instead of developmental process.

Psychological competence is a more clinically useful term because it emphasizes the development of coping skills throughout the life span; however, it lacks the interdisciplinary usage of the other terms. A more recent term, *hygiology*, includes both the promotion of psychologically healthy behaviors and the prevention of psychopathological behavior, and thereby gives an added dimension to the traditional treatment goal of eliminating psychopathology. The section uses all of the above-mentioned terms.

Hansen and Himes (1980) delineate four conceptual models of normality which are based partly on the earlier work of Offer and Sabskin (1974). The first is a biological model which postulates that normal behavior presupposes normal biological or genetic functioning. Simplistically stated, normal people have mostly normal genes, and abnormal behavior is the expression of abnormal genes. A more complex genetic explanation cited by the authors is one that allows for an array of genotypes, which in turn give rise to many kinds of normal behavior that may shade into abnormal functioning as a result of genetic and environmental conditions.

A second model is a sociocultural one, which includes cultural relativism (i.e., the meaning of the terms *normal* and *abnormal* is embedded in the mores and values of a particular culture) and functionalism. Behavior is evaluated in terms of the function or purpose served in relation to the total personality and societal expectations. In the sociocultural model, the primary criterion of normality is the degree of compatibility between an individual's behavior and the values and expectations of the family and of the larger community.

A third model defines normality as an ideal or goal to be approximated. Hansen and Himes describe two variations. The first is a statistical idea, which assumes that the most common or frequently occurring behavior in a particular population is normal, and the uncommon or infrequent behavior deviates from normality. For example, in the normal (bell-shaped) distribution of personality test scores, the statistical ideal is the midpoint of the distribution curve, and extreme deviations in either direction denote abnormal functioning; although with a quantitative continuum, there is no sharp demarcation between normal and abnormal. The other variation is a clinical ideal, in which the conception of normality is derived from a particular personality theory, and which for most theories is an optimal balance between an individual's needs and values, and environmental constraints (e.g., Freud's psychosexually mature person, Roger's fully functioning person, Maslow's self-actualizing person).

A clinical ideal that is both comprehensive and independent of a particular personality theory is one advanced by Jahoda (1958). Six criteria are identified: (1) a positive attitude toward self and a stable sense of identity; (2) evidence of continued psychological growth, cognitively, emotionally, and socially; (3) integration, which includes maintaining an equilibrium of psychological forces, resistance to stress, and a unifying outlook on life; (4) autonomy and reasonable independence from social influences; (5) adequate perception of reality, which includes empathy and interpersonal sensitivity; and (6) environmental mastery, as evidenced in problem-solving efficiency and interpersonal effectiveness. A more recent formulation by Seeman (1989) is a systems based model in which positive

health is the integration and congruence of the major behavioral subsystems (e.g., biochemical, physiological, perceptual, cognitive, and interpersonal).

The fourth model posits a developmental basis for normality. Successful mastery of the developmental tasks of
each life stage defines normality. Especially important is
an individual's flexibility in adapting to the stress and
strain of moving from one developmental stage to the next.
From a developmental perspective the term *competency*
is gaining wider usage insofar as normality is defined in
terms of the developmental competencies needed to cope
constructively with the biopsychosocial stresses of successive life stages.

Hansen and Himes identify the following commonalities in the four models. (1) Physical health and organic
factors contribute to psychological well-being. (2) The psychologically healthy person is able to establish effective
and satisfying relationships with others, and has appropriate and satisfying thoughts and feelings about self.
(3) Being productive is an important criterion of psychological well-being, and is age-based in terms of mastery
of increasingly complex developmental tasks. (4) Psychological well-being requires a modicum of accommodation
to familial, social, and cultural expectations. (5) Psychological health is a dynamic rather than a static concept,
that is, an ongoing process that shows "normal" variations
over time and in response to situational events. To round
out the above, the following points might be added: that
problems of living are to be expected; that each individual
has a unique style of coping; and that psychological health
is more than the absence of symptoms. Commenting on
this last idea, Kazdin (1993a) underscores both the negative and positive formulations of psychological health; the
negative being the absence of symptoms that lead to
impairment or dysfunction in critical life areas, and the
positive referring to the strengths and competencies that
promote optimal functioning in critical areas of living; and

each partially defines the diagnostic categories in the current classification of mental disorders in the *Diagnostic and Statistical Manual of Mental Disorders* (DSM-IV; American Psychiatric Association, 1994).

In addition to theoretical formulations of normality, the concept has been studied empirically in terms of correlations with specific variables. Following is a summary of findings obtained for eight variables.

EDUCATION

Educational achievement is positively related to personal adjustment, particularly self-esteem, and educational problems may either contribute to or result from poor psychological adjustment. A causal link between poor school achievement and juvenile delinquency has been noted repeatedly (Tremblay, Masse, Perron, Leblanc, Schwartzman, and Ledingham, 1992, p. 64), and the developmental pathway between limited education on the one hand, and marginal employment, poverty, and impaired psychological health on the other hand has been referred to repeatedly. In addition to being a significant component in educational achievement, intelligence also contributes to psychological health inasmuch as it reflects an individual's cognitive capacity for adaptation (Hansen and Himes, 1980).

VOCATION

Satisfactory progress in vocational development is also associated with psychological well-being. Over the years, a number of investigators have delineated the relations between employment and one's physical and psychological health. Super (1957) delineates developmental stages in vocational adjustment and explains how the mastery of vocational tasks in each developmental stage impacts on other areas of adjustment. Again, there is the familiar developmental pathway that leads from school problems to vocational problems, to chronic unemployment, to demoralization, and ultimately to psychological health problems. Certainly job loss, especially if prolonged, poses a serious threat to a person's mental health status. As Osipow and Fitzgerald (1993) emphasize, being employed may be related to one's mental health status in a manner that may be quite different from the way that unemployment is related to mental health.

ETHNIC–RACIAL STATUS

By itself, ethnic or racial status does not account for mental health or mental illness (Hansen and Himes, 1980); however, in conjunction with discrimination, poverty, and value conflicts between majority and minority cultures, racial–ethnic status can pose a threat to psychological health. Thus, it behooves a mental health professional to become informed about the range of adaptive functioning in African American, Hispanic, Asian American, Native American, and other minority groups, and to avoid imposing the dominant culture's norms for psychological health and criteria for mental disorder. This takes on added significance in the light of demographic projections that minorities will constitute one-third of the U.S. population by the year 2000 (Hammond and Yung, 1993; Highlen, 1994), and by the year 2056, non-Hispanic whites will number less than half of the population (Highlen, 1994).

SOCIOECONOMIC STATUS

Earlier research that showed an inverse relationship between mental illness and socioeconomic status has come under critical scrutiny (Hansen and Himes, 1980). Although social and economic advantages are likely to enhance psychological well-being, there is no clear-cut relationship between socioeconomic status and normality, except where very low socioeconomic status is associated with oppression and family disorganization. The advantage of improved socioeconomic status is the greater accessibility to professional resources that assist in reducing psychological impairment and strengthening adaptive coping patterns.

GENDER

Both biology and socialization (first in the parent–child relationship and later in same-sex social groups) shape an individual's psychosexual orientation, and deviations from the norm create formidable obstacles to attaining a stable and satisfactory gender identity. In addition, gender role dynamics have been implicated in susceptibility to various types of disorders (Sobel and Russo, 1981); for example, obesity in women, antisocial behavior in men. Furthermore, Gilbert (1981) has underscored dangers inherent in a socialization process that fosters sex role stereotypes, which in turn limit the kinds of roles, behaviors, and personality characteristics that society endorses for each sex (e.g., women are expected to be nurturers and caretakers, men are expected to be providers and to be poorly suited to the role of a custodial parent). However, over time gender role differences have become less rigid and more flexibly defined, as a result of corrections and modifications having been made in the traditional gender role models constructed in the past by white male professionals.

Furthermore, a number of studies have addressed the concept of androgyny, whereby a person blends traits and behavior of both sexes and displays what is appropriate for each situation instead of conforming to stereotypic expectations. In a review of studies on androgyny, Gilbert (1981) concludes that androgyny is an important component of healthy psychological functioning for both men and women, and that "sex typing is not the most adjusted state—particularly for feminine women" (p. 35).

Another aspect of gender is sexual orientation and sexual life-style choice. Estimates (e.g., Fassinger, 1991) of the percentage of the population who are gay or lesbian vary between 10 and 15 percent. As another oppressed minority, lesbians and gay men have struggled to remove the stigma of mental illness from their sexual orientation. In 1973, the American Psychiatric Association agreed to remove homosexuality from the official classification of mental disorders (Morgan and Nerison, 1993), and the American Psychological Association followed suit almost immediately by passing a resolution that homosexuality is not ipso facto synonymous with psychological impairment or dysfunction, and that psychologists should work to remove the stigma of mental illness from homosexual orientation.

AGE

The relationship between age and normality clearly reflects the notion of normality as an ongoing process of change. Within each age period, an individual must adjust to physical and psychological changes, as well as to environmental changes in the form of a new set of age norms. The outcome of each developmental transition depends on the fit between current challenges and the individual's resources for coping with challenges (Peterson and Hamburg, 1986).

Erikson (1963) and Havighurst (1972) have outlined developmental stages throughout the life span. Give or take a couple of stages, the major ones are infancy/early childhood (0–6 years); middle childhood (6–12); adolescence (13–19); early adulthood (20–35); middle adulthood (35–60); and later adulthood. Within each stage, mastery of developmental tasks fosters psychological growth and provides a sound basis for coping with the tasks of subsequent stages. Generally, developmental tasks are defined in terms of physical skills, cognitive skills, emotional regulation, social skills, attitudes toward self and reality, and formation of stable values (Hansen and Himes, 1980). For adult development, Levinson (1977) has described four major periods from young adulthood to old age, each with a developmental period consisting of a stable stage and a transitional stage; the task common to all periods is to decide how to attain life goals and how to be true to cherished values.

Because of the continued lengthening of the average life span in the population, the "later adulthood" or advanced age stage has lengthened and necessitates substages differentiated on the basis of differences in physical and psychological health status. And currently, "the most rapidly growing segment of the American population is the oldest old; those over 85 years of age" (Morgan, 1992, p. 1). Interestingly, while the biopsychosocial risk factors of advanced age stages differ somewhat from younger age stages, the psychological coping mechanisms are quite similar to those of earlier age periods. Morgan (1992) takes to task a common myth that the oldest old have only half as many neurons in their brain as they did when they were young. Since the brain is estimated to have a trillion neurons, even if an individual were to lose 100,000 neurons a day (a frequently quoted estimate) for each day of the 36,000 days in a 100-year life span, "that would still be only 0.5% of the total we started with, hardly a significant loss" (p. 5). Nevertheless, an advancing life span does increase the risk to physical and psychological health. The incidence of depression rises steadily over a lifetime and is a common disorder among the elderly, along with various forms of dementia; in fact, by the middle of the next century the cost of caring for the elderly with brain disorders is expected to be the largest single item in the federal health budget, larger than the cost of all other disorders (Morgan, 1992).

The other transitional age period that has lengthened is adolescence. With the average age of marriage increasing and a greater delay in permanently leaving home, the period of dependence on one's family has lengthened, though other variables such as socioeconomic status, rural versus urban living, subcultural traditions about familial connectedness, also affect the transition to independent adult status (Kazdin, 1993a). Because of experimentation that seems to be the signature characteristic of adolescents, this age period ushers in many risk factors, as well as risk-taking behaviors. Some 15 to 30 percent of adolescents do not complete high school and the highest arrest rate occurs among this age group (Eccles, Midgley, Wigfield, Buchanan, Reuman, Flanagan, and MacIver, 1993). The prevalence rates for substance abuse, mental disorder, suicide, homicide, unintended and/or unwanted pregnancies, and sexually transmitted diseases remain alarmingly high (Takanishi, 1993). Yet it is also the period of promise, opportunity, and some would say high purpose, and moving forward, staying stuck, or regressing is determined by the ratio of promise and opportunity to risk factors and vulnerabilities.

Within the developmental framework, crises are not necessarily inevitable; if present, they are most likely to be the result of discrepancies between an individual's lifestyle and a socially expected role (LaVoie, 1980). Moreover, crises are not necessarily growth-inhibiting; the optimal amount of stress for growth and development varies among individuals; and the process of coping with problems and conflicts may enhance psychological health. Even in adolescence, where there is change in every dimension of growth and in every important social context, the large majority of adolescents increase their psychological competence (Peterson and Hamburg, 1986).

SOCIAL ROLES

Two social roles that have commanded considerable research attention are marriage and parenthood, although the relationship to normality is complicated by other variables such as age, education, gender, socioeconomic status, and physical health. The fact that over 90 percent of the population marry at some time during the life span and approximately 80 percent of divorced people remarry (Barker, 1984, chapter 2) may represent conformity to strong social pressures. On the other hand, the statistics may also indicate that the institution of marriage contributes to psychological well-being by providing a practical way to satisfy basic psychosexual needs. Noteworthy is the finding that separated and divorced people are at high risk for emotional illness, and the rate of hospitalization for mental illness among the divorced is 8 to 12 times the national average (Garfield, 1982). In a review of studies on marital adjustment, L'Abate and Goodrich (1980) report that as a group married couples have a lower incidence of mental disorder than the unmarried, and that women are more susceptible than men to both marital stress and marital satisfaction. Moreover, among those who never marry or do not remarry, women appear to be better adjusted than men, especially in the older age population (LaVoie, 1980).

On the other hand, the trend over the past few decades of later onset of marriage and an earlier onset of sexual activity poses challenges to both psychological and physical health. Poppen and Reisen (1994) cite demographic changes, such as a sixfold increase in the past 20 years of households consisting of unmarried men and women, many of whom are in a cohabiting relationship, and a 75 to 55 percent decline of households of married couples with a corresponding increase in single gender households. The authors draw the obvious conclusion that with fewer restrictions on sexual activity and a greater range of partners, there is increased likelihood of physical and psychological sequelae of sexually transmitted diseases.

Like marriage, the relation between parenthood and abnormality is also strongly influenced by many other variables. The trend today is to examine parenthood within a developmental framework. Parental effectiveness or competence is a function of the skills, knowledge, attitudes, stress, and environmental resources associated with each developmental stage, as well as the successes and failures of the preceding stages (Kaplan, 1980). Much of the literature on the association between psychological health and parenthood addresses the impact of parents' behavior on a child's psychological health. There is no mistaking the critical determinants of children's mental and emotional health. Whether a single or two-parent home (and if the latter, marital compatibility is an additional determinant), first is the absence of parental psychopathology, particularly the chronic, severe forms; second is the expression of parenting behaviors such as firm, consistent, age-appropriate discipline, dependable involvement in and support of children's school and social activities, and a parent's emotional availability. As most parents would attest, their personal resources are sorely tested during the early and middle adolescent years. As expected, optimal parenting practices during this period fall between a laissez-faire, default, or relinquishment of control on the one hand, and harsh discipline and unbending control on the other (Eccles et al., 1993). Finally, an area that continues to be neglected is the effect of a child's behavior on the mental health of a parent, and how a child's behavior can differentially affect the psychological stability of a parent.

PERSONALITY TRAITS

Although there is a consensus that at least several personality traits predict psychological adjustment, the importance of a particular trait varies with the developmental period. Rather than catalogue all the traits which have some association with normality, four are singled out for comment.

The first is temperament, a general trait that subsumes a number of more specific traits, among which are emotionality, activity level, impulsivity, sociability, distractibility, persistence, adaptability to change, and sensory alertness. Strong evidence exists for the inheritability of traits of temperament (Buss and Plomin, 1975). Rowe (1980) concludes that as a global trait, temperament appears early in a child's development, has some genetic basis, and remains stable at least through young adulthood. Thomas and Chess (1977) also conclude that temperament traits are moderately inheritable, emerge early in life, and are subject to gradual change of the environment. High or low degrees of temperament traits (e.g., sociability, fear, activity level, aggressiveness) can facilitate or interfere with family and social relationships, magnify or attenuate environmental stressors, and reduce or exacerbate interpersonal conflicts (Rowe, 1980). Especially important in a child's psychological development is how the environment, particularly the family milieu, responds to his or her temperament.

A second trait is tolerance of ambiguity and uncertainty, or the degree to which an individual copes effectively with unstructured or open-ended situations, and can accept experiences that are at variance with preconceptions or conventional reality (Foxman, 1980). The trait appears to be stable through most of the life span; interindividual differences appear to be independent of gender, intelligence, education, and vocational background; and through the correlation with other adaptive traits, such as emotional resiliency, it appears to be a stable component of psychological health.

A third trait is personal responsibility, or the degree to which an individual accepts and is responsible for his or her behaviors, and is willing to initiate self-change. The trait shows a developmental progression up to adulthood; cuts across gender, socioeconomic, ethnic–racial, and educational–vocational variables; and is a necessary, albeit insufficient, component for coping successfully with problems of living (Genthner, 1980). A longitudinal study of male children found that in comparison to children rated low on understanding, children rated high on interpersonal understanding: (1) focused more on how a conflict is perceived by all parties involved instead of how it is settled; (2) share responsibility for conflicts and problems instead of externalizing responsibility; and (3) were more willing to work through conflicts rather than to withdraw from or reject others (Gurucharri, Phelps, and Selman, 1984).

A fourth trait is attachment, or the degree to which an individual develops and maintains close relationships. The trait has its foundation in the frequency, intensity, duration, and quality of early parent–child bonding. With age progression comes breadth and diversity of attachments, from parents to peers and older persons (e.g., relatives, mentors), and perhaps later to a mate and children. If there is a strong consensus in the field, it clearly has to do with the far-reaching implications of peer attachments from middle childhood through middle adolescence. Cichetti, Toth, and Bush (1988, cited in Ollendick, Weist, Borden, and Greene, 1992) assert that "success with peers may be a prophylactic for ensuring competence in the face of adversity, despite seemingly deleterious biologic and environmental circumstances" (p. 28). Asher and Wheeler (1985) report that in comparison to socially neglected children (i.e., without friends but not disliked), rejected children (i.e., without friends and actively disliked) are more likely to continue in their rejected status and to be highly susceptible to adult maladjustment. More recently, in a five-year longitudinal study of three hundred fourth grade children sociometrically classified as average, controversial, neglected, popular, or rejected, Ollendick et al. (1992) reported that compared to both average and popular children, the rejected children were not only perceived by peers and teachers as being less likable and more aggressive, but also were more likely to have school conduct and sub-stance abuse disorders as well as community delinquent offenses, and were more likely to have failed grades and dropped out of school. Children classified as controversial tended toward or approached the risk status of the rejected ones. On the other hand, those classified as neglected dif-fered little from the popular and average children. As Hartup (1989) points out, rejected children are left to seek out other rejected children as friends, and "the road to deviance, then, does not begin with associates who are deviant; rather it is the final stage on a road that begins with social failure and being disliked" (p. 125).

Most of us can say with conviction that our best mo-ments in life are the ones we share with someone special to us. Close attachments satisfy many of our basic psy-chological needs, not the least of which is self-esteem, and when in distress close friends provide us with emotional support. The loss of attachments and the making of new ones are inevitable and reflect sound personal and social adjustment (LaVoie, 1980). Among the elderly, the pres-ence of a confidant is the prime characteristic that sepa-rates those living in institutions from those living in the community (Kalish and Knudtson, 1976); and for a child or adolescent, close attachment with at least one psycho-logically competent family member or other adult can sig-nificantly lessen vulnerability to serious mental disorder.

SOME IMPORTANT IMPLICATIONS

As noted earlier, a clinical psychologist must have a flex-ible and broad conception of normality, not only as a frame of reference for understanding what abnormality is and is not, but also as a basis for appreciating the many vari-ables that contribute to the development, maintenance, loss, and recovery of normal psychological functioning. One suggestion is that clinicians would benefit from study-ing the lives of psychologically competent persons, so that they might develop as much sensitivity and discernment toward a person's strengths and personal resources as they now have for a person's defects and limitations. By spending some career time working with well-functioning persons, they would gain valuable experience in the practice of hygiology; that is, enhancing health aspects of normal individuals as well as preventing the loss of psychological health.

Especially important is a clinician's awareness of how values and beliefs about normality influence assessment and treatment of clients. For example, clinicians must be careful not to deny their own personal responsibility by assigning all responsibility for recovery to their clients, or by making client evaluations that fail to take into account the loss of personal responsibility due to psychological disorder (Genthner, 1980). A clinician who is knowledgeable about temperament traits and their effect on a child's adjustment may alleviate behavior problems by helping parents to adjust child-rearing practices to a particular child's temperament.

Finally, with female clients a male clinician must be careful not to let gender stereotypes interfere with promoting self-independence and self-actualization, which are part of most definitions of normality (Gilbert, 1981). For a female client who is also a minority person, a clinician must appreciate how both gender and race discrimination and oppression can contribute to psychological disorders, and that psychotherapy must be supplemented by educational, vocational, and social services (Olmedo and Barron, 1981). A clinician must overcome the *uniformity myth* (the norms of the dominant culture become the gold standard of normality) that is grounded in a European-American normative perspective, so that verbal and nonverbal behavior of minority or marginalized clients can be accurately contextualized and not mistaken for symptoms of abnormality or social deviancy. In short, ethnicity, race, age, gender, and socioeconomic status are essential to the understanding of the diversity of behavior and to the appreciation of the range of normality.

ABNORMALITY

Like normality, many definitions of abnormality have been proposed, but not a single meaning has gained universal acceptance. Terms such as *mental illness, maladjustment, immaturity, deviance, psychopathology, pathological disorder/dysfunction* are used interchangeably, and all have shortcomings. *Mental illness*, a term based on a medical model of abnormality, implies an involuntary and organically based intrapsychic condition. *Immaturity* denotes a developmental lag, with a pejorative connotation. *Deviance* is often associated with legal and/or moral judgments. *Maladjustment* is a narrow-band term that refers to problems of minor or moderate severity, and sometimes is a euphemism for more serious disturbances. *Psychopathology* is a term that: (1) encompasses a wider range of abnormal behavior than adjustment; (2) is relatively value-free compared to *deviance* and *immaturity*; and (3) more clearly denotes psychological etiology than does the term *mental illness*; however, it is too strong a label for common adjustment difficulties or ordinary problems of living. *Psychological disorder* is perhaps the most desirable term, at least for nonmedical clinicians, because it is not beholden to an illness model, and it designates the types of clients for whom a clinical psychologist's diagnostic and therapeutic skills are best suited. In this section the terms *abnormal behavior, mental illness/disorder, psychopathology,* and *psychological disorder/dysfunction* are used interchangeably.

Unlike the statistical definition of abnormality which is based on behavior that occurs most frequently in society, abnormal behavior refers to infrequently occurring behavior. Despite oft-cited limitations of a statistical definition of normality and abnormality, such as a bias favoring the majority subculture in society and a lack of criteria to distinguish between adaptive and maladaptive statistical deviations from the norm (Sue, Sue, and Sue, 1994, p. 6), psychodiagnostic evaluations and diagnostic classifications are based to some extent on deviations from a statistical norm.

Nevertheless, the saliency of abnormal behavior is due not only to the lower frequency of occurrence, but more importantly to the presence of one or more of the following psychosocial properties: suffering-distress; irrationality or incomprehensibility; unpredictability and loss of control; vividness and unconventionality; observer discomfort; violations of moral and legal standards of conduct; and interference with the goals and needs of the individual and/or society (Rosenhan and Seligman, 1984). Millon (1981) identifies three distinguishing features of abnormal behavior: (1) maladaptive inflexibility, or a few coping strategies which are applied rigidly and inappropriately; (2) a vicious circle in which habitual coping methods create new problems or intensify already existing ones; and (3) tenuous emotional stability, or lack of resiliency under stress with accompanying loss of control over emotions.

In addition to the issue of which term or label for abnormality is more accurate and useful, assessment of abnormality is complicated by the fact that not all of the distinguishing properties are present at any one time, or overtly displayed for that matter. Moreover, there is no sharp demarcation between normal and abnormal behavior; an individual may function normally in some areas of life (e.g., vocational or educational), and not in other areas (e.g., marital or family); and personality traits that are adaptive or at least neutral in one developmental period may prove to be maladaptive in another developmental period. Finally, behavior that is considered normal in one community or section of the country may be labeled as abnormal in another part of the country. For instance, in the late fifties one of the authors (MHR) was teaching in a southern university at the time a young African-American man, high-school diploma in hand, entered the campus to register for courses. He was promptly and unceremoniously taken into custody and committed to a state hospital on the grounds that he must be mentally ill to have behaved in that manner. Within that community in that era, he did display some of the critical properties of abnormality identified by Rosenhan and Seligman (1984), such as producing observer discomfort, unconventionality, violation of the community's moral and legal standards, even though he was not experiencing acute distress, not evidencing irrationality and loss of control, nor interfering with his goals and needs and those of society at large.

To have a definition of abnormality that is sufficiently inclusive to satisfy a large and varied group of mental health professionals, the authors of the DSM-IV (American Psychiatric Association, 1994) have proposed the following definition, which is almost identical with the definition in previous editions, but with the proviso that the concept of mental disorder simply lacks an acceptable operational definition.

> [A] clinically significant behavioral or psychological syndrome or pattern that occurs in an individual and that is associated with present distress (e.g., impairment in one or more important areas of functioning) or with significantly increased risk of suffering, death, pain, disability, or an important loss of freedom. In addition, this syndrome or pattern must not be merely an expectable and culturally sanctioned response to a particular event, for example, the death of a loved one. Whatever its original cause, it must currently be considered a manifestation of a behavioral, psychological, or biological dysfunction in the individual. Neither deviant behavior (e.g., political, religious, or sexual) nor conflicts that are primarily between the individual and society are mental disorders unless the deviance or conflict is a symptom of a dysfunction in the individual, as described above [p. xxii].

Like it or not, this has become the official definition of
mental disorders because it bears the imprimatur of the
authors of the most widely used diagnostic classification
system.

PREVALENCE OF PSYCHOPATHOLOGY

Of all the health conditions, mental disorders are the most
likely to limit one's ability to work; and they are the third
most limiting health condition (preceded only by cancer
and stroke) with respect to carrying out major daily activities (Welch, 1994). According to a National Institute
of Mental Health survey (see APA, 1989), slightly more
than 15 percent of adults suffer from a mental disorder or
substance abuse disorder in any given month, with higher
rates among those under age 45, except for severe brain
impairment (e.g., Alzheimer's disease). The most common
conditions are anxiety disorders such as phobias, panic,
obsessive-compulsive, generalized anxiety, and bipolar
and affective mood disorders such as depression, manic-
depression, and dysthymia. Males were found to have
higher rates of substance abuse and antisocial personality disorders, while females were found to have higher
rates of affective, anxiety, and somatoform disorders (e.g.,
hypochondriasis). Not unexpectedly, substance abuse disorders were found to be more common at younger ages of
15 to 30, with the rate declining after age 30 for women
but remaining fairly stable for men.

With respect to children and adolescents, prevalence
rates for psychological disorders range from approximately
10 to 15 percent (Kazdin, 1989); other prevalence studies
identify some 14 million children suffering from a diag-
nosable mental disorder (Welch, 1994). Despite the prevailing conception of adolescence as a period of heightened
vulnerability, the incidence of psychopathology is only
slightly higher than it is in childhood and adult life (Peterson and Hamburg, 1986). The authors note that about

half of the disorders in adolescence are a continuation of childhood disorders. For example, delinquency and antisocial disorder continue from childhood, peak in adolescence, and begin to decline in early adulthood. Only about one-third of the antisocial disorders in childhood develop into antisocial disorders of adulthood, and as Peterson and Hamburg as well as other researchers and practitioners conclude, depression appears to be a key variable in the continuation of antisocial behavior into adolescence and adult life. For that matter, at any age the presence of more than one disorder (e.g., substance abuse coexisting with depression, eating disorder, or schizophrenia) is a strong likelihood. Other disorders that show an increase during adolescence are depression, attempted suicide, eating disorders, and schizophrenia (though the peak period is early adulthood). Gender differences vary across studies, but generally prevalence rates for mood and affective disorders are higher for adolescent females, and prevalence rates for acting out and antisocial disorders are higher for adolescent males. Notably lacking in prevalence studies, however, are the differential rates of psychological disorders among the minority subcultures of society, along with information about the range of adaptive functioning within the different minority groups.

CLASSIFICATION
OF PSYCHOPATHOLOGY

The current classification system for psychopathology is the DSM-IV (1994). This most recent edition was designed to be compatible with the preparation of the chapter on "Mental and Behavioral Disorders" of the tenth revision of the *International Statistical Classification of Diseases and Related Health Problems (ICD-10)*, developed by the World Health Organization (WHO, 1992).

To employ the DSM-IV, a clinician makes a diagnostic designation on each of five axes. Axis I encompasses clinical disorders (e.g., mood disorders, organic mental disorder, schizophrenia, eating disorders), as well as conditions that do not meet all the criteria for a mental disorder but may be the focus of clinical attention (e.g., relational problems, abuse or neglect problems). Axis II includes personality disorders and retardation (e.g., borderline, paranoid, avoidant personality disorders, mental retardation). Axis III identifies current medical conditions associated with axis I and II disorders. Axis IV refers to psychosocial and environmental stressors that are likely to influence assessment, therapy, and prognosis of axis I and II disorders. Axis V is a judgment about current psychological, social, and occupational functioning as rated on a 100-point scale of the Global Assessment of Functioning (GAF) Scale (American Psychiatric Association, 1994, pp. 30–31). The following illustrates how a clinician might formulate a multiaxial diagnostic evaluation (with diagnostic code numbers given for the axis I and II disorders).

Axis I: 296.22 Major Depressive Disorder, Single episode,
          Moderate Severity
          305.00 Alcohol Abuse
Axis II: 301.60 Dependent Personality Disorder
Axis III: HIV Positive
Axis IV: Loss of job and threat of loss of partner
Axis V: GAS = 65 (current)

On axis I, the first diagnosis is considered the principal one in terms of clinical management and treatment planning.

As Wenar (1994) and others assert, the major function of DSM is to provide brief, explicit, behavior-specific criteria for defining diagnostic categories. Additional goals are to stimulate research on the delineation and differentiation of psychological disorders, and to assist in the teaching of psychopathology and the training of clinicians. The current revision is more empirically grounded than the previous revisions; as a consequence, the diagnostic reliability of the DSM-IV is improved over previous revisions. Descriptive validity (differentiating individuals in one diagnostic category from those in another category) has improved; outcome validity (predicting the future course of an individual's disorder) is still less than hoped for. However, an assortment of criticisms has been leveled at the current version of the DSM, and for that matter at any diagnostic classification system. The DSM-IV is still medicalized, to the chagrin of many nonmedical clinicians who would prefer a cognitive–behavioral or interpersonally based diagnostic classification; however, no other diagnostic classification has achieved the DSM's acceptance and widespread use. Questions continue to be raised about sexist and cultural bias. In response to past criticisms, the DSM-IV has made an effort to examine multicultural variables and gender-specific issues. Realistically, any human behavior classification system will reflect the cultural orientation, personal beliefs, and professional values of those who construct it. However, one cannot help but wonder if the continued omission of a classification for anger disorders reflects a gender and/or cultural bias on the part of those who decide what to include in or exclude from each revision. Another limitation of the current manual is that the developmental dimension is neglected (Wenar, 1994); both research and conventional clinical wisdom indicate that for many disorders both the symptom picture and the prognosis may change over the course of successive developmental stages. Perhaps the most relevant and common criticism of any diagnostic classification is the use of labels to describe and understand individuals. As the authors of the DSM-IV hasten to point out, the DSM-IV does not classify people; the manual classifies disorders that individuals have (p. xxii), and labels are the shorthand descriptors that are the essence of classification. On the other hand, as the illustrious English physician Sir William Osler commented some hundred years ago, "it's more important to know what kind of patient has a disease than what disease a patient has." Additional points about diagnostic classification are addressed in the next chapter.

ETIOLOGY: AN OVERVIEW OF FOUR EXPLANATORY MODELS

Biological Model

Psychopathology is viewed as an organic process that may be germ-based, anatomical/neurological, genetically transmitted, or biochemical. A frequently mentioned example of a germ-based explanation is the discovery of parasitic microorganisms in which general paresis, an organic brain disorder, develops; another example is dementia and other psychiatric sequelae associated with late-stage HIV disease. Examples of anatomical–neurological impairment are tumors, cerebral strokes, long-term effects of alcohol or other drugs, and traumatic head injury.

With regard to genetic transmission, a body of research has accumulated to support a genetic susceptibility to a variety of psychopathological conditions such as certain subtypes of schizophrenia, mood disorders (especially bipolar type), and particular forms of mental retardation (cited in Rosenhan and Seligman, 1984; Sue et al., 1994; and Strider, 1980); early infantile autism, hyperactivity, alcoholism, and antisocial personality disorder (cited in Schwarz, 1979); as well as some of the anxiety disorders, for example panic disorder (cited in Schwarz, 1979). Silver and Segal (1984) offer the following observation: "It may seem likely that over the next decade geneticists and molecular biologists will be capable of mapping parts of the human genome. Substances thus localized may serve, in turn, as markers for inherited disorders that are caused by derangements in specific areas of the genome" (p. 805). Schwarz (1979) avers: "I am beginning to suspect that all forms of psychopathology that are not clearly due to traumatic, toxic, or infectious conditions of the brain are significantly influenced in likelihood and age of onset not only by environmental factors, but also by genetic variation among individuals" (p. 879). Although a technical update on this topic is beyond the scope of the chapter, a nontechnical summary is provided in Plomin (1989) and Rosenhan and Seligman (1995, pp. 686–688).

Finally, spurred by the introduction of psychoactive medication in the 1950s that paved the way for groundbreaking neuropsychopharmacology research, biologically based etiology has strong currency in professional circles that focus on biochemical changes, especially biochemical imbalances in certain neurotransmitters in the brain. Silver and Segal (1984) single out studies that have used PET-scans to detect hypofrontality in schizophrenia, decreased metabolism in Alzheimer's disease and other forms of dementia, and alterations of metabolic activity in affective and anxiety disorders following administration of psychoactive medication. Research on disordered neurotransmitter systems, abnormal metabolites, and diminished or excessive levels of one or more transmitters, suggests at least a contributory role in the etiology of affective and schizophrenic disorders (Strider, 1980; Rosenhan and Seligman, 1984). An example of how excessive or deficient levels of the neurotransmitter dopamine lead to vulnerability for quite different but serious disorders is that deficiency protects against schizophrenia and excess protects against Parkinson's syndrome (Morgan, 1992).

Although biological findings are promising, at times impressive, organic causation has been limited largely to severe forms of adult psychopathology which comprise only a limited segment of the broad spectrum of psychological disorders and dysfunctions. Genetic explanations, though having important implications for a larger range of disorders, indicate a genetic susceptibility rather than direct, specific genetic transmission. Still to be clarified is how genetic susceptibility to psychopathology is mediated by

other inherited characteristics, and how genetic susceptibility interacts differentially with familial and social influences, and developmental and situational crises. Despite
advances in the study of biochemical correlates of psychopathology, the explanatory hypotheses are based to a large
extent on how disorders respond to biochemical interventions such as the psychoactive medications.

As many have commented, psychology and other behavioral sciences (including the rapidly expanding hybrid
discipline of cognitive sciences) have large untapped contributions to make in terms of understanding and ame-
liorating the impact of psychopathology on the broad
spectrum of an individual's behavior across the life span.
At this stage, for many psychological disorders as well as
the ordinary problems of living, psychological etiology and
intervention have more to offer than exclusively biological theories or interventions. For instance, the approach
to health psychology, which assists individuals to cope
better with medical conditions and to develop healthy life-
styles, can be utilized by clinicians to assist persons to cope
constructively with genetic susceptibility, neurological
defects, or biochemical excesses or deficiencies. As an aside,
even the chronic stress and turmoil that characterize a
schizophrenic disorder may be responsible for the observed
high levels of the neurotransmitter *dopamine* rather than
the schizophrenic disorder being the result of excessive
dopamine levels (Sue et al., 1994, p. 41). Like biology, psychology is also not the whole equation, but it has been and
still is on the cutting edge of progress in the assessment,
rehabilitation, and prevention of psychopathology.

Sociocultural Model

A common theme in sociocultural explanations is that
psychopathology is a response to prevailing cultural expectations and social influences. As Dohrenwend and
Dohrenwend (1969) note, "Symptom items themselves

have different meaning and hence different implication for persons in different subcultures" (p. 169). Two common hypotheses are (1) the *drift* hypothesis; that is, socially and economically deprived areas of society attract and hold individuals from all socioeconomic classes who have seriously dysfunctional personalities and marginal life adjustments, thereby accounting for the higher incidence of abnormality in deprived areas, and (2) the *breeder* hypothesis; that is, depressed, oppressed, and disorganized environments with high rates of unemployment, dehumanization, and hopelessness are fertile ground for the development of abnormality (Strider, 1980). In commenting on living environments, Strole (1972) concludes that due to the greater prevalence in slum areas of parental psychopathology, poverty, and family disorganization, both metropolitan and rural slums are more psychopathogenic for children than are nonslum neighborhoods.

Those who hew to a strong cultural relativistic position contend that abnormal behavior can best be viewed as a reflection of the cultural values, life-styles, and world views of particular groups or populations; for example, the aggressive, hostile behavior observed in some mental disorders are much more frequent in the United States than in Asia (and even in Asian Americans) (Sue et al., 1994, p. 7). Instead of utilizing an individual frame of reference, sociocultural concepts are designed to explain how large units (e.g., families/extended families, social groups, ethnic/racial subcultures) contribute to the development and maintenance of psychopathology (Millon, 1981). This change of focus from intrapsychic and interpersonal levels to a suprapersonal level of explanation may contribute to the fact that sociocultural models have been less prominent in recent years. For extended discussion of the relation between culture and psychopathology, the reader is referred to Draguns (1985).

While the sociocultural model has a long tradition, only in the past decade has the multicultural model appeared in the literature. The premises of the model are that being culturally different is not synonymous with being disordered or deviant; each cultural group has strengths and limitations that must be understood and respected; and, most importantly, behavior must be judged from the perspective of a group's value system as well as other standards in use to arrive at judgments about normality and psychopathology (Sue et al., 1994, pp. 32–33). To illustrate, suspicion and distrust in an individual from a minority group which has a history of being oppressed by the majority culture might better be explained in terms of a survivalist state of mind than a paranoid state of mind. In some minority subcultures the value attached to reliance on the extended family and the church might erroneously be labeled as overdependence, enmeshment, or lack of healthy individuation. In other minority subcultures conformity, passivity, lack of emotional expressiveness, and avoidance of direct eye contact might be inaccurately attributed to interpersonal dysfunction, whereas in fact the behavior may well reflect time-honored cultural values regarding respect and consideration for others.

Psychological Model

Following is a summary of five psychological models: psychodynamic, humanistic, cognitive and behavioral, systemic-structural, and developmental, all of which have overlapping features. The psychodynamic model, which includes classical psychoanalytic theory and neoanalytic modifications, is based on (1) childhood conflicts which arise when needs cannot be satisfied due to external constraints or conscience, and produce (2) conscious or unconscious anxiety, and defensive mechanisms which are designed to eliminate or decrease anxiety (Strider, 1980; Rosenhan and Seligman, 1984). Defense mechanisms almost always involve cognitive distortion of self-awareness or external reality. Defenses against anxiety undergo

developmental progression compatible with matura-
tion of sensorimotor, perceptual–cognitive, affective–
motivational, and interpersonal processes. Anxieties of
the earlier developmental stages become reactivated by
stressful situations of adult life, and psychopathology is
the outcome of escalating anxieties pressing against inadequate or weakened defenses, which is manifested in
symptoms of intrapsychic and interpersonal impairment.
The humanistic approach subsumes person-centered,
existential, and gestalt theories. Common to these theories is the assumption that abnormality develops when an
individual's feelings, needs, values, and intentions run
counter to familial and social pressures, and as a consequence the individual experiences pervasive and protracted conflict, which eventuates in self-estrangement
and self-alienation. The disturbance in self-identity interferes with developing realistic and accurate perceptions
of others, which in turn impairs interpersonal functioning. A core belief is that subordinating one's identity to real
or imagined expectations results in a failure to live productively and with satisfaction (Rosenhan and Seligman, 1984).
   The third group includes behavioral approaches and
cognitive approaches (as well as current hybrids of the
two). Traditionally, the behavioral model contends that the
basis for development, maintenance, and generalization
of maladaptive behavior is the same as for normal behavior, and abnormality refers to behavioral excesses and deficiencies that an individual has learned in order to cope
with stressful developmental events. Abnormal behavior
may be acquired by (1) classical conditioning, in which
abnormal responses become associated with external
events; or (2) operantly conditioned processes, in which
abnormal behavior becomes positively or negatively reinforced. While the source of behavioral deficits and excesses
is to be found in the methods of child rearing and child
management, once formed, the deficits and excesses create environmental contingencies that strengthen and

perpetuate abnormal functioning (Rosenhan and Seligman, 1984). In general, the cognitive model explains abnormal behavior in terms of (1) information-processing
deficits that result from and are maintained by faulty assumptions (the current term is *schemas*) about self and
others instilled during critical developmental stages;
(2) cognitive and perceptual distortions (e.g., misinterpre-
tations, selective perceptions); and (3) arbitrary conclusions (e.g., over- and undergeneralizations). Moreover,
emotional control problems and dysfunctional interpersonal actions are responses to, as well as reinforcement
of, faulty assumptions, perceptual–cognitive distortions,
and other errors of thinking.

The systemic–structural model grew out of several
mainstream family therapy approaches which shared a
systemic view of human behavior. The basic tenet is that
abnormality develops from and continues to be a reflection of one's family legacy. Family legacy, in turn, consists
of several interlocking structures: family composition; recurrent or intergenerational family problems; tension,
conflict, and changes in family subsystems; official and
unofficial family member roles; spoken and unspoken
family rules and expectations; implicit and explicit family values and beliefs; and the interplay of family communication styles (specific source unknown). Therefore,
the source of one's personal identity, self-esteem, and perception of reality is in the interplay over time of the various components of the family legacy. The mandate is
clear: Psychopathology must be understood (and treated)
within an interpersonal rather than intrapsychic context.

The fifth type of psychological model is a developmental one; and developmental psychopathology "refers
to . . . clinical dysfunction in the context of maturational
and developmental processes . . . and encompasses the
entire life span" (Kazdin, 1989, p. 180). Kovacs (1989)
states that developmental theories focus on three areas:

(1) extent to which characteristics of a person mediate what disorders develop and what forms they may take; (2) extent to which psychopathology interferes with age-appropriate behaviors; and (3) continuity or discontinuity of disorders across age periods (i.e., a problem at one age, such as opposition, may disappear and be replaced by a different but related problem at a later age, such as teenage delinquency).

Implicit in the developmental conception of normality and abnormality is the notion of critical periods of development, in which success or failure to cope successfully with the expectations and maturational tasks of one age period facilitates or hinders mastery of age-appropriate competencies of subsequent developmental stages. Developmentally based abnormality assumes an ongoing interaction between (1) risk factors, either in the person or in the environment; (2) vulnerability within a person that intensifies the response to a risk factor; (3) protective factors which can be in the individual or in the environment; and (4) protective mechanisms which refer to the helping activities of self, others, or professionals (Wenar, 1994). It is the interplay between and among these four factors that is largely responsible for a person staying on a normal developmental pathway, being diverted to an abnormal developmental pathway, continuing on an abnormal developmental track, or returning to a more normal developmental track.

Etiologically, Cohen (1974) hypothesizes two types of developmentally sequential interactions. The first interaction is between organismically based characteristics (e.g., sex, size, attractiveness, intelligence, psychophysiological reactivity), and socializing influences and pressures such as family, school, neighborhood, and peers. From this interaction, critical thought-feeling-motivation-action patterns evolve that constitute a predisposition to psychopathology. The stage is then set for the second or developmentally later interaction between specific predispositions and precipitating events that occur at different developmental periods (e.g., the stress of coping with normal developmental tasks as well as accidental stresses such as loss of significant others, failures, physical traumas, illnesses). A familiar illustration is the *diathesis-stress* theory (Zubin and Spring, 1977) in which abnormality is determined by the ratio of the strength of an individual's vulnerability or predisposition, and the frequency, intensity, and duration of psychosocial stressors; both treatment and prevention strategies are directed toward reducing the psychosocial stressors and/or increasing an individual's ability to manage stressors better.

The five psychological approaches can be grouped under three superordinate orientations: the illness orientation, which includes the psychodynamic approach, the social learning orientation which includes the cognitive approaches, and the actualization orientation which includes the humanistic approach. The systems-structural approach falls partly under the social learning orientation and partly under the actualization orientation; and the developmental approach falls partly under each of the three orientations. Despite some differences, central to the three orientations is the basic paradigm of personal distress/interpersonal dysfunction generated by defensive–protective reactions to conflict-centered anxiety, anger, or sadness. The symptoms of the illness orientation are the cognitive and behavioral deficits and excesses of the social learning orientation, and the relational and communication failures of the actualization orientation.

Although differing, perhaps only semantically, on the issue of whether abnormality is quantitatively or qualitatively different from normality, the three orientations generally accept a severity continuum of psychological disorders without a sharp demarcation between normal and abnormal functioning. The three orientations also acknowledge a distinction between predisposing and precipitating factors, though there is less agreement on the former because the concept of predisposition has always been embedded in philosophical assumptions about etiology. Nevertheless, Zubin's (1977–1978) futuristic statement on etiology speaks to all three orientations.

> One solution is to look for the common denominator running through all three models . . . elicited by either exogenous or endogenous life events which produce sufficient stress to elicit an episode. . . . We need to find and differentiate markers of vulnerability from markers of the presence and absence of episodes. . . . The latter wax and wane with the episodes and disappear with the end of the episode, while the former persist in and out of episodes [p. 7].

Although the search for a single, all-inclusive orientation continues, the availability of three viable orientations not only provides the necessary checks and balances to correct for each orientation's selective over- and underemphases, but also accommodates the diversity of professional beliefs, values, and personal world views.

Finally, as discussed in chapter 4, the effort to integrate multiple, competing rival treatment perspectives, instead of relying on a single school of thought, has become a robust trend over the past decade. A case in point is the failure of any one model to address the etiological complexity of schizophrenia, especially brain dysfunction. Although the biogenetic model is congruent with the growing evidence for some type of brain dysfunction (even in the absence of particular brain pathology), the biogenic model is singularly incomplete with respect to the role of environmental components and risk and protective factors during critical developmental periods. With that in mind, a persuasive illustration of the trend to integrate multiple etiological perspectives is the increasing endorsement of a biopsychosocial model which integrates biological susceptibility, psychological vulnerability, and sociocultural conditioning (Johnson, 1989).

CURRENT AND FUTURE ISSUES

Political and ethical concerns notwithstanding, it is the economics of mental health treatment that rivets the attention of lawmakers, health care corporations, and taxpaying citizens. As many professional commentators have observed, mental health costs have been rising annually since the early 1980s, with an increasing percentage consumed by inpatient care. Kiesler (1993) concludes that over 70 percent of mental health dollars is spent on inpatient psychiatric care, even though a large majority of those receiving inpatient care could be treated less expensively, and even more effectively, in alternative care facilities outside the hospital. And Paul and Menditto (1992) are quick to point out that despite substantial changes coming in the wake of deinstitutionalization and cost-containment legislation, for the most part the changes have not translated into increased effectiveness of inpatient treatment.

However, to focus only on mental health expenditures is to overlook savings in productivity and total health care costs that are gained from successful mental health treatment. While per capita expenditures on mental health across states range from a high of about $67 to a low of about $8 with a national average of approximately $24, a more compelling statistic is that as many as eight out of ten people with a mental disorder can resume a normal productive life if they receive timely and appropriate treatment (Delano Clinic, 1989). Another compelling statistic: Those with mental disorders average twice as many visits to primary care medical doctors as do those without mental disorders; and when they do receive mental health treatment, there is often a reduction in overall health care costs. In fact, with mental health intervention, cost offset studies show a reduction in total health care costs, even when mental health intervention costs are included (Welch, 1994).

Smith, Schwebel, Dunn, and McIver (1993) comment that "one of the most remarkable events in psychiatric health care in the United States in this century was the national deinstitutionalization of people with chronic mental illness" (p. 966). On a percentage basis, the census in state and county mental hospitals declined nearly 80 percent from the early 1950s to the late 1980s (Smyer, Balster, Egli, Johnson, Kilbey, Leith, and Puente, 1993, p. 396). The impetus for deinstitutionalization came from the confluence of two major developments: first, the advent of antipsychotic medications in the 1950s, which reduced symptomatology sufficiently for large numbers of chronically mentally ill (CMI) persons to be given continuing care in their community; and second, the implementation of the federally funded community mental health movement in the 1960s, which was designed to provide follow-up treatment in community facilities for those who were released from hospitals, as well as alternative treatment for those who heretofore would have been hospitalized. Because community facilities were sometimes underfunded and often underprepared for their role in deinstitutionalization, the community mental health movement, at least the deinstitutionalization component, was only partly successful.

Due to confusion about the nature of chronic mental illness, seriously mentally ill persons typically have not been well understood and therefore not well matched to treatment services. Chronic mental illness has three defining characteristics: duration, diagnosis, and disability (Bachrach, 1988, cited in Smith et al., 1993). The duration characteristic has to do with a gradual onset, indefinite duration with threat of relapse, and unlikelihood of a return to pre-illness mental status. Diagnosis has to do with the nature of the disorder, for instance, schizophrenia which almost by definition is chronic (for an exceptional article on treatment and rehabilitation of schizophrenia, refer to Liberman, Kopelowicz, and Young, 1994) especially with the likelihood of a coexisting substance abuse disorder; and given the nature of a mental illness and family and societal response to it, significant financial, social, occupational, educational, or personal disabilities are inevitable (Smith et al., 1993). A frequent misunderstanding about the CMI is the purported association of chronic mental illness and violence. Those suffering from mental illness are no more likely to commit violent acts than persons with a medical condition. The personality makeup of the person, rather than the disorder itself, has more influence on the likelihood of violence (Delano Clinic, 1989). Monahan (1992) eloquently and incisively rebuts the equating of mental illness with violence: "None of the data give any support to the sensationalized caricature of the mentally disordered served up by the media, the shunning of former patients by employers and neighbors in the community, or regressive 'lock em all up' laws proposed by politicians pandering to public fears" (p. 519). Monahan then concludes: "Clearly, mental health status makes at best a trivial contribution to the overall level of violence in society" (p. 519).

Although the etiology of chronic mental illness is still based primarily on a biological model, other models are becoming increasingly important in addressing the needs of this population (see Smith et al. 1993): the diathesis–stress or vulnerability model; a cognitive model based on assessment and correction of information-processing deficits; a case-management model to assist with the acquisition and maintenance of basic life management skills; a rehabilitation model to ameliorate various kinds of impairment; and a psychoeducational model to inform, support, and advise families of the CMI. With the exception of the biological model, there are ample opportunities for clinical psychologists to make significant contributions in each of the models.

As expected, the federal government has been and continues to be a major player in providing financial support to improve treatment and prevention of psychological disorders. There are several areas for which the National Institute of Mental Health has already set high priorities for research attention and funding (Silver and Segal, 1984). One is the developmental area, which Silver and Segal describe as "exploring the continuities and transformations whereby individual personalities become vulnerable or invulnerable to psychopathology at various stages in the life span" (p. 808). The authors also comment on the new generation of research strategies and methods for longitudinal study. The new strategies and methods enable long-term patterns of personality functioning to be examined with respect to both biological factors and sociocultural influences, which it is hoped will lead to a useful taxonomy of environments and life situations.

Another promising area is the family context of normality and abnormality. As Kazdin (1989) and others have concluded, many disorders clearly run in families (e.g., obesity, antisocial behavior, some mood disorders, alcoholism). Silver and Segal (1984) outline three lines of research. The first is sociocultural, which examines how families, particularly disadvantaged ones, cope with problems and how support networks facilitate their coping efforts. The second is biobehavioral, which investigates how family living styles interact with biological influences (e.g., temperament) to shape psychological competence in young children. A third line of research focuses on how specific family variables (e.g., family communication styles) contribute to normal and abnormal development. In reviewing family influences on psychopathology, Doane (1978) identifies the following significant differences between normal and dysfunctional families: patterns of conflict, family coalition patterns, flexibility versus rigidity, family effectiveness and efficiency, and habitual communication styles among family members.

The relation between cumulative stress in the family environment and susceptibility to childhood psychopathology has become of prime importance in designing prevention programs. Magnussen (1980) identifies six stress factors that have been found to be strongly associated with childhood disorders: (1) severe marital discord; (2) low social status; (3) overcrowding in the family living environment; (4) paternal criminality; (5) maternal psychiatric disorder; and (6) the family placed under the jurisdiction of local authorities, and we would add to the list, substance abuse disorder in one or both parents. When only one of the six factors is present, a child is no more likely to develop serious problems than any other child. When two of the factors cooccur, the risk of abnormality increases fourfold, which is a persuasive argument for prevention programs to improve the interpersonal environment of the family, ameliorate socioenvironmental conditions such as poverty, homelessness, and violence, and develop skills in family members to cope with developmental as well as accidental crises. In short, home-based, early-in-life prevention programs can reduce risk factors and increase protective factors for childhood psychopathology; and school-based prevention programs for adolescents can significantly reduce at-risk behaviors like school drop-out, chemical dependency, teen pregnancy, delinquency, and strengthen protective factors such as improved academic performance, social skills, and peer support groups (Kazdin, 1993a).

A current issue of considerable import is the failure to stem the soaring rate of violence. Lykken (1993) frames the issue in a way that should challenge the most complacent: "The United States has the highest per capita incidence of interpersonal violence of any nation not actively engaged in civil war" (p. 13).

More recently, the alarming statistics on the frequency of child sexual and physical abuse, and the various forms of child neglect, including the plight of homeless children who are often repeatedly victimized, have led to a high priority for treatment and prevention programs at national, state, and local levels. The frequent association between parental psychopathology and child abuse has been documented repeatedly. Recurrent child abuse sends a strong signal that the family environment is characterized by chronic and pervasive psychopathology, and the serious psychological impairment that is evident later on in adulthood likely reflects not only the childhood abuse experience, but also the day-to-day impact of parental psychopathology (Nash, Hulsey, Sexton, Harralson, and Lambert, 1993). To its credit, psychology has been quick to respond with a coordinated effort from its Practice, Science, Education, and Public Interest Directorates which have demonstrated a willingness to work collaboratively within an interdisciplinary format.

Granted that mental health care for children and adolescents may not be noticeably different today than it was at the turn of the century with 15 to 20 percent needing to be served but 70 to 80 percent of that proportion not being served (Tuma, 1989), the federal government continues to take corrective initiatives. Tuma (1989) cites three promising federal initiatives: first, the Federal Child and Adolescent Service System Program of 1984 to assist state mental health agencies in coordinating care for seriously disturbed children; second, training grants available to graduate and professional schools that are tied to an integration of services to children and adolescents; and third, the State Comprehensive Mental Services Plan Act of 1986 which funds state programs for comprehensive services for the CMI of all ages. However, all three initiatives may be set aside by fiscal reforms.

Another alarming statistic that has mobilized professional and lay persons alike to advocate for well-funded, innovative programs for early detection, treatment, and prevention is the pervasiveness of substance abuse/ dependency. Middle-class use of drugs, adolescent drug use, acquired immunodeficiency syndrome (AIDS), and crime involvement are some of the main forces that have compelled society to accept chemical dependency as a bona fide social and health problem (DeLeon, Freudenberger, and Wexler, 1993). While substance abuse disorders are widespread from the second decade of life on, the prevalence rate is highest in adolescence and in the 21 to 40 age range. Although it is difficult to map out the etiological pathway from experimentation, to recreational use, to eventual abuse and later dependence, family history (both biological and environmental predispositions) is clearly the strongest predictor for developing an addictive disorder. Not to discount biological susceptibility, Shedler and Block's (1990) study of adolescent drug abusers, experimenters, and abstainers, revealed significant psychological differences between the three groups, and the differences could be traced directly to the earliest years of childhood, especially to the quality of parenting received.

Not surprisingly, the incidence of substance abuse is disproportionately higher in society's disadvantaged groups, particularly those of Native American ancestry who have become the nation's most "unserved, underserved, and inappropriately served" group. Moreover, within the young adult CMI population (18–40 years), the role of substance abuse exceeds 50 percent—twice the rate in the general population—and presents a formidable obstacle to accurate diagnosis and effective treatment (Brown, Ridgely, Pepper, Levine, and Ryglewicz, 1989). Matters are made worse by a lack of knowledge about substance abuse among significant numbers of mental health practitioners, which can be attributed to the fact that the addiction field remained outside the mainstream of mental health professionals until the 1980s. Since then, rapid strides have been made. Within the past few years, clinical work with addictive disorders has become an official subspecialty of professional psychology, and has been granted division status within the American Psychological Association. Already professional psychology has made significant contributions to diagnosis and treatment through teaching, practice, and research. And in doing so, it has become evident that there are multiple etiological variables in substance abuse (e.g., a high rate of coexisting mental disorders such as personality disorders, mood disorders, anxiety disorders, and even medical disorders such as sexually transmitted diseases). It has also become evident that the traditional one-treatment-fits-all philosophy must be replaced by an informed matching of client/patient to treatment intervention. Unpredictable shifting federal priorities notwithstanding, currently there is considerable optimism for significantly increased funding for research, prevention, and treatment through the National Institute of Drug Abuse.

To return to the issue of future prospects for the CMI population, a problem of pressing urgency is how to correct deficiencies in treatment programs that are alternatives to state hospital placement. As evidence of the need to improve treatment programs, Teplin (1984) cites research findings which indicate that deinstitutionalization has not significantly reduced the overall rate of hospitalization and rehospitalization; that the incidence and prevalence of schizophrenia is increasing due in part to the greater proportion of younger persons in the population, as well as to the increase in coexisting substance abuse and dependence; and that increasing numbers of the mentally ill are being processed through the criminal justice system instead of the mental health system.

Although touted by many as a forward-looking solution to problems in service delivery to the seriously mentally ill, privatization, or the shift of service delivery from the public to the private sector, is at best a tradeoff. A notable example of privatization is that inpatient mental health care is increasingly provided by for-profit private psychiatric hospitals owned by large health care corporations; however, patient selection (sometimes referred to as "skimming off the cream") is based on the ability to pay (or to afford insurance coverage that reimburses) which of course excludes a large number of the indigent CMI (Beckman and Dokecki, 1989). Other examples of privatization are board-and-care facilities and nursing homes where half or more of the beds are occupied by those with serious mental disorders, and where care is custodial and no more rehabilitative than that which existed in state hospitals before deinstitutionalization (Shadish, 1989). The argument for privatization is based on its potential for making services more cost effective and innovative, that it is an effective response to the drastic reduction in state hospital patient census as a result of the deinstitutionalization movement, and that the concept has a good deal of political currency today (Simons, 1989). Yet to be addressed, however, is the need for quality care and rehabilitation for the indigent CMI population, most of whom remain dependent for care on their families and/or the social welfare system. In short, as Shadish (1989) succinctly notes, in the shift from public-sector to private-sector care, most of our CMI population has been transinstitutionalized, not deinstitutionalized.

However, there is always some basis for optimism. For the first time the CMI population has a strong consumer advocate group, the National Alliance for the Mentally Ill (NAMI). NAMI's rapidly growing membership of families of the CMI has mounted a strong educational program to support research on biological causes of mental illness, and to remove the stigma from families with mental illness; in fact, having to cope for years with a mentally ill family member can cause serious medical and psychological complications in other family members.

Because of expertise in various types of skill training and in psychoeducational consultation with groups, psychology is taking a promising role in the rehabilitation of the mentally ill and in the prevention of problems in family members. Following a stress–diathesis model (Zubin and Spring, 1977), which assumes that a biological vulnerability to mental illness is triggered when the level of environmental stress exceeds an individual's tolerance threshold, psychologists are teaching patients stress-coping skills, in addition to improved adherence to medication management. Families are also being instructed on ways to make the living environment of a mentally ill family member less stressful (Bellack, 1986). Optimism has also been generated by recent advances in the neurosciences that strengthen support for a neurodevelopmental basis of mental disorders; by the development of psychosocial programs that assist adult patients and their families with the personal and social aspects of mental illness; and by the spectacular growth of NAMI as a strong consumer advocacy group for the mentally ill (Johnson, 1989).

To conclude the chapter, not only has our understanding of normality relied too much on extrapolation from the study of psychopathology, but also our knowledge of psychopathology has relied too much on clinical and research findings from already existing psychological disorders. More longitudinal research is needed on developmental variables that predispose an individual to adaptive functioning, along with a taxonomy of environments and life situations that facilitate or inhibit adaptive functioning. Finally, because a comprehensive understanding of normality and abnormality encompasses all of psychology as well as other behavioral sciences, clinical psychologists do not know their own specialty if they know only that.

PERSONAL CONSIDERATIONS

To assist the reader to move toward a "personalized" meaning of normality and abnormality, the following points may be helpful. First, a key element in the terms *normality* and *abnormality* is *norm*, which can be defined as a standard or criterion. Although related to a host of variables described earlier in the chapter, and subject to gradual change over time, a norm, standard, or criterion of appropriate behavior is nevertheless essential to differentiating normal from abnormal behaviors.

In clinical practice there are two norms to be considered: an external or societal norm, and an internal or personal norm. Some individuals are referred involuntarily for mental health services because their behavior, as judged by others, deviates too much from the societal norm. On the other hand, many more individuals seek mental health services voluntarily because they are not functioning in accordance with their personal standard of normality. Thus, the clinical practitioner must address both types of norms to determine how best to assist a client to live his or her life in accordance with both personal and societal standards. In this context, normality denotes success and abnormality denotes failure (as judged by personal and/or social norms) to adapt one's behavior to the changing conditions and exigencies of the psychosocial environment (Robertson, 1980).

Chapter 2

Clinical Assessment and Diagnosis

The father had sought the services of an independent practitioner of clinical psychology. As he described the situation:

> About six years ago, just as I was finishing my college degree, my marriage fell apart. We had a few marriage counseling sessions, but it was hopeless. We had a newborn son, and the thought of giving him up almost destroyed me, but I knew I had to serve four years in the military and had little choice but to let my ex-wife have custody of him. We didn't have much money, and I didn't even get an attorney, I just relied on what her attorney told me. Now I'm out of the military, remarried, and making a good income. I want my son back! I have filed for a modification of custody. What has happened though is that my ex-wife's attorney had her take our son to the clinic that does psychological evaluations for the courts. The psychologists and social workers there spent hours with my ex-wife and my son, interviewing them, giving them tests, observing them together, and even going to her apartment to see how they live. My attorney arranged for me and my second wife to go to the clinic too. They spent about 30 minutes talking to us, and then put my son and me into a room to play together for 15 minutes—we were in the place less than an hour. The clinic sent a report to the court saying that my ex-wife is a far better parent than I am, and recommended that she be allowed to keep custody of my son. Somehow that just doesn't seem like we were treated equally.

Indeed, that may be the case, and for a variety of reasons, ranging from professional standards and ethics to legal principles. The one reason, however, that should be emphasized for purposes of this chapter is that being a diagnostician requires reliable and valid methods, and data collected from a brief interview and a play session of still shorter duration would likely yield "data" of dubious reliability and validity, and would certainly seem less adequate than the data that would come from extensive interviewing and observations, comprehensive psychological testing, and a home visit.

Assessment and diagnosis form the distinguishing cornerstone for the practice of clinical psychology. In a survey of clinical psychologists, Moreland and Dahlstrom (1983) found that 91 percent of the respondents performed assessment. Looking at clinicians' services in the 1980s, Norcross, Prochaska, and Gallagher (1989) found that the mean percentage of time spent doing diagnosis and assessment had increased from 10 percent in 1973 to 16 percent in 1986, with 75 percent of the responding clinical psychologists being involved with diagnosis and assessment to some degree. Phares (1992) says, "All practicing clinicians engage in assessment in one form or another" (p. 10).

This same prominence for assessment has been present throughout the history of clinical psychology and, notwithstanding the increasing array of services provided by clinical psychologists, shows little or no diminution. Matarazzo (1992) predicts that the twenty-first century will embrace continued and expanded use of assessment: "I *predict for the types of today's established individually and group administered tests*, few *radical* changes in either the types of tests or test items that will be used in the measurement and assessment of individual differences in mental abilities, as these abilities relate to success in some aspects of everyday living" (p. 1008).

The reason that assessment has maintained a primary place comes from the fact that psychologists are the only clinical professionals trained to use certain psychological tests. As Abeles (1990) puts it: "It is my contention that one of the unique contributions of the clinical psychologist is the ability to provide assessment data. Providing assessments is again becoming a highly valued and respected part of clinical psychology and in my opinion is coequal with intervention and psychotherapy as a vital activity of clinical psychology" (p. 4).

While psychiatrists, clinical social workers, and other mental health professionals are prepared to conduct evaluations, they must rely on appraisal methods other than psychological tests. State licensing laws for psychologists commonly proscribe or limit the use of psychological tests by other than a licensed psychologist. Also, the publishers of tests typically restrict the sale of certain tests, particularly those that are clinically oriented, to psychologists.

Psychological tests have not received unquestioned acceptance. From concerned parents, to Congressional subcommittees, to the courts, there have been many condemnations of and inquiries about the use of psychological tests. These criticisms have centered on the client's right to privacy, discrimination because of cultural distinctions, the reliability and validity of the instruments, and the kinds of decisions that are based primarily or exclusively on test data. On the latter, the concern is whether too little consideration is given to the unique sociocultural background of the client versus too much importance is placed on numbers. In some instances, a given test has been banned from use in a school system because of content (e.g., asking about values that, by public policy, are deemed to be under the exclusive aegis of the family and exempt from governmental or institutional scrutiny).

Such criticisms should not be viewed as illogical, hostile attacks. Often there has been just reason for questioning the use of a particular test. Too often, decisions have relied on test data when, from a validity point of view, there has been no scientific connector between the data and the criterion for the decision.

Since this is a critical problem, let us give it emphasis by considering three examples. First, candidates for jobs are often screened according to tests that have minimal, if any, predictive validity for the job functions. This problem is highlighted by the use of integrity or honesty tests which, despite great demand for their usage by consumers (e.g., employers), have yet to earn confidence by behavioral science standards: "Researchers have generally agreed that there is insufficient evidence to reach definitive conclusions on some aspects of integrity testing and that the underlying construct of integrity itself is poorly understood" (Camara and Schneider, 1994, p. 117). Second, with exceptional children, placements in special education programs have been made without benefit of test data directly relevant to the placement decision. Third and finally, in child custody proceedings, psychological opinions are often made according to test data that are not known to be valid measures of the factors relevant to distinguishing parents' contributions to the best interests of the child. Brodzinksy (1993) states that, "Unfortunately, psychologists routinely overstep the boundaries of their professional role by offering opinions about custody and visitation matters based to a great extent, and sometimes exclusively, on the results of psychological testing" (p. 214). This is done, notwithstanding the fact that "the standard psychological tests used in custody evaluations were not developed for forensic purposes . . . we do not know how valid they are in addressing those issues that are of primary concern to the court" (p. 214).

There are many reasons underlying abuse of test data. Sometimes the reason may have been rooted in a conscious wish to discriminate, but more often the reasons have been due to a faulty understanding of testing and an ill-formulated wish to appear "professional" in the decision-making process—unfortunately, the outcome in such cases is anything but professional. Even the well-meaning professional may share in the guilt of abusing test data. Since the profession creates a "publish or perish" dictum, particularly if the clinical psychologist is employed by a college or university, there is a never-ending quest to generate research for publication in professional journals. In order to attain the degree of originality that is necessary to win a journal editor's acceptance of a research manuscript, there seems to be a tendency to create tests; many times these tests are poorly developed. In providing an annotated bibliography or compendium of behavioral measurements, Reichalt (1983) asserts that tests are developed so rapidly that they frequently have not been adequately researched, noting that "approximately 70% of instruments are only used by their developer" (p. 341), yet they end up as part of published research.

These slipshod test development practices and the conscious or unconscious abuses have not gone unchecked. Both statutory and case law have imposed strong restraints on testing practices, particularly by specifying the qualities a test must have and the decisions that can be made therefrom. These restraints will likely increase in the future.

Perhaps employment and special education provide the two best examples of how the law has recognized the need to impose standards on the use of psychological assessment. Both areas are founded on protections guaranteed by the Constitution of the United States.

For employment, Bartol and Bartol (1994) summarize:

In the Civil Rights Act of 1964, Congress addressed the broad spectrum of discriminatory practice in its many forms. Specifically relating to employment, under Title VII of the Civil Rights Act it is illegal to discriminate against an individual or class of individuals on the basis of race, color, gender, religion, or national origin. The law (with its subsequent amendments) makes it clear that employees and prospective employees are protected against

discrimination related to hiring and promotion. As a result, psychological tests which lack adequate validation
data or which base classification and cut-off scores on
norms developed from a culturally advantaged population
are particularly susceptible to lawsuits. When the Civil
Rights Act was first passed, many psychological tests,
especially of the cognitive ability (IQ) variety, came under heavy social and legal attack [p. 50].

Bartol and Bartol also point out how the Equal Employment
Opportunity Commission (EEOC) continues to impose guidelines on employment tests. "The guidelines pertain to any
test used to select, transfer, promote, train, refer, and retain
employees" (p. 50). More recently, the Americans with Disabilities Act (ADA) has also specified limitations on the use
of psychological tests (Research Institute of America, 1991).

In the area of special education, L. C. Swenson (1993)
states: "Federal and state laws contain rules controlling
fairness in diagnosis and placements. The federal Education for All Handicapped Children Act initially passed in
1975 both specifies procedural due process safeguards and
guarantees an appropriate education for all handicapped
children. It forbids tests and other evaluation procedures
that discriminate ethnically or racially" (p. 391). As
Swenson also points out, Public Law 94-142, the Education for All Handicapped Children Act, ensures, among
other things, that there will be a correct and proper evaluation for any child designated as being handicapped
(Woody, La Voie, and Epps, 1992).

Case law has also had an impact on assessment for
special education. For example, the California case of
Larry P. v. *Riles* (343 F.Supp. 1306, 1972) revealed that
intelligence tests had been applied in such a manner that
a disproportionately large number of African-American
children had been classified as mentally retarded. The
court enjoined the San Francisco school district "from
placing black students in classes for the educable mentally
retarded on the basis of criteria which rely primarily on

the results of I.Q. tests as they are currently administered, if the consequence of use of such criteria is racial imbalance in the composition of such classes" (p. 1315). Note that some wags have chosen to interpret this legal decision incorrectly as being a ban on intelligence testing. First, the decision applies, at the most, to California, but second, the decision (quite correctly) bans discriminatory use of intelligence tests, not the tests per se. However, there are cases from other jurisdictions, including those from federal courts (which could potentially have a more far-reaching influence than a state court's decision) that create similar legal mandates for testing practices. Carpignano (1987) describes subsequent related legal actions, which revealed "legal, political, social and economic pressures from a number of sources" (p. 1).

From the point of view of the clinical psychologist, the statutory and case legal decisions are joined in importance by disciplinary dictates. An important treatise is *Standards for Educational and Psychological Testing* produced jointly by the American Educational Research Association (AERA), the American Psychological Association (APA), and the National Council on Measurements Used in Education (NCMUE) (1985). By its title alone, it is apparent that authoritative standards are set forth to contradict the criticisms that have been directed, justly or unjustly, at psychological testing. Moreover, the "Ethical Principles of Psychologists and Code of Conduct" (APA, 1992) provides that strict standards relevant to appropriate use of assessment methods be maintained; test construction embrace "scientific procedures and current professional knowledge for test design, standardization, validation, reduction or elimination of bias, and recommendations for use" (p. 1603); and "Psychologists who perform interventions or administer, score, interpret, or use assessment techniques are familiar with the reliability, validation, and related standardization or outcome studies of, and proper applications and uses of, the techniques they use" (p. 1603).

In keeping with the legal principle of informed consent (whereby a client has a right to know the positive and negative qualities of an intervention and to accept or reject it accordingly), the APA ethical principles state:

> Unless the nature of the relationship is clearly explained to the person being assessed in advance and precludes provision of an explanation of results (such as in some organizational consulting, preemployment or security screening, and forensic evaluations), psychologists ensure that an explanation of the results is provided using language that is reasonably understandable to the person assessed or to another legally authorized person on behalf of the client [p. 1604].

Extending from the base created by statutory and case law (e.g., on employment and special education) and complementing professional ethics and standards, some states have adopted regulatory rules on psychological testing, such as under the law for licensing psychologists. For example, the Florida Board of Psychological Examiners (1995) adopted Rule 59AA-18.004, which states:

1. The Board finds that the inappropriate use of test instruments is harmful to consumers. The Board finds further that a need exists to set out the minimum standard of professional practice maintained and required of psychologists who use test instruments in the psychologist's practice of psychology.
2. A psychologist who uses test instruments in the psychologist's practice of psychology:
   a. must consider whether research supports the underlying presumptions which govern the interpretive statements which would be made by the test instrument as a result of its completion by any service user;
   b. must be able to justify the selection of any particular test instrument for the particular service user who takes the test at the instruction of the psychologist;
   c. must integrate and reconcile the interpretive statements made by the test instrument based on group norms, with the psychologist's independent

professional knowledge, evaluation and assessment of the individual who takes the test [p. 2118].

Moreover, some states are incorporating by reference the APA ethics, and many other states make at least implicit reliance on them, thereby bracing those assessment-related standards with the authority of the law. All of this is well and good. To be sure, it is probable that such authoritative statements are honored, at least in essence, by the large majority of clinical psychologists. If a clinical psychologist does not honor them, he or she could be subjected to disciplinary sanctions by ethics committees, state licensing boards, and courts (since ethical principles are part of the standard of care for the profession, and a breach of them could lend credence to a malpractice action against the practitioner). On the other hand, the likelihood that all clinical psychologists will, in fact, "indicate any significant reservations that they have about the accuracy or limitation of their interpretations" (as required by APA ethics, p. 1603) to each and every client seems rather slight. In the end, the only "policeman at the elbow" (to rely on an old legal guide) has to be the internalized values, ethics, and standards of the individual practitioner. Of course, this underscores the importance of high quality training before entry into clinical psychology, and continual updating and professional development throughout one's career.

FUNDAMENTAL CONCEPTS

There are two vantage points for viewing a person, either (1) intrapersonal distinctions, or (2) interpersonal comparisons. The principles of individuality are referred to as being *idiographic*, whereas seeking laws that apply to all persons and/or making comparisons of the individual to groups of people is termed *nomothetic*.

Clinical psychologists use both idiographic and nomothetic approaches. When a set of psychological needs are gleaned from personality tests, it is usually an idiographic profile of the client. When the test scores are presented as percentiles, they offer a nomothetic comparison of how the client performed in relation to a normative group performance. The idiographic and nomothetic concepts will receive further clarification throughout this chapter.

Terminology is a common troublemaker in professional literature. For example, it is sometimes difficult to distinguish between the terms *testing*, *measurement*, *evaluation*, *appraisal*, and *assessment*. Mehrens and Lehmann (1991) tell us: "The terms test, measurement, evaluation, and assessment are occasionally used interchangeably, but most users make a distinction among them" (p. 4). This section shall provide both definitions and distinctions.

The first term, *testing*, refers to an instrument or strategy for collecting information or data. For legal purposes, the Florida Board of Psychological Examiners (1995) provide a definition in Rule 59AA-18.004:

> "Test instruments" are standardized procedures which purport to objectively measure personal characteristics such as intelligence, personality, abilities, interests, aptitudes, and neuropsychological functioning including evaluation of mental capacity to manage one's affairs and to participate in legal proceedings. Examples of such tests include intelligence tests, multiple aptitude batteries, tests of special aptitudes, achievement tests, and personality tests concerned with measures of emotional and motivational functioning, interpersonal behavior, interests, attitudes and other affective variables [p. 2118].

As Hanson (1993) puts it: "a test is a representational technique applied by an agency to an individual with the intention of gathering information" (p. 19); and "a test is a special sort of investigation in which the information that is collected is not itself the information that one seeks but is instead a representation of it" (p. 18). Incidentally, Hanson is concerned about the social consequences of the examined life, noting that: testing is making "increasingly minute distinctions" (p. 15); "the testing situation nearly always places test givers in a position of power over test takers" (p. 19); and "several forms of authenticity and intelligence testing pose a threat to the autonomy and dignity of the individual and my suggestion for countering that threat has been to do away with many of the most offensive tests" (p. 314).

Measurement is a rather broad term, yet reasonably easy to define. Aiken (1989) says: "*Measurement*, the assignment of numbers to events, is one of the foundations of science. Almost any effort to describe and classify natural phenomena involves measurement of a sort, albeit sometimes a rather crude level of measurement" (p. 35). Hamersma (1972) states: "Measurement basically is the use of numbers, or numerals, and the way in which the numbers are assigned to data" (p. 6). Mehrens and Lehmann (1991) go further:

> *Test* is usually considered the narrowest of the four terms; it connotes the presentation of a standard set of questions to be answered. As a result of a person's answers to such a series of questions, we obtain a measure of a characteristic of that person. *Measurement* often connotes a broader concept: We can measure characteristics in ways other than by giving tests. Using observations, rating scales, or any other device that allows us to obtain information in a quantitative form is measurement. Also, measurement can refer to both the score obtained and the process used [p. 4].

Thus, *quantitative data* is a key term to remember.

Measurement is commonly sequenced into four scaling levels. Level 1 is the nominal scale, where data are simply classified or named. Level 2 is the ordinal scale, where data are ranked or ordered according to some priority system. Level 3 is the interval scale, which relies on units that are presumably equal distances apart. Level 4 is the ratio scale, where the data have a zero value and progress upward with equality. Table 2.1 clarifies the levels of measurement.

TABLE 2.1 Levels (Scales) of Measurement*

Level (Scale)	Procedures Involved	Restrictions	Appropriate or Permissible Statistics	Examples
I. Nominal	Classify or name data by using numerals	Only counting procedures; no arithmetic	1. Number of cases (Chi-square) 2. Mode 3. Contingency correlation 4. Nonparametric test—Fisher exact probability test, Cochran Q test, X^2 for two or k independent samples	Numbers on football or baseball jerseys, coding in research
II. Ordinal	Ranking or ordering	Only ranking allowed; no arithmetic involved	1. Median 2. Percentiles 3. Nonparametric tests—Kolmogorov-Smirnov, one-sample runs test, Wilcoxon matched-pairs signed ranks test, Mann-Whitney U, Wald-Wolfowitz, Moses test of extreme reactions, Friedman two-way analysis of variance, Kruskal-Wallis, Kendall rank correlation coefficient, Kendall partial rank correlation, Kendall coefficient of concordance, Spearman rank correlation coefficient	Ranking for graduate school selection, quality of cloth, etc.

TABLE 2.1 Levels (Scales) of Measurement* *(continued)*

Level (Scale)	Procedures Involved	Restrictions	Appropriate or Permissible Statistics	Examples
III. Interval	Establishing equal-of units or differences	Addition and Subtraction allowed	1. Mean 2. Standard deviation 3. Rank-order correlation 4. Product-moment correlation 5. Nonparametric tests—Walsh test, Randomization test for matched pairs, Randomization test for two independent samples	Temperature, calender dates, measurement of energy
IV. Ratio	Equality of units and a true "zero" point	No restrictions: addition, subtraction, multiplication, and division are all possible	1. All previously mentioned statistics are permissible including nonparametric statistics 2. Coefficient of variation 3. Logarithmic transformations 4. Nonparametric tests—all possible	Weight, height, volume, money, etc.

* From Hamersma (1972), with permission.

The following are examples of the different levels of measurement in a clinical psychology context. If a clinical psychologist divides a group of subjects according to "normal" versus "abnormal" (with an established data-based definition for the dichotomy), it is a nominal measurement. If a clinical psychologist observes a classroom and ranks the students for being well behaved (in sequence from being well behaved to being poorly behaved), for example, it is ordinal scaling. If a clinical psychologist considers intelligence quotients for a group of subjects, it is interval scaling: "Intelligence quotients (IQs) usually are considered examples of interval scale scores" (Kleinmuntz, 1982, p. 5). If a clinical psychologist does research on the incomes of clients, the money constitutes ratio scaling. Clearly, each of the levels of measurement is used in clinical psychology, but, "In personality assessment, most numerical findings are expressed in ordinal or approximate interval scales" (Kleinmuntz, 1982, p. 5).

The distinction between the terms *evaluation*, *appraisal*, and *assessment* is not as clear as for the term *measurement*. For example, the word *evaluation* has often been given a rather broad definition. Mehrens and Lehmann (1991) acknowledge that evaluation may have at least three foci: reference to the process associated with information used for judging decision alternatives; "the determination of congruence between performance and objectives" (p. 4); and "a process that allows one to make a judgment about the desirability or value of something" (p. 4), with the latter evaluation relying on either qualitative or quantitative data. Evaluation has also been connected to analysis of programs, such as estimating how well a mental health facility fulfills its program objectives.

The word *appraisal* has tended to be defined in qualitative terms, such as quantifying skills for a selection process or developing a mental status report. It seems to convey a connotation of being for a singular task. At one time, it seemed to reflect a subjective synthesizing of case-related information, but that definition no longer has a monopoly on the meaning of appraisal. *Assessment* has become the preferred term for clinical psychology. Matarazzo (1990) asserts: "Competent practitioners in psychology learn from clinical role models during apprenticeship training and from their own subsequent experiences that objective psychological testing and clinically sanctioned and licensed psychological assessment are vastly different, even though assessment usually includes testing" (p. 1000).

There is no shortage of definitions for the term *assessment*. To start with a brief definition, Maloney and Ward (1976) state: "A simple definition for an extremely complex process is that *psychological assessment is a process of solving problems (answering questions)* in which psychological tests are often used as *one* of the methods of collecting data" (p. 5). Kleinmuntz (1982) indicates: "Most psychologists would probably agree on the following definition: Assessment includes all systematic (or standardized) and objective procedures (or devices) for obtaining observations and scores reflecting samples of psychological behavior" (p. 6). Focusing on personality, Sundberg (1977) offers: "For our purposes personality assessment may be defined as *the set of processes used by a person or persons for developing impressions and images, making decisions and checking hypotheses about another person's pattern of characteristics which determine his or her behavior in interaction with the environment*" (pp. 21–22).

It is important to realize that clinical assessment is more than psychological testing. Maloney and Ward (1976) make the distinction:

> Psychometric testing refers to the systematic study of individual differences among people along specified traits or dimensions. The essence of the psychometric test is that the description of people is done in objective, standardized, quantifiable ways. Psychological assessment, on the other hand, is generally a process of solving problems. The basic

differences in the purposes, goals, and methodologies of
these two operations can be illuminated by considering the
following propositions: (1) psychometric testing is primarily measurement oriented, while psychological assessment
is primarily problem oriented; (2) psychometric testing is
primarily concerned with describing and studying *groups*
of people, while psychological assessment focuses on a
description and an analysis of a particular *individual* in a
problem situation; (3) psychometric testing demands little
if any clinical expertise other than that of a psychometrist,
while the role of the clinician or expert is crucial and integral to the process of psychological assessment [p. 38].

Kleinmuntz (1982) points out that psychological assessment encompasses virtually all types of psychological
tests, as well as procedures for "systematically recording
behavior observations and scoring and quantifying data
gleaned from personal documents, case histories, interviewing, and behavioral analysis" (pp. 6–7). Woody (1980a)
emphasizes four critical points: "First, clinical assessment
is not restricted to objective, standardized, quantifiable
procedures. For example, many of the data might come
from interviews or observations. Second, clinical assessment is individually focused. . . . Third, clinical assessment
is problem oriented. Fourth, the diagnostician, that is, the
assessor, has the responsibility of applying and maintaining astute clinical acumen" (p. xxxi).

Assessment does not, however, include unsystematic
or informal techniques, unless they can, in some way, attain
legitimacy by being processed through the clinical acumen of
the psychologist. Assessment must be predicated on scientifically derived notions, concepts, strategies, and methods.

In a nutshell, assessment is, thus, defined as the application of behavioral science methods, techniques, or strategies to garner information, as will be useful for problem
solving. In the context of clinical psychological services, assessment is joined with therapeutic interventions, consul-
tations, program development, supervision, and evaluation
of services.

CLINICAL VERSUS STATISTICAL PREDICTION

As will be discussed in the next section on clinical judgment, it is important to recognize, as Matarazzo (1990) reminds us: "Rather than being totally objective, assessment involves a subjective component. Specifically, it is the activity of a licensed professional, an artisan familiar with the accumulated findings of his or her young science, who in each instance uses tests, techniques, and a strategy that, whereas also identifying possible deficits, maximizes the chances of discovering each client's full ability and true potential" (p. 1000). In considering this quotation, it is prudent to give special consideration to the terms "assessment involves a subjective component" and that the psychologist is deemed an "artisan." This subjectivity or artistry has spawned one of the greatest debates in clinical psychology, namely clinical versus statistical prediction.

The debate, for the most part, started with Meehl's (1954) treatise, wherein he attacked Allport's (1942) assertion that "psychological causation is always personal and never actuarial" (p. 157), reviewed empirical comparisons of clinical and actuarial predictions, and concluded "in all but one . . . the predictions made actuarially were either approximately equal or superior to those made by a clinician" (p. 119).

For basic definitions, Wierzbicki (1993) indicates: "The clinical method involves learning as much as one can about the individual, constructing some abstract model to explain the individual's psychological functioning, and using this model to derive predictions concerning the individual's future functioning (e.g., response to one treatment versus another, likelihood of becoming violent)" (p. 131). Then Wierzbicki makes an important distinction: "The statistical method, on the other hand, involves classifying the individual among similar cases. Empirical techniques are then used to determine how this class of similar cases has behaved in the past. Then, it is assumed that the case in point will behave similarly to members of the comparison group, and so a prediction is derived for the individual which is based on the group's behavior" (p. 131). As should be evident, the clinical method is idiographic and the statistical or actuarial method is nomothetic.

To this day, each approach has its antagonists and protagonists. In modern clinical psychology, suffice it to say that both approaches continue, with the practitioner's allegiance to one or the other probably dictated by the principles within his or her early training. Note that there is reason to believe that, unless contradicted by clear and convincing evidence, the clinician is apt to adhere to the primacy principle, that is, what is first learned on a particular topic (e.g., psychological assessment) is weighted more heavily than most subsequent learning relevant to the same topic. Nonetheless, the clinical versus statistical debate has likely fostered, at the minimum, a bit of chastened and wisened reflection by clinical psychologists during their assessment services, because they "now attend more closely to the criterion variable they attempt to predict" (Wierzbicki, 1993, p. 150).

CLINICAL JUDGMENT

The scientist–practitioner model maintained and coveted by clinical psychology encounters considerable friction from the human factor inherent to assessment. Stated bluntly, the human condition sometimes rubs science the wrong way!

While for the most part the experimental psychologist can be assured of scientific results by restricting data collection to tabulations of observable behavior or quantifiable performance, the clinical psychologist commonly filters data through his or her subjective ability to recognize, analyze, and interpret (i.e., clinical acumen or expertise). Thorne (1961) states: "The same laws and principles discovered by basic science psychology in relation to psychophysical judgments, perceptual discriminations, etc., also appear to apply to clinical judgments, which are not qualitatively different but simply represent quantitative complications due to the greater complexity of clinical factors requiring judgment" (p. 1).

Clinical psychologists offering assessment services must constantly make judgments, often without clear criteria for the objective under consideration. In other words, the clinical psychologist makes an individualized judgment, yet must fulfill professional standards, which means safeguarding against idiosyncratic preferences or biases.

Clinical judgments can only be made by a professional—a seemingly comparable decision by a layperson is merely a personal opinion. Through such public policy avenues as laws, society has ordained people with certain qualifications to be "professionals." Be it with engineers, medical personnel, clinical psychologists, or other professionals, this ordination may occur without the benefit of impeccable science or proof of quality, but: "professions in which practitioners' (artisans') work products are judged by society to be valid (usable) for many services, despite the absence of the necessary research, primarily on the basis that common experience (of legislators, professional peers, patients, clients, and others) suggests some utility from their services" (Matarazzo, 1990, p. 1015).

The cloak of professionalism carries both benefits (e.g., status, income) and liabilities (e.g., duties, accountability for malpractice). At the present time, professionalism is being revised significantly, with the previously dominant academic/intellectual thrust being augmented, and thus paradoxically diminished, by "influence of markets and private sector employers on the practices of professionals" (Brint, 1994, p. 17). The authority and control being manifested by governmental regulators (with commitment to societal objectives other than promoting the professional discipline per se) creates a press for accountability to nonprofessionals (e.g., government and insurance industry personnel) that will undoubtedly result in redefinition of the term *professionalism*. Perhaps foremost, professional self-determination for services is weakening: "Professions do not necessarily hold unchallenged authority over an area of functional expertise" (Brint, 1994, p. 25).

For the clinical psychologist, clinical judgment is a core ingredient for claiming professional status: "*clinical judgment* properly refers simply to the correctness of the *problem-solving thinking of a special class of persons*, namely clinically trained persons with special levels of training, experience and competence" (Thorne, 1961, p. 7). The success or failure of clinical judgment in satisfying a societal expectation may determine the degree of professional status granted to the specialty in general and, within the profession, to the practitioner in particular. In other words, professional status reflects an awarding of "special class," and clinical judgment is the key to entering that domain.

The highly personal nature of clinical judgment, even with the best-trained clinical psychologist, is always open to variability or error. It would be nice if a clinical psychologist could achieve 100 percent consistency (reliability) or accuracy (validity) with his or her judgments or in comparison with other clinical psychologists, but such does not occur. It is axiomatic that "people in general make biased judgments when under conditions of uncertainty, many studies have demonstrated that clinicians are subjected to the same biases" (Wierzbicki, 1993, p. 146). This is one of the fallibilities of the assessment process that contributed to the clinical versus statistical debate.

Why is inconsistency or inaccuracy allowed in the judgments of clinical psychologists? The answer is that society has recognized that: (1) someone must make clinical judgments to accommodate social order and development; (2) the person should be qualified in some manner; and (3) the profession of clinical psychology produces candidates best suited to meet the needs of society. As mentioned, however, the special status is subject to revision; for example, there will be a diminution of status (and opportunities) if the profession fails to successfully fulfill a societal expectation.

While research reveals difficulties with clinical judgment, it is a pragmatic creation of and for society. As Thorne (1961) states: "Even in view of the admitted invalidity or relative inefficiency of many clinical decisions, society must depend upon clinical decisions because of the practical and economic limitations of life situations" (p. 23).

Professionalism mandates that there be a constant search for scientific support and validation, with a "complete" status probably never being attainable. Further, the practitioner should only assert that he or she is doing the best that can be: (1) done at this particular point in the societal–professional evolution; and (2) offered under the existing conditions, in the particular contextual framework, and to the specific client being served.

RELIABILITY

Reliability refers to the consistency of a measurement or judgment. The lack of reliability is a plague to many procedures in clinical psychology. For example, the development of a psychological test requires proof that the instrument will measure the same thing in the same way twice. The test must have "content reliability," meaning that the test items measure the same factor or construct. There are various statistical formulas for estimating content reliability; these include analysis of the scores after the same test has been administered on two (or more) occasions (called test-retest or temporal reliability), and a division of the test into parts (called the split-half or odd–even reliability).

Cicchetti (1994) provides a useful discussion of test reliability, and offers guidelines for interpreting the significance of a reliability coefficient.

Given the subjectivity of judgments, clinical psychology has special concern about scorer reliability. Here there are two forms: intrajudge and interjudge reliability.

Early research by one of the authors (RHW) exemplifies these two types of reliability. In doing his Ph.D. dissertation on the use of electroencephalography (EEG), the measurement of electrical brain wave activity, and mental abilities tests, he was struck by how the EEGer could rapidly review page after page of tracings and come up with judgments about factors that supposedly delineated the presence or absence of brain dysfunction. A search of journals revealed little evidence to assure that the EEGer would, in fact, evaluate the same EEG protocol exactly the same way twice (i.e., that there would be intrajudge reliability). The EEGer was open minded to examining his functioning, and agreed that it was just assumed that a professional well trained in the use of EEG would be able to make exactly the same judgment twice. He cooperated with a study (Woody, 1966) that presented him with 15 EEGs from behavioral problem boys and 15 EEGs from well-behaved boys (all personal cues regarding the EEG subjects were eliminated), and he judged a series of factors that were commonly relied upon for diagnostic purposes. Eight months later, he rejudged the same EEGs (without knowledge of how he had judged a particular EEG the first time). Without going into all of the findings, suffice it to say that there were indications of problems with intrajudge reliability. As one specific finding, the EEGer was asked to classify each overall record as being in one of five well-defined categories (normal, borderline, mildly abnormal, abnormal, and markedly abnormal). The statistical analysis revealed that the initial rating and the rerating were not significantly related—there was poor intrajudge reliability, even though this was a well-trained, highly experienced EEGer operating under standard conditions.

As might be expected, this poor intrajudge reliability raised the question of interjudge reliability; that is, would two or more EEGers agree with each other? Again, a search of the journals failed to yield any answer, and a trip to one of the most prestigious neuropsychiatric institutes to interview the director (an M.D. neurologist) met with the answer: "There's really no need to study an issue like that, we physicians know what we're doing, of course we agree with our own judgments and with those of our colleagues—the results of your first study must have been due to the EEGer's being poorly trained."

To investigate the matter further, a second study (Woody, 1968) was conducted, wherein three EEGers (with strong credentials) were hired to judge EEG protocols. The second research design was much the same as in the first (intrajudge) study, but this time the focus was on how well the EEGers would agree with each other (i.e., interjudge reliability). Again, there were problems, this time in the realm of interjudge reliability. For example, the three EEGers were asked to simply assign each EEG protocol to either a "normal" or an "abnormal" classification (they had agreed on detailed definitions and criteria for these two classifications). Using only a normal–abnormal dichotomy, the three judges had complete agreement on only 53 percent of the cases; two-judge combinations had complete agreement on 60 to 86.7 percent of the cases. Since EEG plays such a critical role in neurological diagnosis and treatment, these findings certainly raised doubts about the reliability of clinical judgments in this area.

To be sure, clinical use of EEG has progressed since these studies were conducted. There is, however, still reason to question the reliability of judgments for EEG protocols and, indeed, any kind of clinical data (albeit that the contemporary application of computer analysis to EEG and other clinical data assures reliability).

The message should be clear: even well-trained, highly experienced professionals may get involved in judgmental tasks that defy adequate intrajudge or interjudge reliability. But as was pointed out earlier, society can authorize professional practices that are less than perfect, and notwithstanding questionable reliability for clinical assessment procedures, there is public policy endorsement for the clinical judgments. As Thorne (1961) views the public policy endorsement: "The clinicians have the responsibility to go on making decisions in any situation where their predictions are even 1 or 2% better than common sense or pure chance choices" (p. 23).

VALIDITY

There is an old assessment saw that says: "You can have reliability without having validity, but you can't have validity without having reliability." This means that it is possible for, say, two clinical psychologists to agree with each other on some diagnostic notion (there would be interjudge reliability), yet their agreed-upon notion could be false (there would not be validity). But conversely, a judgment based on a diagnostic notion that is true (i.e., one that validly reflects a particular matter) must be consistently appraised (there must be reliability or else the validity does not obtain).

For a definition of validity for clinical assessment in general, the fundamental premise is: Validity is the most important psychometric characteristic or technical attribute of a test or measurement (Kamphaus, 1993; Hoy and Gregg, 1994). The somewhat overused definition is that validity is the degree that a measure, in fact, achieves what it is supposed to accomplish; that is, a test measures what it is supposed to measure. Or as Kaufman and Kaufman (1993) state: "the validity of a test is defined as the degree to which it accomplishes what it was designed to do" (p. 84). Fleshing this out a bit, Salvia and Ysseldyke (1988) say:

Validity refers to the extent to which a test measures what its authors or users claim it measures. Specifically, test validity concerns the appropriateness of the inferences that can be made on the basis of test results. A test's validity is not measured; rather, a test's validity for various uses is judged on a wide array of information, including its reliability and adequacy of its norms. The process of gathering information about the appropriateness of test-based inferences is called *validation* [p. 132].

Mehrens and Lehmann (1991) state: "Validity can best be defined as the extent to which certain inferences can be made accurately from—and certain actions should be based on—test sources or other measurement" (p. 265).

While it is easy to assert that all clinical assessment procedures must be valid (i.e., they must measure what they purport to measure), there are pitfalls. It must be remembered that "Unlike reliability, which is influenced only by unsystematic errors of measurement, the validity of a test is affected by both unsystematic and systematic (constant) errors" (Aiken, 1988, p. 104). Achieving reasonable control of errors in test construction is the backbone of psychological testing. Unfortunately, there are numerous methods or techniques used in clinical assessment that are not predicated on statistically based test construction safeguards, again giving fuel to the clinical versus statistical debate.

There are several types of validity. Let us examine types that have the most relevance to clinical psychology. In the next few paragraphs on validity, the example of psychological tests will be used, but principle applies to other diagnostic strategies as well.

Face validity refers to the fact that the test "appears" to be true. For example, the test items on a depression test look or seem, by a psychologist's subjective judgment, as if they are the kinds of questions that should be asked about depression. While "Whether a test 'looks good' for a particular purpose (face validity) is certainly an important consideration in marketing the test" (Aiken, 1988, p. 104), obviously this offers limited behavioral science proof of validity for justifying professional usage: "face validity is *not* a genuine type of validity at all but albeit an enviable ingredient of a test" (Hamersma, 1972, p. 66).

Content validity comes from logic supporting the test. Like face validity, content validity is, for all practical purposes, a nonstatistical judgment about the test or measurement, albeit that content validity involves a more detailed examination by the expert to determine whether the items "tap the depth and breadth of the area of interest" (Hoy and Gregg, 1994, p. 73). There is usually a "textbook justification" for the material. As Aiken (1988) puts it: "The procedure involves the judgments of subject-matter experts; if they agree that the test looks and acts like a measure of the skill or knowledge it is supposed to assess, then the test is said to possess content validity" (p. 104). While potentially applicable to various assessment strategies, "Content validity has been most closely associated with the development of tests of academic achievement for use in school settings" (Kamphaus, 1993, p. 112). Like face validity, the absence of statistical analysis means that content validity provides, at best, limited proof of validity, but at least there is some expert screening.

Moving to statistical analysis, factorial validity refers to a factor analysis supporting that a test is a relatively pure measure of a given matter. Criterion-related validity encompasses the empirical, concurrent, predictive, and construct forms of validity (Kamphaus, 1993). Empirical validity suggests the relationship between, say, a test and a standard of observable performance. Concurrent validity refers to the agreement between two assessment methods or instruments that claim to be measuring the same factor(s). Nietzel, Bernstein, and Milich (1994) state: "When two assessment devices agree about the measurement of the same quality, they are said to have *concurrent validity*. Predictive and concurrent validity are subtypes of criterion validity, which is a measure of how strongly an assessment result correlates with external criteria of interest" (p. 83). Thus, *criterion validity* reveals the correlation between the score from one test and another measure (such as correlating IQ with grade point average), and moves toward, but does not fully attain, predictive power. Predictive validity has, by this point in the continuum of types of validity, entered the picture, and is, according to Aiken (1989), "of greatest concern in situations involving occupational or educational selection and placement" (p. 85). Caution should be stated, however, that predictive validity is relevant and important to various other assessment purposes as well.

Construct validity is akin to criterion validity (Hamersma, 1972). For definition, Aiken (1989) indicates:

> The *construct validity* of a psychological assessment instrument refers to the extent to which the instrument is a measure of a particular *construct*, or psychological concept, such as anxiety, achievement motivation, extraversion–introversion, or neuroticism. The construct validity of a test, which is the most general type of validity, is not determined in a single way or by one investigation. Rather it involves a network of investigations and procedures designed to discover whether an assessment instrument constructed to measure a certain personality variable is an effective measure of the variable [p. 85].

Aiken opines that construct validity is of greater concern to personality assessment than to educational selection and placement assessment. Mehrens and Lehmann (1991) say that: "Construct validity is important for tests purportedly measuring such characteristics (constructs) as intelligence, motivation, assertiveness, compulsiveness, paranoia, and others" (pp. 269–270).

For construct validity, the clinical psychologist accumulates research findings, formulates hypotheses, and tests statistically for whether there is, in fact, a relationship between a test score and a behavior that it purports to measure. As Lyman (1963) describes it: "With construct validity, we predict the results which logically should be obtained if the test is valid. The prediction is stated concretely enough and precisely enough so that it can be tested statistically. In this way, we actually are checking the validity of both the test and its underlying theory" (p. 30). Lyman (1991) also says: "Construct validity involves an effort to understand the psychological meaningfulness of both the test and the rationale that lies behind the test. Increasingly the term is coming to refer to the entire body of accumulated research on a test" (p. 21).

Construct validity accommodates important statistical analyses and, therefore, generates and merits behavioral science confidence. To go a bit further with the statistical processes, construct validity embraces convergent and discriminant validation:

> To possess construct validity, an assessment instrument should have correlations with other measures of (or methods of measuring) the same construct (*convergent validity*) and low correlations with measures of different constructs (*discriminant validity*). Evidence pertaining to the convergent and discriminant validity of an instrument can be obtained most convincingly by comparing correlations between measures of (1) the same construct using the same method, (2) different constructs using the same method, (3) the same construct using different methods, and (4) different constructs using different methods [Aiken, 1989, p. 86].

Note that "different constructs using different methods" is referred to as the multitrait–multimethod approach.

Construct validity seems to be the preferred standard for psychological tests in this day and age. Federal guidelines still seem to accept the content, construct, and criterion-related forms of validity, depending upon the circumstances. The more stringent accountability being imposed on clinical psychologists by public policy clearly supports that construct validity is the method of choice, and would likely be the prevailing standard in any sort of ethical or legal proceeding associated with the appropriateness of a particular assessment service.

STANDARDIZATION AND NORMING PROCEDURES

Standardization and norming procedures are crucial to the reliability and validity of a psychological test. Using intelligence tests to exemplify standardization, Cicchetti (1994) asserts that "any test of intelligence needs to be based on systematic stratification on the following variables: age; gender; education, occupation, or both; geographic region; and urban versus rural place of residence" (p. 284). Norming involves using psychological test data from the subjects in the systematic stratification; the process involves: "Applying appropriate methods, raw test scores are converted into several primary derived scores: standard scores, national percentile ranks, and age equivalents" (p. 284).

PSYCHOLOGICAL TESTS VERSUS OTHER DIAGNOSTIC STRATEGIES

There is an important distinction between psychological tests based on standardization and norming and certain other diagnostic strategies that lack standardization and norming. Taking an example from personality testing, while the Minnesota Multiphasic Personality Inventory-Second (MMPI-2) yields scores based on large samples of criterion-referenced groups of human subjects (it has been standardized via normative sampling), the Thematic Apperception Test (TAT) offers no standardized scores and relies on the subjective interpretation of the clinical psychologist (both the MMPI-2 and the TAT will be discussed in chapter 3). To a limited degree, these other diagnostic strategies, such as the TAT, have been standardized, in that there is a set way to: (1) administer the test; (2) collect and formulate the data; and (3) produce clinical interpretations. But for the most part they do not have the benefit of numerical–empirical references to large samples of human subjects.

As will be discussed in chapter 3, the foregoing distinction between psychological tests and certain other diagnostic strategies does not, in any manner, mean that diagnostic strategies that are nonstandardized or nonnormative do not merit inclusion in clinical psychology. Rather, it only means that these other diagnostic strategies are different in nature from psychological tests, and the data obtained by them must be viewed and treated for what they are—nonstandardized data that must be interpreted without the benefit of norms.

NORM-BASED INTERPRETATIONS

When a psychological test is developed, the statistical analysis leads to norms; that is, there is a statistical summary of how the human subjects performed on the test. Consequently, certain statistics are computed (such as the mean, the standard deviation, and other estimates of central tendency) that provide objective signposts for the clinical psychologist's interpretation. The common bell-shaped curve that reflects the normal distribution of test scores is presented in Figure 2.1.

The standards of the American Educational Research Association/American Psychological Association/National Council on Measurement in Education (AERA/APA/NCME, 1985) have specific requirements for how normative data are established. In addition to the normative data that initially establish a test, norms should be updated, and care should be taken to avoid using the test with a client or for a diagnostic issue that would not be compatible with the standardization or normative data.

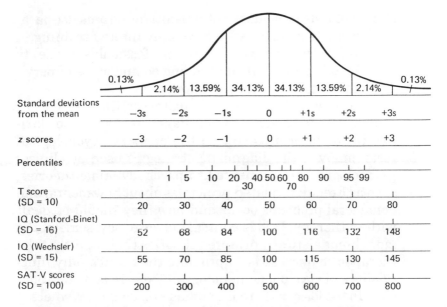

Figure 2.1. Relationships Among Derived Scores. Adapted from *Methods of expressing test scores, Test Service Bull.* No. 48. New York: The Psychological Corporation, January 1955, p. 2.

DIAGNOSIS

Historically, being a diagnostician carried special prestige. To this day, many mental health treatment programs require: (1) a senior-level professional to evaluate every case, perhaps by chairing an interdisciplinary case conference (wherein, for example, diagnostic ideas from a psychiatrist, a clinical psychologist, a clinical social worker, and others are pooled to formulate a comprehensive diagnostic picture); (2) the formulation of an individualized treatment plan, with the senior-level professional's assuring that the approach is appropriate for and in the best interests of the particular client or patient; and (3) the assignment of the case to a therapist, one who has the skills specifically needed and who is often (but not always) a junior-level professional working under the supervision of a senior clinician. Indeed, some mental health programs use para-professionals (persons who have only limited training in human services and who are not professionals per se) to provide follow-up treatment, doing so under the supervision of the senior-level professional.

To be sure, there are differing theoretical views about the importance and nature of diagnosis. As will be clarified in the later material on the primary psychological tests, many of the diagnostic strategies used by clinical psychologists are connected to psychodynamic theories, such as Freudian-related principles about how mental and behavioral problems occur and how they should be dealt with in therapy. This is contrasted with, say, some of the more humanistically oriented theories that posit that the therapeutic purpose is to promote the client's fully functioning self via a phenomenological "be here now" relationship. In the former, there is emphasis on diagnosis, whereas in the latter there is minimal, if any, consideration given to diagnosis (some humanistic therapists believe it is inappropriate to diagnose because to do so would be to tamper with and impede the client's existential flow).

While all sorts of theories and, consequently, views about diagnosis abound in clinical psychology, the prevailing stance is that psychological assessment (encompassing diagnosis) is the foundation on which treatment ideas are built. Thus, being a diagnostician is an inextricable part of being a clinical psychologist.

Diagnostic awareness of mental conditions was probably present in the Stone Age and has continued through the centuries and in virtually every society and culture (Menninger, 1944). In describing the history of "mental healing," Bromberg (1975) identifies a 7000-year-old framework that was "influenced indirectly, and sometimes directly, by political philosophies, religions and neo-religions, mythologies and folklore, science and theories of ego function, as well as economic and cultural realignments" (p. 1). Hippocrates classified mental disorders into mania, melancholia, and phrenitis. Plato studied a variety of mental cases, including those of individuals who committed criminal acts. Aristotle questioned whether mental disorders were caused by psychological factors (e.g., frustration and conflict) and tended to view them as being a reflection of underlying organic difficulties (Coleman, 1956). Through the Middle Ages, demonology, mass madness, and witchcraft prefaced a more modern awareness of mental illness.

In 1400, the Bethlem Royal Hospital (Bedlam) was established in London (the citizenry could come and view the patients for a penny a look), and other countries followed suit. Hospitals were opened in Mexico in 1566, France in 1641, Russia in 1764, and Austria in 1784.

In the United States, Benjamin Franklin guided the development of the Pennsylvania Hospital in Philadelphia (which opened in 1756 with a few cells or wards for the mentally ill). In 1773, Williamsburg, Virginia, was the site of the first United States hospital exclusively for mental patients (Coleman, 1956). Obviously, diagnostic awareness is nothing new.

In clinical psychology, the term *nosology* refers to the naming and classification of human diseases or conditions. Throughout the evolution of mental health services, there has been a press to have a system for classifying the mental disorder or condition.

One of the first ancestors of modern-day psychiatric nosology was Emil Kraepelin (1856–1926), a German psychiatrist who conceptualized symptoms into clusters or syndromes, using the labels manic-depressive illness and dementia praecox (Kraepelin, 1907). Eugen Bleuler, another German psychiatrist, later changed the name of the dementia praecox syndrome to schizophrenia (Bleuler, 1912). The Kraepelin–Bleuler efforts were the onset of a series of nosological systems embraced by diagnosis.

In dissecting the meaning of diagnosis, it should be underscored that it is more than nosology: "a diagnostic point of view fosters a way of approaching clinical issues and conceptualizing them" (Shevrin and Shectman, 1973, p. 467). Nosology provides terms or labels that are connected to carefully thought out diagnostic syndromes, categories, or classifications. Classifying persons has always received criticism: "Of course, there will always be those who resent any attempts at classification or who, for example, favor dynamic-Freudian systems rather than descriptive-Kraepelinian ones" (Phares, 1992, p. 142). Aside from theoretical considerations, there is concern that: "(a) diagnostic labels can harm a client; and (b) diagnostic labels serve little purpose in the treatment of a client" (Wierzbicki, 1993, p. 97).

There are, however, benefits from a classification system, such as for facilitating proper treatment decisions, research, and interprofessional communications (Nietzel, Bernstein, and Milich, 1994). As Phares (1992) puts it:

> Classification systems are necessary; otherwise, our experience and our consciousness become a chaotic array of events. By abstracting the similarities and the differences among the events of our experience, we can establish categories of varying width and purposes that allow us to generalize and predict. If our categories are too broad, then they may not be functional. . . . A major problem is that clinicians have come to expect too much from psychiatric classification systems [p. 144].

Care must always be exercised when making use of a classification, namely the clinical psychologist should not go beyond the purposes of classification. More will be said on this caveat shortly. Even critics of the reliability of diagnosis accept that classification systems have social and professional utility, maintaining logically that: "The criticism that diagnostic labels may harm a client must be weighed against their potential benefit to the client" (Wierzbicki, 1993, p. 101).

Related to misuses of diagnostic labels, there has long been concern about the heavy reliance placed on classifications by service facilities and insurance companies (Miller, Bergstrom, Cross, and Grube, 1981), using the labels to have a means for keeping track of cases via a set classification system and assuring that the therapy for which health insurance reimbursement is sought is predicated on a relevant diagnosis. In recent years, with the expansion of third-party payment sources for health care, the issue of whether a disorder is eligible for coverage commonly hinges on the classification assigned by the clinician.

The issue of not expecting too much from or going beyond the purposes of a classification system deserves emphasis. Of importance, the American Psychiatric Association's (1994) *Diagnostic and Statistical Manual of Mental Disorders* (DSM-IV) makes it clear that:

> In DSM-IV, there is no assumption that each category of mental disorder is a completely discrete entity with absolute boundaries dividing it from other mental disorders or from no mental disorder. There is also no assumption that all individuals described as having the same mental disorder are alike in all important ways. The clinician using DSM-IV should therefore consider that individuals sharing a diagnosis are likely to be heterogeneous even in regard to the defining features of the diagnosis and the boundary cases will be difficult to diagnose in any but a probabilistic fashion [p. xxii].

The DSM-IV points out that "A common misconception is that a classification of mental disorders classifies people, when actually what are being classified are disorders that people have" (p. xxii).

Diagnosis is usually viewed as being concerned about psychopathology. After all, seldom is a diagnosis formulated for anyone not seeking treatment. Diagnosis should, however, carry an awareness of health or hygiology as well. There should be an accommodation of normality along with recognizing abnormality.

Persons seeking the services of a clinical psychologist, even those needing psychotherapy, are not to be viewed as categorically or permanently "abnormal" or "mentally disturbed." An important attainment for our society is that there is no reason to be ashamed of needing therapy. Indeed, the term *mental illness* is secondary to the term *mental health*. Moreover, about 25 percent of the "normal" population suffers from a significant degree of emotional disturbance (M. J. Goldstein, Baker, and Jamison, 1980). Since there is a substantial amount of mental disturbance among "normals," comparisons of the test results from clients with those of everyday folk do not always reveal abnormal distinctions; nonetheless, psychological testing of normal characteristics can aid in understanding the clinical issues.

Diagnosis has a nexus to classification, but is much more than labeling. Diagnosis accommodates interprofessional communication and treatment planning and predictions: "diagnosis conveys information and permits professionals to make predictions about the client's symptomatology, etiology, psychophysiology, treatment, and prognosis" (Wierzbicki, 1993, p. 100).

Diagnosis is a multifaceted process. Woody (1969) sets forth three requirements: "the present functioning or characteristics should be evaluated and described; possible causative factors or etiology should be posited; and a prognosis should be made and a treatment approach recommended" (p. 77). Determining the recommended treatment approach necessitates, in effect, making a probability statement about how the patient will respond to the various treatment alternatives. The treatment decision includes recognizing and considering the availability of resources. For example, it may be that the client would respond better to intensive psychotherapy, but the financial picture leads to only occasional supportive counseling being available. Beller (1962) posits six requirements for diagnosis: "observation, description, a delineation of causation or etiology, classification, prediction or prognosis, and control-modification or treatment plan" (p. 109). Arbuckle (1965) comments: "Diagnosis may be considered as the analysis of one's difficulties and the causes that have produced them. More clinically, it may be thought of as the determination of the nature, origin, precipitation, and maintenance of ineffective abnormal modes of behavior. More simply, it may be considered as the development by the counselor of a deeper and more accurate understanding and appreciation of the client" (p. 220). Arbuckle has generally been aligned with the humanistic approach to therapy, which (as discussed earlier) tends to value diagnosis a bit differently from the psychodynamic approach.

Diagnosis is dependent upon the qualities of the relationship between the diagnostician and the client: "In the diagnosis of mental disorders the diagnostician, through the *medium of a personal relationship, elicits and observes* a range of *psychological functioning* which he considers *relevant on some theoretical grounds* for understanding the disorder so that he can make a *recommendation* which stands a good chance of being acted on as a basis for dealing with the disorder" (Shevrin and Shectman, 1973, p. 451). Shectman (1973) goes further: *"Diagnosis can work when it is based not on labels but on establishing relationships which permit the observation of psychological functioning and in turn leads to an appreciation of a patient's internal experience and understanding of it and the drawing of proper conclusions"* (p. 524).

Diagnosis is not a permanent framework, be it for the client or for the profession. For the client, it is assumed that a diagnosis can and should change—therapeutic interventions are intended to alter emotions and behaviors and, therefore, the diagnosis should change accordingly.

For the profession, diagnosis is simply a product of the evolutionary processes of professionalization. Part of the public policy mandate for the mental health professions calls for diagnosis—just as public policy changes, so do the tenets of diagnosis. For example, the criteria for various DSM categories have been changed throughout the four editions (actually, five editions, the third edition was revised before it was replaced by the DSM-IV) to accommodate public attitudes (e.g., those regarding alcoholism, homosexuality, and so on). Rosenhan (1975) states: "Unlike most medical diagnoses, which can be validated in numerous ways, psychiatric diagnoses are maintained by consensus alone" (p. 464).

The foremost present-day nosological system is that of DSM-IV (American Psychiatric Association, 1994). The basic purpose is to provide definitions of and criteria for psychiatric nomenclature, as would facilitate medical record keeping and differential diagnosis. While differential diagnosis (selecting a particular diagnosis for a given patient from the array of potential diagnoses) is accommodated by the DSM-IV, "Making a DSM-IV diagnosis is only the first step in a comprehensive evaluation" and "the clinician will invariably require considerable additional information about the person being evaluated beyond that required to make a DSM-IV diagnosis" (p. xxv).

Fulfilling the basic purpose is not an easy matter. Stagner (1948) states: "Much of science consists of a search for adequate definitions. This is necessary not merely because man is generally happier when he has a neat system for classifying ideas; increasing precision of definitions frequently results in focusing research more sharply and revealing important truths which had previously been ignored" (p. 1).

When consideration is given to the numerous dimensions of diagnosis (e.g., description of present functioning, an etiological statement, and a prediction- or prognosis-oriented treatment plan, to use a three-dimensional model), it is obvious that the "search for adequate definitions" seems destined to encounter barriers. Since psychiatric nomenclature or nosology is applied with a multitude of professional inputs (e.g., the context of treatment, the type of patient, the disciplinary identity of the professional, and the theoretical orientation of the professional), there is equal surety that there will be continuation of the controversy (described earlier) about the propriety and adequacy of any nosological system, including the DSM-IV.

To the credit of the American Psychiatric Association, the DSM-IV sets forth various caveats about its usage, thereby hoping to prevent distortion of its basic purpose. For example, the DSM-IV acknowledges the limitations of the categorical approach, urges use of expert clinical judgment, prescribes and proscribes certain uses of the DSM-IV in forensic settings, recognizes the importance of ethnic and cultural considerations, and so on.

It should be noted that the DSM system has suffered countless attacks on its adequacy. Nonetheless, it has weathered many storms of controversy. Nathan and Harris (1983) compared the structure of the first two editions. They indicate that the first edition (American Psychiatric Association, 1952), known as the DSM-I, had 104 diagnoses, using the major categories of acute brain disorders (13 diagnoses); chronic brain disorders (25 diagnoses); mental deficiency (6 diagnoses); psychotic disorders (17 diagnoses); psychophysiologic autonomic and visceral disorders (10 diagnoses); psychoneurotic disorders (7 diagnoses); personality disorders (18 diagnoses); and transient situational personality disorders (8 diagnoses). They say that the second edition (American Psychiatric Association, 1968), DSM-II, had 146 diagnoses, using the major categories of mental retardation (6 diagnoses); organic brain syndrome (40 diagnoses); psychoses not attributed to physical conditions listed previously (24 diagnoses); neuroses (11 diagnoses); personality disorders and certain other nonpsychotic mental disorders (33 diagnoses); psychophysiologic disorders (10 diagnoses); special symptoms (10 diagnoses); transient situational disturbances (5 diagnoses); and behavior disorders of childhood and adolescence (7 diagnoses).

The reason for citing each major category and the number of possible diagnoses for each one is to point out the changes in terms and diagnoses over the 16-year period. Does the absence of a first-edition category from the second edition mean that the mental disorder has been cured and eliminated? Does a new second-edition category, one that was not included in the first edition, mean that a new mental disorder has developed and been recognized for the first time in history? Does the fact that the number of diagnoses within a category has changed from the DSM-I to the DSM-II (such as neurotic conditions increasing from 7 to 11 diagnoses) mean that the categorical mental disorder is decreasing or increasing in our society? The answer to each of these questions is no. The changes reflect Rosenhan's (1975) previously cited view: "psychiatric diagnoses are maintained by consensus alone" (p. 464).

In 1994, the DSM-IV further expanded classifications, having 16 major diagnostic classes and one additional section, and numerous diagnostic features, subtypes, and specifiers. Due to the quantity, the captions cannot be presented herein, but every serious student and practitioner of clinical psychology should be familiar with them. Criteria are set forth for the clinical disorders.

The DSM-IV uses a multiaxial assessment model. That is, the assessment considers five different domains of information that can be used to facilitate clinical treatment planning and outcome predictions. The axes and their components are:

Axis I—Clinical Disorders and Other Conditions that May Be a Focus of Clinical Attention
  Disorders Usually First Diagnosed in Infancy, Childhood, or Adolescence (*excluding Mental Retardation*)
  Delirium, Dementia, and Amnestic and Other Cognitive Disorders
  Mental Disorders Due to a General Medical Condition
  Substance-Related Disorders
  Schizophrenia and Other Psychotic Disorders

Mood Disorders
Anxiety Disorders
Somatoform Disorders
Factitious Disorders
Dissociative Disorders
Sexual and Gender Identity Disorders
Eating Disorders
Sleep Disorders
Impulse-Control Disorders Not Elsewhere Classified
Adjustment Disorders
Other Conditions That May Be a Focus of Clinical Attention [p. 26].

Axis II—Personality Disorders and Mental Retardation
Paranoid Personality Disorder
Schizoid Personality Disorder
Schizotypal Personality Disorder
Antisocial Personality Disorder
Borderline Personality Disorder
Histrionic Personality Disorder
Narcissistic Personality Disorder
Avoidant Personality Disorder
Dependent Personality Disorder
Obsessive–Compulsive Personality Disorder
Personality Disorder Not Otherwise Specified
Mental Retardation [p. 27].

Axis III—General Medical Conditions (with ICD-9-CM codes)
Infectious and Parasitic Diseases (001–139)
Neoplasms (140–239)
Endocrine, Nutritional, and Metabolic Diseases and Immunity Disorders (240–279)
Diseases of the Blood and Blood-Forming Organs (280–289)
Diseases of the Nervous System and Sense Organs (320–389)
Diseases of the Circulatory System (390–459)
Diseases of the Respiratory System (460–519)
Diseases of the Digestive System (520–579)
Diseases of the Genitourinary System (580–629)
Complications of Pregnancy, Childbirth, and the Puerperium (630–676)

Diseases of the Skin and Subcutaneous Tissue (680–709)
Diseases of the Musculoskeletal System and Connec-
tive Tissue (710–739)
Congenital Anomalies (740–759)
Certain Conditions Originating in the Perinatal Period
(760–779)
Symptoms, Signs, and Ill-Defined Conditions (780–799)
Injury and Poisoning (800–999) [p. 28].

Axis IV—Psychosocial and Environmental Problems
Problems with Primary Support Group
Problems Related to the Social Environment
Educational Problems
Occupational Problems
Housing Problems
Economic Problems
Problems with Access to Health Care Services
Problems Related to Interaction with the Legal System/
Crime
Other Psychosocial and Environmental Problems [p. 30].

Axis V is Global Assessment of Functioning, which is based
on a scale (ranging from "Superior functioning in a wide
range of activities" to "persistent danger of severely hurt-
ing self or others" and "Inadequate information"). Psychological, social, and occupational functioning are considered
on a hypothetical continuum of mental illness (physical
and environmental limitations are not included). As mentioned before, the various disorders have criteria that must
be satisfied to justify use of a particular classification, with
general consideration being given to temporal factors (e.g.,
age of onset, frequency of occurrence), specific symptoms,
and supportive and/contradictive conditions and considerations (as would be useful for differential diagnosis).

It seems highly probable that the DSM-IV will dominate clinical diagnosis for years to come given its prominence in mental health services. It will not, however, be
the permanent nosological system. Due to shifts in public
attitudes, professional politics, and research advances
(e.g., relevant to the efficacy of treatment alternatives),

the DSM system will continue to evolve. Frank (1975) asserts: "Yet despite the many revisions . . . we have never seemed to find a truly satisfactory system of classification of psychopathology" (p. 5).

Given the previously mentioned reasons for changes in the DSM system (i.e., shifts in public attitudes, professional politics, and research–academic advances), concern is justified as to whether the DSM system has been structured, at least in part, to exclude nonmedical professionals. Schacht and Nathan (1977) suggest that DSM-III may be a promotion of psychiatry's control over the other mental health professions, as opposed to being an honorable attempt to meet the mental health needs of our society. Nathan and Harris (1983) acknowledge a psychiatric denial of this alleged motive but conclude "suspicion persists among some psychologists" (p. 309). To date, the DSM-IV is too new to have generated substantial analysis and criticism relevant to possible ulterior or nefarious motives.

Controversy based on disciplinary dominance, such as psychiatry over psychology, has minimal, if any, public policy benefit: "The message seems to be that the classification of emotional and behavioral disorders will receive a great deal of professional attention in the foreseeable future, but regrettably that attention may be motivated by professional self-interest (such as political and legal power to increase economic rewards to practitioners) rather than by the desire to develop a classification system that could be used for the benefit of patients" (Woody, 1980a, p. xxxvi).

While there is controversy about and criticisms of the DSM system, it is still the approach to classification and diagnosis that is most relied upon by clinical psychologists. Whatever the approach to classification, including the DSM system, a realistic view must be maintained: the clinical psychologist should keep the nosological system subservient to the diagnostic processes. An essential mandate is: "Clinicians should use labels in such a way as to avoid dehumanizing clients. They should base their diagnoses on objective evidence in order to minimize the potential of subjective perceptual bias" (Wierzbicki, 1993, p. 101). Furthermore, diagnosis should use classification in a technical–adjunctive manner, rather than classification dictating or controlling the diagnosis.

Finally, it is important to accept that diagnosis can no longer be an isolated event, an "end product." Rather, diagnosis in clinical psychology is to be used as a conceptual-analytic framework and source of data-based formulations for individualized treatment planning (see Woody, 1991, for guidelines for individualized treatment planning).

PSYCHOLOGICAL REPORTS

Within clinical psychology, what function provides the psychologist with the greatest satisfaction? Obviously the answer to that question will be determined, to some degree, by the characteristics and preferences of the individual psychologist.

Subjectively and all things being equal, the all-encompassing nature of the scientist–practitioner model supports that the ultimate reward might come from contributing new behavioral science knowledge for the well-being of society and professionalism (e.g., conducting a research project and authoring a scholarly article for a learned journal). If that be so, perhaps the penultimate reward is producing a psychological report.

When clinical psychologists gather and talk about their work, whether it be therapy, assessment, or otherwise, it seems that their comments inevitably center on what should be included in a psychological report. The typical clinical psychologist tends to view the psychological report as the culmination of effort, a documentation of the quality of service. Commonly, considerable time and personal concern are committed to the preparation of the psychological report, because it evidences the psychologist's expertise.

In general, it seems that the psychological report is most often thought of as being assessment oriented. This is due, no doubt, to the fact that, among mental health and other health care practitioners, psychologists have unique assessment skills. About a half-century ago, the reknowned psychiatrist William Menninger (1948) declared: "the diagnostic function of the clinical psychologist is now well established" (p. 389)—and so it continues to this day.

Since assessment serves an umbrella for most (if not all) other clinical psychology services (e.g., individual treatment planning requires a diagnosis that emanates from assessment), the results of the assessment must be communicated effectively to the client and other professionals. In this era when the clinical psychologist is an integral part of the total health care team, psychological assessment reports are considered crucial and awarded elevated importance in multidisciplinary clinical decision making.

The psychological report is not confined to assessment data per se. It may also be the vehicle for communicating about virtually any aspect of clinical psychology. That is, a psychologist may prepare a report based solely of therapeutic interventions, which may, of course, have had a prefacing assessment that was reported previously and/ or will receive consideration in the report about treatment.

In general, the psychological report has at least four definite purposes:

1. to answer referral questions as explicitly as possible, depending on how well defined the questions are;
2. to provide the referring agent with additional information when it is relevant to his or her work with the client and when it is appropriate to the use the report will be put to (this includes providing a general description of the client);
3. to make a record of the assessment activities for future use;
4. to recommend a specific course of action for the report's recipient to follow in his or her work with the client [Ownby, 1987, p. 16].

In other words, the psychological report should have practical utility. It provides information that will justify present services and enhance subsequent services to the client.

The theoretical framework for the psychological report is constructed from principles of behavioral science. That is, reliance is upon, among other things, information that is reliable and valid. The clinical significance of the information is, of course, determined subjectively by the psychologist, as guided by academic and scholarly notions. Whenever clinical judgment is involved, there is the risk of bias; the psychologist must strive to avoid any statement that is not supported by the facts of the situation.

The theoretical framework will be influenced by the professional viewpoints of the psychologist. From the plethora of theories pertaining to the human behavior, the psychologist will posit statements, factual and opinion, that describe the client, as necessary for subsequent professional purposes (e.g., the sort of services that should be provided in the future). Here again, the risk of biasing statements must be monitored and minimized, and ideally eliminated. For example, certain theories may accommodate zealous promotion of ideas that are different from what would be embraced by other theories; apostolic allegiance to any singular theory could jeopardize the scientific elements of the report—the psychologist must prevent such contamination in the report.

Exactly what should be contained in the psychological report will be determined to a large extent by the needs of the particular client. Perhaps most exemplary, each client comes to the psychologist with a referral question (be it posed by another professional or by the client) for which an answer is sought. The psychologist's services, especially in the realm of assessment and diagnosis, are directed toward formulating an answer. Even if the services are primarily therapeutic (i.e., not assessment per se), there is still a "question" underlying the intervention, which will merit an "answer" when feedback is given, whether it is to the client in the form of a verbal report or in a formalized psychological report. The all-important referral question may well be the determinant of the subsequent strategies that are implemented, and certainly necessitates coverage in the psychological report. To accommodate the idiosyncratic needs of the client, there can be no uniform structure and contents of the psychological report cannot be preordained. Beyond the client, there will be influence from the psychologist's theoretical position and competencies. The setting in which the services occur will also influence the structure and contents. For example, a report from a mental health clinic might be quite different from what would come from a school, even though the purpose (e.g., the referral question) and the child were the same in both contexts.

Structurally, the various influences must be accommodated. In general, Wolber and Carne (1993) indicate the format should include:

    I. TITLE AND DEMOGRAPHICS
   II. SOURCE AND REASON FOR REFERRAL
  III. ASSESSMENT INSTRUMENTS AND EVALUA-
       TIVE PROCEDURES
   IV. BACKGROUND INFORMATION (HISTORY)
    V. BEHAVIORAL OBSERVATIONS
   VI. ASSESSMENT RESULTS
       A. INTELLECTUAL AND COGNITIVE FUNCTION-
          ING
       B. PERSONALITY FUNCTIONING
          1. EMOTIONAL
          2. INTRAPSYCHIC
          3. INTERPERSONAL
       C. IMPRESSIONS
  VII. SUMMARY AND RECOMMENDATIONS [p. 11].

If the report is primarily diagnostic, Ownby (1987) believes the report should include the reason for the referral, background information (previous assessment results, school and social history, and so on), observations (from diverse contexts), assessment tools and results, and summary and recommendations.

The contents of the report will be shaped by the same influences that determined the structure. Ownby (1987) seems to give emphasis to "middle-level constructs," described as: "terms which are commonly used in explanation of clients' behavior but which often do not have precise shared definition" (p. 37). This would include terms like *intelligence, perceptual skills, anxiety,* and the like. Tallent (1993) appears to allow the contents to flow from the "case focus," meaning the conceptualization of the report whereby: "The psychologist must adapt these general interpretive meanings to the specific case and mission, determine the central and pertinent topics with which to deal, and develop the interpretations (conclusions) in these topic areas as the mission requires" (pp. 135–136). He organizes the report around central themes, with the psychologist unabashedly "supplying appropriate emphasis to content as literary creativity will permit" (p. 139). Interestingly for the latter, Tallent cites certain techniques clearly intended to promote persuasion in the mind of the reader: "These include the order of presentation, the skillful and appropriate use of adjectives, and the use of vivid illustrative material. Less often the psychologist might resort to the use of underlining, capitalization, dramatic presentation (such as is produced by a clipped statement), or an exclamation point" (p. 139). This raises an important point. The psychological report should be tailored to influence the mind of the reader; indeed, it may be appropriate to actively seek to persuade the reader to accept a particular viewpoint. To the contrary, it is easy to recognize that a quest to be persuasive carries the risk of over-emphasis. Care must be exercised to be sure that the message is, in fact, empirically based.

Another important point relevant to the contents of the psychological report is the language used. Especially problematic is the inclusion of psychological terms. Needless to say, there are certain words, particularly diagnostic or nosological labels, that can be stigmatizing, and should be avoided as much as possible. While power words about aberrant or bizarre behavior might be provocative, or highfallutin phrases might seemingly aggrandize the stature of the psychologist, the purpose of the report can be best accomplished by language and word choices that are compatible with the needs and characteristics of the reader. Seldom, if ever, will a psychological term be irreplaceable.

Also relevant to the language and words used, the overall importance attributed to the psychological report means that it may well be relied upon for, literally, years to come, and it may well be accessed by a variety of sources that cannot be knowledgeably contemplated or identified at the time that the report is written. For example, while the report may be written for, say, a referring pediatrician, there is the possibility that the report will eventually be used in a child custody legal proceeding. The foregoing does not mean that the report should suppress or exclude information that is important to the purpose; it means only that consideration must be given to maximizing the benefits for the client, and this objective commonly is dependent upon the language and words used.

Special emphasis should be given to the summary or conclusions. In other words, after presenting the array of information factually and setting forth interpretations, it is critical for the clinical psychologist to integrate all of the material and issues into a cohesive conclusion. While this section will certainly have to be idiosyncratic to the client and the purpose, the scope should include: (1) the immediate and future needs of the client; (2) other medical and nonmedical/psychological evaluations that are needed; (3) the options for intervention, perhaps with a probability statement about the benefits that may be possible from each option; (4) the client's strengths and weaknesses (e.g., degree of insight, motivation for change, systemic supports and other resources, known or likely

barriers to progress); (5) ways to draw help from significant others (e.g., family, friends, coworkers, other professionals); (6) adjunctive services or activities; (7) prognosis
(being as specific as possible); (8) recommendations for
reevaluations and follow up services; and (9) any other
recommendations.

As is readily apparent from the foregoing issues, the
psychological report represents the overall quality of the
clinical psychologist's services. Therefore, report writing
requires careful cultivation, whether during training or
advanced practices.

Chapter 3

Psychological Assessment Methods and Tests

Mike's performance in sales and public relations had been outstanding. At the middle level of management, he had been trustworthy and tireless in his efforts for the company. The Chief Executive Officer (CEO) concluded that Mike should be rewarded with a promotion, but being prudent, she decided to give him the title "Acting Director" of a large department before finalizing the appointment. To the amazement and chagrin of all, Mike floundered hopelessly in the new role. The CEO telephoned the clinical psychologist, saying: "I just can't understand it, Mike has always done so well. He deals with clients and coworkers with qualities that I would be pleased to possess. He has been aggressive and committed to our organization. He has seemed bright and up-to-date in his ideas. I thought that he was a natural for the job of director, but he acts totally differently. It's as if he isn't intelligent enough to handle it." When Mike came to see the clinical psychologist, he was understandably upset, but spoke logically about wanting to find out what was happening. He acknowledged that he just could not grasp the data that he had to work with all day. As it turned out, he had to access the data by computer. In fact, the entire department was heavily reliant upon computerized systems, and this was the first time that Mike had encountered computerization. After taking his case history, the clinical psychologist had no clear-cut clues to go on. One of the first psychological tests to be administered was the Wechsler Adult Intelligence Scale-Revised. While Mike's overall intelligence was well above average, the pattern of the eleven subtests made the clinical psychologist suspicious of a possible neurological problem. Use of neuropsychological tests seemed to confirm the hypothesis. Retracing Mike's history resulted in his recalling, "Oh, yes, I was in an automobile accident about eight years ago. I had a pretty nasty bump on the head, but I got over it okay. I'm sorry I forgot to mention it when you asked me about injuries." The psychological assessment supported the presence of neurological damage, and Mike was referred to a neurologist for further evaluation. The psychological and neurological data were consonant—Mike had apparently suffered a closed-head injury that was restricting his ability to learn new concepts and to deal with computerized data. The CEO was helpful. She knew Mike was a valuable asset to the company, and recognized that he was in the wrong job. After talking with Mike, she tactfully channeled him to another high level position—one that capitalized on his ability to communicate well with people. In a follow-up session with the clinical psychologist, Mike seemed pleased at what he called "the brain detective work" and was happy with his success in his most recent assignment.

While the preceding chapter discussed an academically oriented framework for psychological assessment and diagnosis, this chapter is devoted to describing the assessment methods, techniques, and instruments that are employed in clinical psychology. The focus will be on the ways in which clinical data are collected, analyzed, interpreted, communicated, transformed, and integrated into clinical psychology services.

As a preface, clinical assessment has borne the brunt of much criticism because of its subjectivity. In *Clinical versus Statistical Prediction*, Meehl (1954) examined the theory and method inherent to psychometric (i.e., statistical) and nonpsychometric (i.e., clinical) data sources. His views, which many behavioral scientists found to be convincing, supported the supposition that psychological test results could best be interpreted by a set of rules or an actuarial method. He asserted that interpretations dependent upon the subjective or clinical acumen of the diagnostician would be vulnerable to greater error.

Subsequently, there have been four decades of scholarly research debate (which, on occasion, defensive emotions have rendered "pseudoscholarly"). Wierzbicki (1993) provides an astute review of this continuum of debate. Suffice it to say that there is, indeed, reason to be skeptical of a clinician's subjectively derived judgments. From the preceding chapter, recall the discussion of clinical versus statistical prediction and clinical judgment in general and the electroencephalography (EEG) reliability studies in specific (Woody, 1966, 1968). Consequently, there is a mandate to objectify clinical interpretations as much as possible.

This mandate is leading to more computer analyses of case data, such as with personality tests. There is a trend toward computer-generated psychological reports. The motive for this trend may be economic (computer analyses are cheaper) as much as or more than being an assurance of reliability and validity.

Short of a computer analysis, the diagnostician must adhere to clear-cut criteria for judgments. For example, there should, whenever possible, be a set of criteria that are checked off to ascertain the most appropriate clinical judgment.

In an era when there is a computer on every desk, it is tempting to side with the actuarial approach. Unfortunately, this would be an affront to the public policy that has allowed the development of clinical psychology as a profession. That is, while science may be at the point where a machine can replace a human, society has not reached the stage where it will universally accept such a replacement.

Clinical psychology is one of the *human services*. The full meaning of the term is that humans are served by humans. Science and technology should be used to the optimum level, but to date this does not mean at the exclusion of the diagnostician's clinical judgment.

It is important to recognize that there is no single strategy or instrument that is adequate for any one diagnostic task. Every assessment method and every psychological test has weaknesses. For example, there will be limits to reliability and validity, and this might be evident in the wrongful use of a test. That is, there is often research to suggest that a test developed and standardized for one purpose can probably be used for another purpose (such as estimating intelligence from a single-factor perceptual test). But under most circumstances, all but the wary could be led astray if they used the test in such a way.

Clinical assessment is best performed by relying on multiple sources for collecting data. This would include having more than one method to assess the same quality, such as having two measures of depression to cross-validate a judgment about the presence or absence of the mood.

Not only should there be multiple sources, there should be different types of data-collection sources. When a computer analysis of a personality test is made, it will be reliable and as valid as the interpretations that are programmed into it. On the negative side, a computer analysis is restricted by its program—it cannot accommodate the client's idiosyncratic features. Of course a clinical psychologist can be restricted to his or her "mental program" (i.e., the fixed ideas that dominate diagnostic thinking and concept formation). The solution is to cultivate a diagnostic set that will allow the clinical psychologist to maintain reliable and valid indices, yet integrate any idiosyncratic feature of the client that deserves consideration.

Data-collection sources could include, for example, using data from standardized personality tests to formulate tentative ideas or diagnostic hypotheses that are then checked out or "tested" against the information obtained from a clinical interview and/or life history questionnaire (a second type of data-collection source). Thus, if a personality test score reflected social introversion, yet anecdotal information from a clinical interview or from a life history questionnaire reflected social extraversion, there would be reason to inquire further as to which data source, if any, was reliable and valid on the introversion versus extraversion question.

If there is any universally accepted notion in diagnostics, it is that clinical assessments should make use of multiple psychological tests, not just a single test, no matter how powerful it may be. A battery of tests is preferred for differential diagnosis (Schafer, 1950), because it can eliminate the deficiencies of a single test. Rapaport, Gill, and Schafer (1968) point out: "The advantages of such a battery of tests are that indicators that for some reason are absent from one or several of the tests are likely to be present in others; that indicators in the different tests are likely to support and supplement each other; and that the presence of indicators in some of the tests may call attention to more subtle indicators in others which might otherwise be overlooked" (p. 48).

Of special note, the economy of the psychological assessment battery is often more determinative than what might be best according to professional standards. That is, the time of a clinical psychologist creates an expense (e.g., to the employer and/or the client). The time required for conducting the psychological assessment becomes of pragmatic importance. J. D. Ball, Archer, and Imhoff (1994) provide survey data on the time requirements associated with administering, scoring, and interpreting the most commonly used tests.

It is logical that a test battery should be selected for the particular case, with an allowance for improvisation (additions to or deletions from) as new considerations emerge (Lezak, 1983). Certainly it is axiomatic that the psychological assessment should be tailored to promoting effective treatment, which would mean that the treatment implications of psychological assessment should be weighted heavily when deciding on the test battery (Haynes, 1993).

Notwithstanding the logic of idiosyncratic determinations, the preferences of the clinical psychologist (i.e., his or her "favorite" instruments) and expediency (i.e., the "economy" or cost factor) will be influential. While not speaking well of psychologists' professionalism, Canter (1985) alleges: "The more cumbersome or apparently cumbersome the method seems to be, the more likely the clinician is inclined not to use it" (p. 225).

From surveys of assessment practices (Prout, 1983; Lubin, Larsen, and Matarazzo, 1984; Piotrowski and Keller, 1984; Rosenberg and Beck, 1986; Reschly, Genshaft, and Binder, 1987; Archer, Maruish, Imhof, and Piotroski, 1991; Hutton, Dubes, and Muir, 1992; J. D. Ball et al., 1994) and professional experience, it would seem that the seven main dimensions of a clinical assessment should be:

1. Personal History
2. Behavioral Observations
3. Intelligence
4. Academic Achievement
5. Perception
6. Neuropsychology
7. Personality

In selecting assessment methods and psychological tests to be used as examples of the seven dimensions, there has been reliance on Woody's (1980b,c) encyclopedic review of clinical assessment, as well as the previously cited surveys of assessment practices.

PERSONAL HISTORY

Clinical assessment is predicated upon the client's personal history. While some humanistically oriented psychologists might allege that knowledge of the client's personal history could preordain a diagnostic impression (i.e., knowledge of certain past events could be overvalued), most clinical psychologists believe that every assessment strategy should be tailored to the particular client and that this can best be established by considering the psychosocial history. As Kleinmuntz (1982) states: "The fundamental assumption underlying the collection of case history data is that a person's present personality is part of a continuous process of development" (p. 187). Or as Sundberg (1977) indicates: "Each assessor is to some extent a historian, analyzing the meaning of the person's background for the purposes of today's decisions" (p. 85).

The personal history can be obtained in several ways. For present purposes consideration will be given to: (1) record analysis; (2) use of a life history questionnaire; and (3) clinical interviewing.

Record analysis involves obtaining all relevant professional materials on the client that predate the clinical psychologist's intervention. Relevance would, of course, be defined by the needs and characteristics of the particular client, but usually it requires obtaining educational, psychological, and medical records. Since such records will not be released without the client's approval (or by legal process), it is typically necessary for the client to sign a written release of confidential or privileged communication and to transmit it to the previous service facility or professional.

Upon receipt of these records, the clinical psychologist analyzes the documents for the purposes of: (1) gaining an understanding of the influences (positive and negative) in the client's psychological makeup; (2) identifying any special considerations; (3) evaluating the findings of other assessment data sources; (4) weighing the efficacy of past interventions (i.e., how successful or unsuccessful they have been); and (5) formulating a psychodiagnostic preface for the client that will allow subsequent assessment strategies and other interventions to be optimally beneficial and efficient.

Since the client's records may contain assessment data quite similar in nature to what the clinical psychologist will collect, the selection of strategies or psychological tests for the present evaluation can be based, in part, on omissions in the psychosocial data. Eventually, there can be a comparison of the earlier data with the contemporary data. Thus, the records can create a psychosocial profile that will assist in assessment and that can serve as a baseline for interpreting the present findings.

Records vary considerably in quality. It is often impossible to know the reliability or validity of a comment in a record. Thus, any record analysis is limited to tentative impressions, but they can then be cross-checked by other data sources.

To acquire an up-to-date factual picture, a life history questionnaire may be used. This is usually composed of a set of questions developed by the individual clinical psychologist that covers what is regarded as being essential information.

Generally the questions cover factual matters: the client's name, address, telephone number, employer, social security number, health insurance carrier, spouse's name, names and ages of children, other persons in the household, and so on. Also, it is likely that there will be questions about educational, employment, marital, and health histories. From this point on, the questions will be tailored according to three considerations: (1) the theory espoused by the clinical psychologist (e.g., a clinical psychologist who is a behaviorist would pose questions that would reveal reinforcement contingencies, whereas one who is psychodynamically oriented would pose questions that would reveal emotional conflicts and ego defense mechanisms); (2) the context in which the client is being seen (e.g., a sexual dysfunction clinic would make use of questions about health, marital, and sexual behavior, whereas a vocational counseling center would make use of questions about work, education, training, aptitudes, and interests); and (3) the special needs of the client (e.g., there could be alternative questionnaires, with one being for clients seeking individual therapy and another being used for those coming for family therapy).

The life history questionnaire is usually a document that is either mailed to the client prior to the first appointment or that is completed in the waiting room upon his or her first arrival. A secretary or psychological assistant may oversee the answers. For example, if the client has limited ability to read or write in English, the questions may be asked and the client's oral answers written down by the secretary or psychological assistant. In these instances, the life history questionnaire has become, in a sense, a structured interview.

To return to the issue of reliability and validity for the life history questionnaire (and this also has relevance to clinical interviewing), it should be underscored that any inferences based on these data sources should be regarded as tentative. Studies reveal that there are numerous errors in personal history information given by clients and their family members; often the incorrect information is given in the belief that it is true, but sometimes the error is a result of psychological reasons (e.g., conscious or unconscious dissembling, paranoid exaggeration, and so on) (Kleinmuntz, 1982).

Clinical interviewing is a continuation of the acquisition of life history data, but it is also more. The first contact between the clinical psychologist and the client may, in fact, be the most significant influence on the entire therapeutic formulation, for it is at this time that both parties create a lasting impression of each other. While there will surely be changes in these mutual perceptions as the relationship evolves, the first impression is of crucial importance. Consequently, the clinical psychologist is careful to use the first session to, among other things, foster "facilitative conditions," those qualities in the relationship that will maximize rapport and communication between the two of them, as well as promote psychological growth for the client:

> Facilitative dimensions in communication are those behaviors whereby a message is sent from one person (or speaker) to another person (listener). Successful communication is facilitated by speakers through *owning of feeling* (identifying and disclosing their reactions to themselves and others), *commitment to change* (resolving to work at maintaining and improving communication), *differentiation of stimuli* (identifying and discrimination between various sources of affect and anxiety and the corresponding reactions they stimulate), and *internalization* (immediate awareness of their actions and feelings, with appropriate recognition of the effects and impact of their behaviors). Listeners facilitate communication through *empathic understanding* (responding clearly and directly to the speaker so as to demonstrate hearing and understanding of what the speaker is saying), *concreteness* (responding so as to aid speakers in identifying and discussing their most relevant concerns), *genuineness* (demonstrating spontaneous and congruent reactions in a constructive manner), *respect* (the communication of regard and caring for the speaker's worth as a person), *confrontation* (constructively confronting the speaker with inconsistencies or conflicts which the listener experiences in the interaction), and *immediacy* (the expression of an awareness of dynamics between speaker and listener at any point in the relationship) [Schauble, 1980, pp. 1035–1036].

These facilitative conditions, therefore, accomplish both the collection of data for clinical assessment purposes and therapeutic growth for the client from the first contact with the clinical psychologist.

The first clinical interview is commonly referred to as the *intake*. The term connotes that the client is being taken into the clinical fold. From that initial point on, there is a professional responsibility to the client.

The structure of the clinical interview can vary greatly, essentially for the three reasons stated earlier as the bases for the contents of the life history questionnaire (namely the theoretical orientation of the clinical psychologist, the context of services, and the needs of the client).

A standardized or structured interview follows the same format (i.e., the same general questions are used) with every client. While this may yield a lot of information (of which some could be quantified by the interviewer), it is rather rigid, may foster an interrogation-type of communication, and does not accommodate individual differences between clients.

The unstructured interview "goes with the flow." While certain general topics will likely be covered with every client, the specific questions and their sequence will be different with each client.

Is either the standardized or unstructured interview superior to the other? Kleinmuntz (1982) believes that: "In summary, the advantages and disadvantages of each form of interview . . . are about equal" (p. 180).

As might be inferred, there are different categories of information that may be obtained by clinical interviewing. For general clinical purposes, these would include (but not necessarily be limited to): identifying data; reason for coming; present situation; family constellation; early recollections; birth and development; health; education and training; work record; recreation and interests; sexual development; marital and family data; self-description; choices and turning points in life; views of the future; and any further material (Sundberg, 1977).

Covering these categories adequately can require varying lengths of time, though Sundberg (1977) points out that "with a talkative adult it could easily take two or three hours" (p. 98). This would be to simply give superficial facts—exploration of the issues, which would mean a clear-cut entry into therapy, would likely take much longer. Further, even the "intake" is not limited to a single session, there can be as many interview sessions as are needed for diagnostic purposes, and diagnosis and treatment blend together in clinical interviewing.

Harry Stack Sullivan is commonly thought to be the "father of clinical interviewing." Sullivan was a psychiatrist, psychoanalyst, and founder of the Washington School of Psychiatry. The crux of Sullivan's (1954) approach is that the psychiatric interview contains the essential character-istics and movements of prolonged therapy. As Houck and Hansen (1972) put it: "The diagnostic interview as seen by Sullivan is in essence a therapeutic interview" (p. 125).

Sullivan emphasizes the relationship between the interviewer and the client. Consequently, his approach can be considered to presage the facilitative conditions which were discussed earlier (Schauble, 1980), and can be aligned with the unstructured form:

> It is the interpersonal events and the pattern of their course which generate the data of the interview; that is, the in-terviewer experiences the ways in which the interpersonal events follow each other, what seeming relationships they have to one another, what striking inconsistencies occur, and so on. Thus the data of the interview may come, not so much from the answers to questions, but from the tim-ing and stress of what was said, the slight misunderstand-ings here and there, the occasions when the interviewee got off the subject, perhaps volunteering very important facts which had not been asked for, and so on [Sullivan, 1954, p. 54].

The foregoing does not mean that the interview is not purposeful. On the contrary: "In other words, the inter-viewer is quite clearly aware of the type of significant data that he may reasonably expect in different phases of the interview; he takes steps to secure these data; he validates, or marks for subsequent validation, anything which seems needlessly indefinite or improbable; and he notes most carefully any occasion when material reasonably to be expected *has not* come forth" (Sullivan, 1954, p 55).

Sullivan conceptualizes the interview into four stages. Stage 1 is the formal inception, wherein there is an exchange of preliminary information, such as would be needed for defining the situation and problems (but no interpretations are given). Stage 2 is the reconnaissance, a survey of factors that contribute (positively or negatively) to the client's psychosocial condition (with a focus on problems); tentative formulations about therapy are made. Stage 3 is the detailed inquiry, where an interpersonal data analysis is made; impressions are validated. Stage 4 is the termination stage, and "the therapist makes a clear, explicit statement of the possibility for therapy and the procedure to be used, including the purposes of the particular procedures and the possibility for progress in therapy" (Houck and Hansen, 1972, p. 129); the statement should be supportive, with an avoidance of negativism.

Sullivan's approach lends itself nicely to the definitions of diagnosis discussed in the preceding chapter. It certainly can provide data that will be useful in psychological assessment, for example, through complementing the results of psychological testing, and it ushers in a therapeutic framework at an early, critical point in the client's contact with health care professionals.

The Sullivanian interview, with the necessary termination statement, has contributed to the popularity of the "case conference" in interdisciplinary settings (of course, there are other reasons for the case conference as well). In the case conference, intake data collected by, for example, a clinical social worker will be presented to an interdisciplinary mental health team. The team will pool diagnostic and treatment ideas. Usually a senior clinician, such as a clinical psychologist or psychiatrist, coordinates or supervises the decision making.

There is also a time-honored allegiance to a so-called "mental status examination." For practical purposes, this may be viewed as a model for a medically oriented diagnosis of a client's psychiatric condition. Goodwin and Guze

(1989) state: "A *mental status* examination . . . deals with the patient's thoughts, feelings, and behavior at a particular point in time" (p. 293). Kleinmuntz (1982) identifies six dimensions for the mental status interview or examination: (1) general appearance, attitude, and behavior; (2) discourse (manner of speaking); (3) mood and affective fluctuations; (4) sensorium and intellect (orientation to place, person, and time; memory; mental abilities); (5) mental content and specific preoccupations (thoughts, obsessions, delusions, hallucinations), and (6) insight (e.g., regarding the need for treatment). The mental status interview or examination is supposed to provide a clear-cut statement, according to the six dimensions, of the client's psychiatric status, that would support a DSM-IV diagnostic classification.

BEHAVIORAL OBSERVATIONS

As a clinical or psychological assessment method, behavioral observations require that there be a scientifically based plan for the monitoring, recording, analysis, and interpretation of a client's behavior. This plan may be informal to some extent, but to qualify as an assessment method there must be a certain degree of academic formality.

In many ways, the data gleaned from behavioral observations will be comparable to that gained through clinical interviewing. The data are anecdotal or episodic and reveal only what the client is willing or able to communicate to the clinical psychologist. Making use of these data is dependent upon an inference that the sampling is a reliable and valid reflection of the client's true psychosocial state. The reliability and validity problems that plague data from clinical interviewing also plague data from behavioral observations.

When doing behavioral observations, the clinical psychologist is an "observer." In order to have access to the most usable behavioral sample, the observer may have to participate in the activity. Thus, the question arises as to whether the observer's presence or participation leads to different client behavior than if the observer were able to sample the client's behavior unobtrusively (i.e., without the client's being aware of the behavioral observation). This is sometimes true and sometimes not. The observer's presence may be partially accountable for the behavior, but it will be difficult or impossible to estimate how much influence observer participation produced.

Observation can be either direct or indirect. Direct observation requires having firsthand access to the client's behavior, whereas indirect observation relies on second-hand accounts, such as questionnaires (perhaps a self-report completed by the client, or a behavior rating by some other person, say a family member or teacher, who is familiar with the client's behavior).

The observational framework can be either naturalistic or controlled. Naturalistic observation is conducted in the client's usual life sphere, such as in the home, on the job, in the classroom, and so on; whereas controlled observation relies on experiences that are contrived by the professional to trigger a kind of behavior that is of clinical interest, such as how the client behaves in a problem-solving group, an interaction with family members, a stress-provoking situation, and so on.

Before beginning a behavioral observation, the clinical psychologist must decide on a scientifically based plan for monitoring, recording, analyzing, and interpreting the client behavior that will be accessed. The initial step is to define the "target behavior," that is, the behavior that is of clinical interest and that motivated the clinical psychologist's implementing the behavioral observation in the first place.

In defining a target behavior there must be enough specificity to be able to distinguish when the behavior does or does not occur; and, of course, for interjudge reliability, it would have to be specific enough to allow multiple observers to identify the behavioral occurrence. Specificity means fulfilling the criteria of objectivity, clarity, and completeness:

> To be *objective*, the definition should refer to observable characteristics of behavior or environmental events. Definitions should not refer to inner states of the individual such as aggressiveness or emotional disturbance. To be *clear*, the definition should be so unambiguous that it could be read, repeated, and paraphrased by observers. Reading the definition should provide a sufficient basis for beginning actual observations. To be *complete*, the boundary conditions of the definition must be delineated so that the responses to be included and excluded are enumerated [Kazdin, 1980, p. 71].

As is evident in this statement, the definition should counteract reliability problems, such as by avoiding emotional states that could be defined differently and promoting clear-cut behaviors.

The recording phase means noting the occurrence or amount of the discrete behavioral response. Frequency counts can be made; this requires recording the number of times that the behavior was demonstrated in a prescribed time frame. This method of "incident sampling" is concerned with occurrence and not with the time of the selected behavior. Here there is an implied assumption that the quality of the behavior is the same, regardless of when it occurs (i.e., a behavior is a behavior), and that the time frame will yield a sampling of the behavior that is representative of the universal occurrence of the behavior. Discrete categorizations can be made. This requires, among other options, rating the quality of a behavior (e.g., degree of application to a specified task), the alignment with a criterion (e.g., appropriate or inappropriate for the stimulus), or distinguishing one behavior from another (e.g., having a list of behaviors, and noting which do and do not occur). The recording can also note how many of a pool of subjects behave in a certain way to a specified stimulus or reinforcing context. Interval recording uses units of time to track behavior (e.g., a time sampling). Relatedly, the amount of time that is devoted to a behavior can be a useful measure.

Selecting a behavioral sampling strategy depends, to a large extent, on the type of behavior being studied. The goal or purpose of the strategy has to be matched with the goal or purpose of the clinical assessment.

A noteworthy behavioral recording strategy, known as Interaction Process Analysis, has been developed by Bales (1950). Without going into the methodological details, suffice it to say that a trained observer watches the interactions between people. The focus could be on how an individual client interacts with others (e.g., the client with family members), or the focus could be on how a group of clients (e.g., a psychotherapy group) interacts. The observer may be in the room with the people in question, or may observe their behavior through a one-way window. Using any one of a variety of sampling techniques (e.g., incident sampling, time sampling, etc.), as discussed previously, the examiner records interactions according to a twelve-category system. Figure 3.1 clarifies the 12 categories, and points out that consideration is also given to the task area (social–emotional positive, neutral, and negative), the problematic nature of each of the twelve categories (problems of communication, evaluation, control, decision, tension reduction, or reintegration), and the thrust of each of the twelve categories (positive reactions, attempted answers, questions, or negative reactions). All of the attendant reliability and validity difficulties that are present with other behavioral sampling strategies are also present with Bales' interaction process analysis.

Olmsted (1959) says: "The recording procedure of interaction process analysis rests on the assumption that the observer can judge the dominant function or meaning of an act and that in the long run the true tendencies of individual and group behavior will be portrayed with

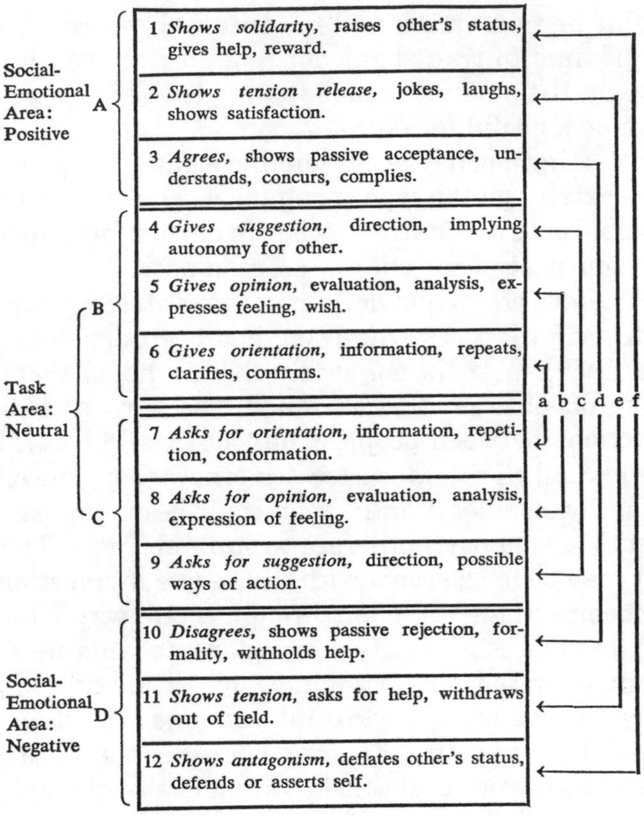

KEY

a Problems of Communication
b Problems of Evaluation
c Problems of Control
d Problems of Decision
e Problems of Tension Reduction
f Problems of Reintegration

A Positive Reactions
B Attempted Answers
C Questions
D Negative Reactions

Figure 3.1. Bales' System of Observational Categories. From Robert F. Bales, *Interaction Process Analysis*, Cambridge: Addison-Wesley Press, 1950, p. 9

acceptable accuracy even though in any given instance the subsidiary function of the act will be lost" (p. 124).

When the interactions have been recorded and classified, an interaction profile analysis can be completed: "A profile is a straightforward summary of how much an individual, or all individuals, in a group gives and receives in the various categories; it can be portrayed numerically or graphically. Inspection of group profiles can show differences between types of groups . . ." (Olmsted, 1959, p. 125). The analysis also reveals channels of communication, phase movement, meaning where the person or group is at a given phase of the life of the group (e.g., early in a session versus late in the session), and role relationships.

Bales' interaction process analysis is singled out for discussion here because: (1) it exemplifies a useful behavioral analysis strategy; (2) it has proven to be one of the more worthwhile approaches for behavioral analysis in clinical psychology; and (3) it can be applied, with a fairly limited orientation, by even the novice at behavioral observation (it is a good strategy for the student of clinical psychology to try out). The Bales' system has been modified by various researchers, and its fundamentals are readily evident in interaction studies to this date.

The foregoing comments underscore the need for objectification for the monitoring and recording phases. For the analysis phase, however, subjectivity reenters the clinical picture. In discussing the use of behavioral observation for the analysis of children's behavior, Palmer (1983) states:

> The analysis of such observations is often more "unstructured" than the sample. In clinical practice (as distinct from research studies), the observed behavior is seldom scored or rated in metric fashion. The fairly reliable rating scales constructed in development research studies have not been adopted in clinical use. The careful assessor who makes detailed notes may be able to detect patterns of repeated

behavior, however. If enough observations in a variety of situations are made, an observer may be able to demarcate recurrent themes in the child's behavior. If the assessor falls back on some intuitive global impression, the conclusions are also likely to be global and nonspecific [p. 99].

In other words, behavioral observation has numerous strategies available to it for objectifying and quantifying the data, yet the analysis is likely to be highly subjective.

As with analysis, the interpretation of behavioral observations is usually without an actuarial guideline. Consequently, the clinical acumen of the observer will determine the reliability and validity of the interpretive ideas. Presumably, the clinical psychologist will base the interpretation of behavioral observations on a scientific rationale; that is, interpretations will draw upon familiarity with the research on the correlates of a behavior. As with so many aspects of clinical assessment, however, there is, unfortunately, no quality assurance for the interpretation of behavioral observations.

The theory supported by the clinical psychologist will, of course, influence how the data from behavioral observations are transformed into services to the client. If the clinical psychologist is committed to behaviorism, the data will provide the basis for establishing reinforcement contingencies to accommodate behavioral modification: "It is conceivable that IQ and/or other tests may provide information about the kinds of events, verbal and nonverbal, that may be effective in modifying the behavior of the patient" (Greenspoon and Gersten, 1967, p. 851). But if the clinical psychologist is committed to a psychodynamic approach, the data will be formulated into a profile of emotional dimensions.

INTELLIGENCE

The evaluation of intelligence or mental abilities was the threshold over which psychologists crossed into the realm of clinical services. Prior to the development of intelligence tests, there had been a few attempts to apply the methods of the psychological laboratory to human behavior, but true clinical psychology obtained its greatest initial impetus from intelligence testing.

There are as many definitions of "intelligence" as there are professionals dealing with the topic. From his review of the history and theories of intelligence, A. J. Edwards (1971) recommends dealing with it as a construct, and the nature of intelligence gains definition by the observable behaviors (which are prescribed by the given intelligence test that is used for measurement).

Intelligence testing began with the hallmark efforts of Alfred Binet (1857–1911), a French pediatrician. From 1892, when he joined the psychological laboratory at the Sorbonne in Paris until his death in 1911, Binet and his colleagues pursued the study of individual differences, particularly as measured by intelligence scales.

In collaboration with Theodore Simon, Binet created a 30-item intelligence scale for identifying mentally retarded schoolchildren in Paris (Binet and Simon, 1905). The Binet scale has been credited with being one of the most critical factors in the development and expansion of clinical psychology (Pinter, 1931). To be sure, being able to evaluate intelligence by standardized instruments did serve to distinguish a psychologist's role in educational and clinical settings; and this distinction remains important to this day.

Binet considered intelligence to encompass ten mental functions: memory, imagery, imagination, attention, comprehension, suggestibility, aesthetic appreciation, moral sentiments, muscular force or willpower, and motor skill (A. J. Edwards, 1971).

While the mental functions delineated by Binet have been refined, renamed, and supplemented, for example by Spearman's (1904) concept of "general intelligence," the gist of these functions has continued. Now, however, specific functions seem more defined by the test contents than by theory per se.

Binet's turn-of-the-century intelligence materials were translated for American use by Lewis M. Terman of Stanford University. In 1916, the Binet-Simon Scale was made available to American psychologists. With the 1937 Revision of the Binet-Simon Scales, the intelligence testing boom occurred: "Probably never again will a single test be as widely used as the 1937 Revision of the Binet-Simon Scales" (A. J. Edwards, 1972, p. 4).

In 1960, another version of the Stanford-Binet Intelligence Scale became available (Terman and Merrill, 1960). The norms were updated in 1972.

Using children's performances on Binet scales, Wilhelm Stern (1914) devised the "intelligence quotient" (IQ), which Aiken (1988) describes as: "An examinee's mental age (MA) and intelligence quotient depended on the number of subtests passed at successive age levels. The IQ was determined from the ratio of the examinee's mental age (MA)—and the total number of months credit earned on the test—to his or her chronological age (CA) in months, multiplied by 100 to get rid of the decimal" (p. 157).

To summarize, the formula for computing an intelligence quotient is: intelligence quotient = the mental age divided by the chronological age, multiplied by 100. While the computation can be made individually (using months to express the numerator and the denominator), the manuals for intelligence tests commonly provide tables for determining the intelligence quotient, making computations per se unnecessary.

Today, the prevailing version of the Binet scales is the Stanford-Binet Intelligence Scale-Fourth Edition (SBIC-IV; Thorndike, Hagen, and Sattler, 1986), which uses 15 subtests to measure four broad areas of cognitive abilities: Verbal Reasoning, Abstract/Visual Reasoning, Quantitative Reasoning, and Short-Term Memory. The construction of the test is described as follows: "the authors adopted a three-level hierarchical model of the structure of cognitive abilities with a general reasoning factor, **g**, at the top. Three broad factors—crystallized abilities, fluid-analytic abilities, and short-term memory—constitute the second level. Three more specific factors—verbal reasoning, quantitative reasoning, and abstract/visual reasoning—make up the third level" (p. 3). The test is applicable to children from the age of 2 on to adults. A Standard Age Score (SAS) is obtained for each of the 15 subtests, as well as a Composite SAS.

The Stanford–Binet IV is commonly viewed as being heavily weighted for verbal mental abilities, and thus some psychologists believe that it is not as useful as other intelligence tests (such as the Wechsler series) for certain types of clients, especially those with limited verbal mental abilities. Yet surveys continue to support that the Stanford-Binet is a frequently used instrument.

At present, the most popular intelligence tests are in the Wechsler series. Without going into the history, the Wechsler series has evolved to three instruments, covering an age span of preschool through adulthood: the Wechsler Preschool and Primary Scale of Intelligence—Revised (WPPSI-R; Wechsler, 1989); the Wechsler Intelligence Scale for Children—Third Edition (WISC-III; Wechsler, 1991); and the Wechsler Adult Intelligence Scale—Revised (WAIS-R; Wechsler, 1981).

The Wechsler tests are very similar in structure and contents (except as relevant to age). Each is based on a point-scale concept (meaning one or more points are earned by successfully answering a question or responding to a task). Items of a like nature are grouped together to form a mental ability subtest. Across the Wechler instruments, essentially the same set of mental abilities are estimated by the coterie of subtests. Finally, each Wechsler test yields subtest scaled scores and three intelligence quotients (a verbal scale IQ, a performance scale IQ, and a full scale IQ).

All of the Wechsler tests are individually administered, which means that time utilization is a concern. J. D Ball, Archer, and Imhoff (1994) report that the time demands for the Wechsler IQ scales, in general, are 75.62 minutes for administrating, 21.61 minutes for scoring, and 24.97 minutes for interpreting (a total of 122.2 minutes). Therefore, while yielding valuable psychological information, a Wechsler test can be financially costly.

THE WECHSLER PRESCHOOL AND PRIMARY SCALE OF INTELLIGENCE— REVISED (WPPSI-R)

Federal legislation plays an important role in determining services to, among other persons, children with disabilities. For example, the Individuals with Disabilities Education Act of 1990 (IDEA) and/or Public Law (PL) 101-476, includes provisions for early intervention services for infants and toddlers. Therefore, the Wechsler Preschool and Primary Scale of Intelligence—Revised (WPPSI-R; Wechsler, 1989) is an important tool for evaluating the intelligence of children between the ages of 3 years through 7 years, 3 months.

Wechsler's approach to intelligence differs from certain others because: "(1) it conceives of intelligence as an overall or *global* entity that is multidetermined and multifaceted rather than an independent, uniquely defined trait, and (2) it avoids singling out any one ability (e.g., abstract reasoning) as overwhelmingly important" (p. 2). This definitional framework led to structuring the WPPSI-R to having Performance (perceptual-motor) and Verbal subtests. The subtests comprising the Performance scale include:

> Object Assembly (arranging puzzle pieces in configurations);
> Geometric Design (distinguishing simple designs and drawing geometric figures);
> Block Design (analyzing and reproducing patterns with colored blocks);

Mazes (solving pencil and paper mazes);
Picture Completion (identifying missing parts from pictures of common objects or events); and
Animal Pegs [an optional subtest] (placing colored pegs in the correct holes).

The subtests comprising the Verbal scale include:

Information (orally revealing knowledge relevant to commonplace events and objects in the environment);
Comprehension (understanding reasons for actions and consequences of events);
Arithmetic (solving quantitative problems);
Vocabulary (orally defining words);
Similarities (understanding commonalities, similarities, and analogies); and
Sentences [an optional subtest] (repeating verbatim verbal stimuli).

The scaled scores for the subtests, individually and in combinations, are interpreted; and the WPPSI-R yields Performance, Verbal, and Full Scale IQs.

THE WECHSLER INTELLIGENCE SCALE FOR CHILDREN—THIRD EDITION (WISC-III)

The Wechsler Intelligence Scale for Children—Third Edition (WISC-III; Wechsler, 1991) assesses intellectual ability for children from 6 years through 16 years, 11 months. The subtests comprising the Verbal scale include:

Information (questions for knowledge of common events, objects, places, and people);
Similarities (pairs of words elicit explanations of similarity of objects and concepts);
Arithmetic (problems solved mentally and responded to orally);
Vocabulary (words defined orally);
Comprehension (questions for solving everyday problems or understanding social rules and concepts); and

Digit Span [a supplementary subtest] (number sequences repeated verbatim forward and backward).

The subtests comprising the Performance scale include:

Picture Completion (identifying missing parts from pictures of common objects and scenes);

Coding (pairing simple shapes and symbols for drawing a sequence of symbols with corresponding shapes);

Picture Arrangement (rearranging mixed-up pictures into logical story sequences);

Block Design (replicating two-dimensional geometric patterns with two-color cubes);

Object Assembly (assembling common objects into meaningful wholes);

Symbol Search [a supplementary subtest, which can substitute only for Coding] (recognizing the presence of target symbols in search groups of symbols); and

Mazes [a supplementary subtest] (using a pencil to solve printed mazes).

Individual and combined subtests can be interpreted. In addition to Verbal, Performance, and Full Scale IQs, the WISC-III provides four optional factor-based index scores, namely Verbal Comprehension, Perceptual Organization, Freedom from Distractibility, and Processing Speech.

THE WECHSLER ADULT INTELLIGENCE SCALE—REVISED (WAIS-R)

The Wechsler Adult Intelligence Scale—Revised (WAIS-R; Wechsler, 1981) has norms based on persons from 16 years through 74 years, 11 months. The WAIS-R has 11 subtests. The subtests comprising the Verbal scale include (using meanings based, in part, on Ogdon [1982]):

Information (questions of facts and events to reveal academic achievement, and richness of environment);

Digit Span (repeating series of numbers forward and backward to measure immediate attention, memory, and recall; anxiety and distractibility may enter into the performance);

Vocabulary (defining words, which is dependent upon learning ability and early educational environment; this may be the best single measure of intelligence);

Arithmetic (solving problems without paper and pencil, which requires concentration, mental alertness, and academic achievement);

Comprehension (solving everyday problem situations, as dependent upon logical reasoning and judgment); and

Similarities (recognizing and expressing relationships between verbal stimuli, necessitating verbal concept formation and logical reasoning; an estimate of true verbal learning potential).

The subtests comprising the Performance scale include:

Picture Completion (identifying a missing part from a picture of an object, which is a nonlinguistic measure of general intelligence and involves concentration, reasoning, and attention to details);

Picture Arrangement (ordering pictures to make a sensible story, revealing an ability to plan, perceive cause-and-effect relationships, and social intelligence);

Block Design (reproducing pictorial designs with colored blocks, demanding visual–motor coordination, perceptual analysis, synthesis, and abstract reasoning);

Object Assembly (fitting puzzle pieces together, bringing out visual perception and organization, sensorimotor feedback, and concentration); and

Digit Symbol (translating a symbol-number code into new learning, requiring visual–motor activity and coordination, concentration, and psychomotor speed).

For each subtest, the items or tasks: (1) start easy and become more difficult; (2) earn varying amounts of points; and (3) may or may not be timed (these three considerations also apply to the other WPPSI-R and the WISC-III).

For the WAIS-R, intelligence quotients are classified according to Figure 3.2, and Figure 3.3 shows the standard deviation and percentile rank for intelligence quotients at five-point intervals.

Figure 3.2. Intelligence Classifications

| IQ | Classification | Percent Included | |
		Theoretical Normal Curve	Actual Sample[a]
130 and above	Very Superior	2.2	2.6
120-129	Superior	6.7	6.9
110-119	High Average[b]	16.1	16.6
90-109	Average	50.0	49.1
80-89	Low Average[b]	16.1	16.1
70-79	Borderline	6.7	6.4
69 and below	Mentally Retarded[b]	2.2	2.3

[a]The percents shown are for Full Scale IQ, and are based on the total standardization sample (N = 1,880). The percents obtained for Verbal IQ and Performance IQ are essentially the same.
[b]The terms *High Average, Low Average,* and *Mentally Retarded* correspond to the terms *Bright Normal, Dull Normal,* and *Mental Defective,* respectively, used in the 1955 *WAIS Manual.*

Figure 3.3. Relation of IQs to Deviations from the Mean and Percentile Ranks

Verbal, Performance, or Full Scale IQ	Number of SDs from the Mean	Percentile Rank	Verbal, Performance, or Full Scale IQ	Number of SDs from the Mean	Percentile Rank
145	+3	99.9	100	0 (Mean)	50
140	+2⅔	99.6	95	−⅓	37
135	+2⅓	99	90	−⅔	25
130	+2	98	85	−1	16
125	+1⅔	95	80	−1⅓	9
120	+1⅓	91	75	−1⅔	5
115	+1	84	70	−2	2
110	+⅔	75	65	−2⅓	1
105	+⅓	63	60	−2⅔	0.4
			55	−3	0.1

INTERPRETATION OF WECHSLER RESULTS

Interpretation of the WAIS-R or the other Wechsler tests is not restricted to the level of intelligence per se. This is, of course, a primary concern, and the contents of Figures 3.2 and 3.3 provide the framework for considering the client's level of intelligence.

An interpretation is also made of the level of each mental ability (Kramer, 1993; Lipsitz, Dworkin, and Erlenmeyer-Kimling, 1993). The subtest scores are analyzed individually and comparatively. For example, subsequent assessment and intervention strategies could be tailored accordingly if scores on subtests that suggest general and/or social learning potential (e.g., Similarities, Vocabulary, Picture Completion, Picture Arrangement) are significantly higher than scores on subtests that suggest verbally oriented academic achievement (e.g., Information, Arithmetic, Vocabulary). In such a case, a diagnostic hypothesis might be that the client has been an underachiever, subjected to a culturally impoverished environment, and/or thwarted in fulfilling his or her intellectual potential by some psychosocial factor (e.g., poor motivation, anxiety, low achievement need).

Consideration is also given to the scatter of subtests. This is similar to a comparative analysis of two or more subtests, but requires considering, among other things, the extent of the variance of the subtests and the particular pattern of highs and lows created by the subtest scores. While there are reference sources upon which a clinical psychologist can rely for guidance in this sort of profile analysis (and there is a growing number of computer programs for profile analysis), there are conflicting research-based opinions about the meaning of particular profiles. Thus, the clinical acumen of the diagnostician remains crucial. As a rule of thumb, the clinical notion is that everyone should have differences in mental abilities (i.e., stronger in one area and weaker in another), but a great deal of subtest scatter or variance can trigger a concern for barriers (cultural, mental disorder, organic) to intellectual development.

A comparison is also made of the level of verbal intelligence and performance intelligence. Again there are varying research-based opinions about what a difference in levels means. As one view, Ogdon (1982) suggests that having a verbal IQ significantly above the performance IQ is characteristic of most mental disorders (including neuroses, psychoses, and organic conditions), whereas a performance IQ significantly above the verbal IQ is found primarily among persons with "acting out" tendencies (including adolescent delinquents, sociopaths, persons with poor academic achievement).

The Wechsler series has gained support for differential diagnosis. That is, while the adult Wechsler is the most popular test for intellectual assessment, research has been amassed to support that it can distinguish emotional conditions and neurological dysfunctioning (Woody, 1969; Sattler, 1974; A. J. Edwards, 1975; Walsh, 1978; Ogdon, 1982; Lezak, 1983; Putnam, Adams, and Schneider, 1992; Karenken and Williams, 1994).

As mentioned earlier a Wechsler test typically requires about two hours (and possibly more, depending upon the response style of the client). In the name of efficiency, efforts have been made to develop a short form. That is, researchers have investigated using only a few subtests to gain the same clinical picture as would come from all of the subtests (Paolo and Ryan, 1993). For example with the WAIS-R, Silverstein (1982) posits that Vocabulary and Block Design can be used for a two-subtest short form, or that Arithmetic, Vocabulary, Block Design, and Picture Arrangement can be used for a four-subtest short form. However, as seems to be true with short forms for other tests, an attempt to shorten the instrument may lead to a sacrifice in reliability and validity. For example,

Ryan, Larsen, and Prifitera (1983) found high correlations between the IQs from Silverstein's short forms and WAIS-R full-scale IQs, but concluded: "short forms should be used with caution where precise IQ measurements are required" (p. 460). Roth, Hughes, Monkowski, and Crosson (1984) applied Silverstein's short forms to patients suspected of having brain impairment, and found that they overestimated full scale IQ (FSIQ). Roth et al. concluded: "short forms do not appear adequate for estimating the FSIQ of patients suspected of brain impairment" (p. 723).

ACHIEVEMENT TESTS

Psychological assessment usually involves some estimate of educational or academic achievement. As mentioned previously, several subtests on each of the Wechsler instruments have a connection to educational achievement (e.g., the Information subtest). When the contents of the tests are linked to the generally accepted ideas about how intelligence is defined, it is not surprising that intelligence and achievement test scores have significant correlations (Henderson, Butler, and Goffeney, 1969).

Academic achievement may also reflect the diagnosis of the client. Sattler (1974) states: "Children placed in learning disability classes usually (a) have normal or above normal intellectual capacity, as indicated by an IQ above 90; (b) display academic deficiencies in one or more of reading, arithmetic, spelling, and handwriting; and (c) have difficulties, other than those noted in (b), associated with syndromes of learning disabilities, such as hyperactivity, deficits in expressive language, or attentional difficulties" (p. 332). Woody (1969) compared the mental abilities and achievement scores of well-behaved and behavioral problem boys (matched groups), and found that the well-behaved boys scored significantly higher than the behavioral problem boys in both reading and arithmetic achievement (the two groups were also significantly different on 7 of 11

Wechsler subtests). Virtually any emotional or neurological condition could impact upon academic achievement, and
thus, while it does not make a differential diagnosis per se,
it should be evaluated.

There are many achievement tests available to clinical psychologists, but none can be considered as being in
a most favored position. Depending on the nature and purpose of the clinical assessment, it is likely that measures
of reading (word recognition or comprehension), arithmetic, and spelling would be useful.

It is important to recognize that academic achievement is not the end goal. Our society is highly oriented
toward achievement, and the achievement motive is powerful in one's personality structure—but there is more to
life. Noted intelligence theorist George D. Stoddard
(1943) commented: "Knowledge indiscriminately gath-
ered in for its own sake has no place in our concept of
intelligence-at-work, nor is it . . . to be highly regarded
as a preparation for life" (p. 432). Also, Albert Einstein
(1936) stated: "The development of general ability for independent thinking and judgment should always be
placed foremost, not the acquisition of special knowledge"
(p. 47). In other words, achievement is necessary for the
welfare of both the individual and society, but the proper
perspective places it in a more diversified psychological
framework. In clinical assessment, therefore, it is but one
of many factors that will enter into the appraisal of the
person.

PERCEPTUAL FUNCTIONING

Perceptual functioning is a dimension of intelligence, and
has implications as well for personality and achievement.
While a brief definition could emphasize thinking, imagination, and perception forming a continuum of perceptual
functioning, perceptual functioning does not accommodate
a succinct definition (Lezak, 1983).

Perception is part of a client's response to virtually any test (and the Wechsler instruments include subtests that purposely rely on perceptual functioning). Surveys of psychological assessment practices reveal the Bender Gestalt test to be one of the most used specialized tests of perceptual functionings. Its creator, Lauretta Bender (1938) sets forth the rationale:

> The gestalt function may be defined as that function of the integrated organism whereby it responds to a given constellation of stimuli as a whole; the response itself being a constellation, or pattern, or gestalt. All integrative processes, within the nervous system occur in constellations, or patterns, or gestalten. Integration occurs not by summation or subtraction or association but by differentiation, or by increasing or decreasing the internal complexity of the pattern in its setting. It appears that an integrated organism never responds in any other way. The whole setting of the stimulus and the whole integrative state of the organism determine the pattern of the response [pp. 3–4].

In order to attain a measure of perceptual functioning, the Bender Gestalt test consists of nine designs, and the client is asked to draw them.

The manner in which the designs are reproduced allows for clinical impressions. There are numerous factors that are considered by the clinical psychologist, including modifications in size (e.g., expanding or reducing the drawings from the size depicted on the standardized cards); the arrangement of the designs (e.g., rigid, methodical, confused, collisions, logical); unusual modes of reproduction (e.g., angulation changes, circles or dots modified, closure difficulties, overlapping, perseveration, reversals, sloping deviations, and so on) (Ogdon, 1982). For a few interpretive examples, angulation changes, perseveration, reversals, rotations, and destruction of a design's configuration might be suggestive of organicity, whereas closure difficulty, circles or dots modified, overlapping, sketching, and expansion or

reduction in size might be suggestive of emotional disturbances (Ogdon, 1982).

The origination of the Bender Gestalt test was predicated on neurological functioning, and it is still used in
conjunction with neuropsychological assessment. Rightly
or wrongly, it has been extended to nonneurological issues
as well. Hutt and Briskin (1960) capture the reasoning:

> Mature, healthy perception, according to the Gestalt school,
> consists of the integration of a triad of factors: (1) the in-
> nate tendency of organisms to organize perceptual data as
> it is affected by (2) temporal factors and (3) maturational
> level. It tends to follow that any other factors, emotional,
> toxic, organic or traumatic, that affect these perceptual pro-
> cesses would also be reflected in some way in the patient's
> response (verbal or written) to his perceptual experience
> [p. 9].

Consequently, Hutt and Briskin offer guidelines for using
the Bender Gestalt test for other than neurological matters (see also Hutt, 1980). Piotrowski and Keller (1984)
found the Bender Gestalt test was the fifth most endorsed
projective personality test used in the training of clinical
psychology candidates.

Despite its professional popularity, there has been
much criticism of the Bender Gestalt test. Too often, no
systematic scoring system is used (even though there are
several scoring systems available whose developers have
made reasonable efforts to establish reliability, validity,
and interpretive guidelines). Too often, a clinical judgment
is based on the Bender Gestalt test results in isolation,
as opposed to being part of a comprehensive psychological test battery.

After critiquing the studies of the use of the Bender
Gestalt test as a singular measure of neurological functioning, Bigler and Ehrfurth (1981) conclude the following about
the instrument (which they refer to as the BVMG, meaning the Bender Visual Motor Gestalt): "Because of its

simplicity, short administrative time, and initial studies of its success, the BVMG rapidly became the revered test for establishing organicity" (p. 562); "continued misinterpretation of much of the data on the BVMG has taken place" (p. 567); and consequently, "The use of the Bender-Gestalt as the only measure to assess organic status should not continue" (p. 568).

Relatedly, the Bender Gestalt test has also been used for assessing intelligence: "the Bender Gestalt Test can be used with some degree of confidence as a short nonverbal intelligence test for young children, particularly for screening purposes" (Koppitz, 1963, p. 50). Salvia and Ysseldyke (1988) consider the Bender Gestalt test to be simply a measure of skill in copying geometric designs, and state: "In our opinion, the BVMT should never be used as, or substituted for a measure of intellectual functioning" (p. 283). In other words, there is no agreement on the use of the Bender Gestalt test beyond its initial purpose, namely a measure of perception as might be related to neurological functioning.

Use of a single test, such as the Bender Gestalt test, for assessing any factor is foolhardy and risking error. In point of fact, experience supports that it is not necessarily the use of the single test per se (be it the Bender Gestalt test or another one) that leads to false positives (i.e, judging a client to possess a clinical condition, such as organicity, when, in fact, he or she does not possess the clinical condition). Rather, it is the clinical psychologist's failure to apply a standardized system of administration, scoring, analysis, and interpretation, whether the instrument be for perceptual function or personality or whatever. Stated as politely and respectfully as possible, it is known, and highly regrettable to report, that some clinical psychologists do not adhere to the standards relevant to the task, such as following the established administration, scoring, and interpretation systems.

NEUROPSYCHOLOGY

Only a few short years ago, a work of this sort would not have included material on neuropsychology. While certain tests, such as the various Wechsler intelligence scales and those that tap into perception, were interpreted for neurological implications, the prevailing view was that the clinical psychologist should studiously avoid direct commentary on neurological functioning—to do otherwise would be to risk an inappropriate excursion into the realm of medicine, namely the practice of neurology.

Care must still be maintained to avoid going beyond the practice of psychology, but it is now generally accepted (including by medical practitioners) that clinical neuropsychology is an appropriate service for clinical psychologists to render. It is recognized that clinical neuropsychology can make a substantial contribution to the practice of medicine in general, and in particular to the practice of neurology; in other words, the clinical neuropsychologist and the physician (such as a neurologist) engage in teamwork.

Clinical neuropsychology is devoted to the psychological assessment of brain-related behavior. Luria (1970) sets forth the fundamental premise of clinical neuropsychology: "First by pinpointing the brain lesion responsible for specific behavior disorders we hope to develop a means of early diagnosis and precise location of brain injuries. . . . Second, neuropsychological investigation should provide us with a factor analysis that will lead to better understanding of the components of complex psychological functions for which the operations of the different parts of the brain are responsible" (p. 66). The assessment challenge becomes: "(1) the presence or absence of neurologically based cerebral impairment, and (2) the lateralization and localization of the lesion" (Walsh, 1978, p. 285).

The clinical neuropsychologist can offer far more than diagnostic test information. While assessment is likely to be ever present, Lezak (1983) points out that there are three basic purposes of neuropsychology: "diagnosis, patient care—including questions about treatment and planning, and research" (p. 8). To exemplify the connection between clinical neuropsychology and treatment, consider the following from Walsh (1978):

> Neuropsychological assessment also provides an important method of evaluating various forms of treatment such as neurosurgical procedures and drug therapy. The neurosurgical procedures include resections for tumor and epilepsy, the insertion of shunts in cases of so-called normal pressure hydrocephalus, and the special procedures loosely referred to as psychosurgery. Assessment is also valuable in checking progress after vascular surgery such as endarterectomy for stenosis of the vessels supplying the cerebrum [p. 285].

As evident in this quote, the clinical psychologist will be required to have training that may or may not be part of the traditional curriculum; more will be said on this matter later on.

The concept of treatment extends into therapy and rehabilitation, and here again the clinical neuropsychologist can play a critical role:

> Rehabilitation of closed head trauma patients is best accomplished when the interdisciplinary team approach is used to provide for the wide variety of behaviors and disabilities exhibited by this population. When possible, team members should routinely include representatives from psychiatry, neurology, speech-language pathology, psychology, physical therapy, occupational therapy, nursing, social service, vocational rehabilitation, therapeutic recreation, medical and other consultants as indicated, and family members or significant persons in the patient's life [Adamovich, Henderson, and Auerbach, 1985, p. 4].

It seems well accepted by the health care professions that the patient with neurological difficulties will usually require rehabilitation services of some form, that the multidisciplinary model of service delivery is the most logical, and that clinical neuropsychology is capable of making a critical contribution to the rehabilitation program, whether it be through assessment, consultation, research, or therapy-counseling (Ylvisaker, 1985).

This is not the place for a detailed discussion of brain-related behavior or the conditions associated with neurological damage or dysfunctioning, but the key dimensions can be recognized. Lezak (1983) states: "Behavior may be conceptualized in terms of three functional systems: (1) *intellect*, which is the information-handling aspect of behavior; (2) *emotionality*, which concerns feelings and motivation; and (3) *control*, which has to do with how behavior is expressed" (p. 18). All three of these systems are within the professional purview of clinical neuropsychology.

Scholarly debate continues as to whether or not psychological tests can reliably and validly measure brain functioning. To counter the critics, neuropsychologists have moved toward statistical documentation of the "hit rates"; that is, how well neuropsychological test results predict a particular brain condition. For example, Golden, Hammeke, and Purisch (1980) cite cross-validation studies (e.g., comparing the test data of brain injured patients with normal-control subjects) for the Luria-Nebraska Neuropsychological Battery (LNNB), and they compared the data from the LNNB with "such medical and laboratory data as the CAT scan, EEG, angiogram, pneumoencephalogram, skull x-rays, neurological history, and/or surgery, according to the patient's condition" (p. 4). While there have been many studies on the reliability and validity of the LNNB and each study has yielded unique results, the general posture taken because of the research is that there are: "hit rates ranging from

62 to 80% for the brain-injured group and from 72 to 98% for the control group" (p. 8).

Some clinical neuropsychologists believe that the best approach is to select numerous single-factor tests to create a battery of instruments designed especially for a particular patient (Lezak, 1983). Other clinical neuropsychologists maintain that reliability and validity are enhanced by having a specific battery of tests designed for brain-related behavior and using the same battery with all relevant patients, thereby allowing the clinical neuropsychologist to build up a common frame of reference for diagnosis, treatment, and rehabilitation.

While there are numerous standardized neurological test batteries (Lezak, 1983) the two foremost batteries are the Halstead-Reitan Battery (Halstead, 1947; Reitan and Davison, 1974) and the previously mentioned LNNB. Without going into all of the subtests within each of the batteries, suffice it to say that each battery consists of a collection of tests that is believed to provide measures of the important facets of brain functioning. The names of LNNB scales reveal the scope of measurement: motor, rhythm, tactile, visual, receptive speech, expressive speech, writing, reading, arithmetic, memory, intellectual processes, pathognomonic (items highly indicative of brain damage), left hemisphere, and right hemisphere (the latter two scales are constructed to estimate lateralization of damage).

Neuropsychological tests go beyond assessment of a brain injured person, such as being useful for evaluating: the development of children (Townes, Trupin, Martin, and Goldstein, 1980); health conditions, such as asthma (Dunleavy and Baade, 1980); the effects of aging (Bak and Greene, 1980); propensities toward violence (Bryant, Scott, Golden, and Tori, 1984); and a host of other human qualities that are essential to clinical assessment.

Neuropsychology requires that the clinical psychologist have an advanced academic understanding of physiological processes and specialized skills. Since clinical neuropsychology is relatively new, training opportunities in this area are still emerging. Golden and Kuperman (1980a) found that at least 30 percent of APA-approved clinical psychology training programs offer enough training in neuropsychology to accommodate specialization. Golden and Kuperman (1980b) provide a list of neuropsychology internships. They conclude: "However, most students do not get adequate training to enable them to claim a specialty in neuropsychology" (p. 917). While the latter may still be true, it should be noted that their survey was conducted in 1978, and it is probable that far more training opportunities have been created since that time.

It seems likely that today's clinical psychology students will be expected to have a greater preparation in neuropsychology than did earlier generations. Indeed, the American Board of Professional Psychology (ABPP) is now conducting examinations for the status of Diplomate in Clinical Neuropsychology. Clinical psychologists face an increasing need to have training in biological bases of behavior, whether it is to accommodate clinical neuropsychology or to be prepared to exercise the emerging privilege of prescribing medications.

PERSONALITY

As with the term *intelligence* and so many other psychological terms, personality has been defined in all sorts of ways. The theoretical orientation of the clinical psychologist (such as psychoanalytic, behavioral, or humanistic) will have a major influence on the definition endorsed, but even within those major rubrics, there are many variations on an orientational theme. Hall and Lindzey (1957) say: "It is our conviction that *no substantive definition of personality can be applied with any generality*" (p. 9); and they add: "Thus, we submit that *personality is defined by the particular empirical concepts which are a part of the theory of personality employed by the observer"* (p. 9).

While the foregoing seems accurate from an academic perspective, it is necessary to establish a practical framework. For present purposes, Maddi (1980) offers a succinct definition: *"Personality is a stable set of characteristics and tendencies that determine those commonalities and differences in the psychological behavior (thoughts, feelings, and actions) of people that have continuity in time and that may not be easily understood as the sole result of the social and biological pressures of the moment"* (p. 10). Placing personality into clinical assessment, Beck (1981) states:

> The task before a psychology of personality is to delineate the forces, the constancies (hypothetical constructs, to be sure), that are the sources of the observables. A corollary from the hypotheses of the constancies is that they enable us to predict the behavior of others. This inheres in the sheer fact that they are constants. In our transactions with one another we are, in fact, always predicting. We are pretty sure regarding what a person is likely to do, sure that what he does today, he will do tomorrow, and on another morrow. These are the judgments of everyday life and its wisdoms [p. 24].

Notice how Beck's tracking of personality into clinical assessment is consonant with the definition of diagnosis set forth in the preceding chapter, especially as is relevant to transforming the appraisal of the past (etiology) and present functioning into a prognostication or prediction.

There are (literally) thousands of personality tests. Recall the comments in the preceding chapter about how many "tests" fail to reach acceptable standards. Partly because of the nebulous nature of and diverse theories for personality, the problem is seemingly more pronounced for clinical assessment of personality than for certain other areas, such as achievement, aptitudes, and vocational interests.

For simplicity, personality assessment tests can be dichotomized as being objective or projective (Graham, 1977; Piotrowski and Keller, 1984). In this context, "objective" does not convey anything about reliability and validity per se, because both objective and projective instruments lay claim to those qualities.

An objective personality test: (1) has specific stimulus items (such as questions about the client); (2) requires the client to give a discrete response (such as true or false, or a rating, say on a 1 to 5 scale, or to choose which of X number of descriptors is preferred most and which is preferred least)—that is, the objectivity comes, in part, from the form of the response; (3) obtains a codification (usually in writing) of the client's responses (such as a self-report); (4) yields numerical measurements; and (5) has been standardized (and likely has norms to assist in the interpretation). It should be noted that an objective test remains subject to scoring errors. Using an error-free computer system, Allard, Butler, Faust, and Shea (1995) checked the hand scoring of an objective personality test, finding that the trained clinic personnel produced frequent mistakes (19% of the tests possessed errors substantial enough to alter the clinical diagnoses).

A projective personality test relies on the psychoanalytic principle of projection. For now, the term *projection* refers to "a method of studying personality by confronting the subject with a situation to which he will respond according to what the situation means to him and how he feels when so responding" (L. K. Frank, 1948, p. 46). This might, for instance, involve having the client look at a picture, and let his or her imagination produce a story. The story will then be analyzed by the clinical psychologist as a product of the client's personality structure.

The selection of personality assessment tests for illustrative purposes will rely on a survey by Lubin et al. (1984), which found that the top three personality tests (in order of frequency of usage) were: (1) the MMPI; (2) the Rorschach Inkblots Method; and (3) the TAT.

THE MINNESOTA MULTIPHASIC PERSONALITY INVENTORY-SECOND (MMPI-2)

The first MMPI was copyrighted in 1942, and credited to Hathaway and McKinley (1967). It was revised in 1989 (Hathaway and McKinley, 1989); the current edition is referred to as the MMPI-2. It is an objective instrument, with 567 true or false items in the test booklet. The client responds to each item to reflect how it does or does not apply to him or her. From a larger pool of statements and a series of standardization studies on both normals and clinical patients, selected items were used to form subtests or scales by criterion keying (meaning that a given clinical scale, say Scale 2 = Depression, was formed by the responses of patients with a particular diagnosis, such as a psychiatric diagnosis of depression).

Just as the Wechsler subtests create a mental abilities profile, the MMPI-2 scales form a personality profile. The patterning of the scales (i.e., the profile) is the basis for interpretation, not just the high or low level of a score for an individual scale.

A unique feature of the MMPI-2 is that there are validity scales that are devoted to detecting unusual or deviant approaches to responding. The "Cannot Say" scale is the total number of omitted items (or those that were marked both true and false), and a high number of these responses could raise doubts about whether the profile can accommodate a meaningful interpretation. The "L" or "Lie" scale can reveal whether the client is trying to answer in a manner that will be overly favorable for him or her (i.e., faking good), whereas the "F" scale can be used to identify the client who does not answer with a normal test-taking attitude (as might invalidate the scale, such as by claiming to be more troubled than is actually true, i.e., faking bad). The "K" scale reveals defensiveness, such as denial of symptoms. The most recent edition also includes: a "Back F" scale, which may identify a client who has stopped paying attention to the test items and adopted an essentially random pattern of responding; and the "VRIN" or "Variable Response Inconsistency" scale and the "TRIN" or "True Response Inconsistency" scale. According to Hathaway and McKinley (1989): "VRIN and TRIN provide an index of the tendency of a subject to respond to items in ways that are inconsistent or contradictory" (p. 27).

While an elevation on any one of these validity scales has potential clinical relevance, the patterning (particularly of the L, F, and K) can yield more refined information about the client's test-taking attitude. Extensive research has been conducted on the validity scales to allow the diagnostician to apply scientifically based guidelines for interpretation.

Before reviewing the clinical scales, methods for interpreting the MMPI-2 should be noted. There are essentially three approaches.

Clinical Judgment. If the clinical psychologist has extensive experience with the MMPI-2 and with clinical assessment, he or she can make the interpretation based on clinical acumen. However, as discussed in the preceding chapter, this can lead to problems in reliability of judgments, and the criteria for a given diagnosis, even if reliably applied, could have dubious validity.

Computer Analysis. If the clinical psychologist has very little experience with MMPI-2 or with clinical assessment, he or she can transmit the client's responses for a computerized interpretation. This service can be obtained from the test publisher, but certain software can be purchased for use in the psychologist's office. The computer option affords the expertise of an eminent MMPI-2 specialist(s), whose interpretations were used in the computer

programming. The advantage is that the interpretive processes will have 100 percent reliability and proven validity. The disadvantage is that the idiosyncratic nature of
the client's case history cannot be incorporated into the
computer's interpretation. *Reference to Cookbooks.* The most common approach
is for the clinical psychologist to rely upon a "cookbook."
There are numerous references, such as those offered by
Gilberstadt and Duker (1965), Lachar (1974), Butcher
(1990), and J. R. Graham (1993).

According to Hathaway and McKinley (1989) the
step-by-step approach for interpreting the basic MMPI-2
profile involves:

1. Evaluating the acceptability of the record for an individual interpretation including some determination of
   the approach that the test subject took in completing
   the inventory and the extent to which this test-taking
   set is consistent with other background information on
   him or her;
2. Examining the clinical scale scores in the standard profile to generate a list of possible lines of interpretation
   about the personality and current emotional status of
   the test subject;
3. Consulting various MMPI interpretive guides for common correlates of the code pattern generated by the
   clinical profile including possible psychodiagnostic alternatives;
4. Determining for the scales that are elevated to at least
   a moderate level the subscale components that are
   primarily contributing to these elevations and noting
   the kinds of issues of greatest concern to the test subject;
5. Noting any significant critical items that may have been
   endorsed to signal special problems or previously un-
   suspected symptoms or concerns;
6. Examining the scores in the content scales to elabo-
   rate on the interpretive hypotheses already generated
   and formulating a coherent summary of the personality dynamics and diagnostic status of the test subject with proper caveats on the dependability of these

conclusions in light of the scores on the various validity indicators [pp. 21–22].

Clearly the interpretation of the MMPI-2 requires advanced clinical knowledge and skills.

In the foregoing set of interpretive guidelines set
forth by Hathaway and McKinley (1989), reference is
made (item 3) to consulting "interpretive guides." Commonly, these guides are referred to as "cookbooks," and
are the offspring of the movement to use actuarial methods in clinical assessment (Meehl, 1954, 1956). This type
of reference provides clinical summaries for combinations
of elevated clinical scales. In implementing a "cookbook
analysis," the clinical psychologist simply: (1) notes the
configuration of the validity scales (and the cookbook will
have summaries for alternative validity scale patterns);
(2) determines the clinical scales that are elevated (any
T-score above 65 is considered to be significant clinically);
and (3) looks up combinations of two and/or three elevated
scales in one of the authoritative references or "cookbooks."
Each of these sources provides a clinical description for
each of the clinical scales individually; but it is clear that
a more refined clinical picture can be obtained by combining scales into two- or three-scale patterns.

At first blush, the use of a cookbook might seem unprofessional, but such is not the case. There are so many
possible two- or three-scale combinations that the clinical psychologist would be taxed if he or she had to memo-
rize all the nuances. Moreover, the clinical summaries in
the cookbooks are based on amalgamations of research,
thereby affording optimal reliability and validity.

There are 10 basic MMPI-2 clinical scales (number 1
through 0). The scales and brief symptomatic definitions,
derived from J. R. Graham (1993), are as follows:

Scale 1 (Hypochondriasis): "preoccupation with the body
and concomitant fears of illness and disease" [p. 56].

Scale 2 (Depression): "The primary characteristics of symptomatic depression are poor morale, lack of hope in the future, and a general dissatisfaction with one's own life situation" [p. 58].

Scale 3 (Hysteria): "involuntary psychogenic loss or disorder of function" [p. 60].

Scale 4 (Psychopathic Deviate): "such delinquent acts as lying, stealing, sexual promiscuity, excessive drinking, and the like, no major criminal types were included" [p. 63].

Scale 5 (Masculinity-Femininity): gender-based preferences, and "most items are not sexual in nature and cover a diversity of topics, including work and recreational interests, worries and fears, excessive sensitivities, and family relationships" [p. 66].

Scale 6 (Paranoia): "ideas of reference, feelings of persecution, grandiose self-concepts, suspiciousness, excessive sensitivity, and rigid opinions and attitudes" [p. 68].

Scale 7 (Psychasthenia): "thinking characterized by excessive doubts, compulsions, obsessions, and unreasonable fears" [p. 69].

Scale 8 (Schizophrenia): "disturbances of thinking, mood, and behavior. Misinterpretation of reality, delusions, and hallucinations" [p. 72].

Scale 9 (Hypomania): "elevated mood, accelerated speech and motor activity, irritability, flight of ideas, and brief periods of depression" [pp. 74–75].

Scale 0 (Social Introversion): "tendencies to withdraw from social contacts and responsibilities" [p. 77].

There are also numerous supplementary scales. Dahlstrom, Welsh, and Dahlstrom (1972, 1975) offer over 450 ancillary scales, from typical clinical matters (e.g., Dominance) to specialized matters (e.g., Success in Baseball). Butcher (1990) and J. R. Graham (1993) provide useful information on the myriad of supplemental scales.

To illustrate how combining MMPI-2 scales works, consider a client with elevated scores (more than two standard deviations above the mean) on the Depression and Psychopathic Deviate Scales, that is, a 2-4 code. In a refinement beyond the symptomatic definitions for the individual scales given previously, Graham's (1993) description of the 2-4 code is:

> When persons with the 24/42 code come to the attention of professionals, it usually is after they have been in trouble with their families or with the law. They are impulsive and unable to delay gratification of their impulses. They have little respect for social standards and often find themselves in direct conflict with societal values. Their acting out behavior is likely to involve excessive use of alcohol, and their histories include alcoholic benders, arrests, job loss and family discord associated with drinking [p. 88].

This is just a partial description, but it captures the essence of a "cookbook" interpretation.

Some of the reference sources provide elements of diagnosis, such as prognosis. For the 2-4 code, Lachar (1974) states: "The depression abates when escape from stress is effective or manipulations promise to be effective. While the insight these persons show may be good and their verbal protestations of resolve to do better may seem genuine, long-range prognosis for behavior change is poor. Recurrence of acting out and subsequent exaggerated guilt are common" (p. 74). He adds: "The modal diagnosis was Personality Trait Disturbance" (p. 75).

The MMPI-2 represents research-based advances that will enhance treatment planning. Butcher (1990) explains how psychological assessment in general and the MMPI-2 in particular can be used for pretreatment planning (e.g., an "outside opinion"), evaluation of ongoing treatment (i.e., progress or lack thereof), and posttreatment evaluation.

Just as efforts have been made to find short forms for the Wechsler tests, clinical psychologists have devised various short or abbreviated forms for the MMPI. Basically, the same advantages and disadvantages for short forms of the Wechsler tests apply to short forms of the MMPI. Butcher,

Kendall, and Hoffman (1980) conclude that it is unwarranted to believe that MMPI short forms are "accurate substitutes for the standard form MMPI in predicting objective measures of psychopathology" (p. 278). Similarly, Helmes and McLaughlin (1983) compared three MMPI short forms, and decided: "the rate of correct classification by all three major short forms is insufficient for clinical use" (p. 787).

From a survey of practicing clinical psychologists, Moreland and Dahlstrom (1983) found limited acceptance accorded to short forms, but a positive reception for computerized interpretations and supplementary scales.

Since research on the original MMPI seemed to overwhelmingly indicate that short forms were inadequate substitutes for the total instrument, the modern view of short forms seems to be: "except when administering the first 370 items in the booklet when only the standard validity and clinical scales are needed, the use of shortened forms of the MMPI-2 is not acceptable" (p. 17). In this age of elevated accountability, it would be foolhardy for the clinical psychologist to use a short or abbreviated form of the MMPI-2. Indeed, the same assertion would seem to hold true for virtually any psychological test.

There was considerable concern about whether the original version of the MMPI was discriminatory or biased, for example, whether it "overpathologizes" African American clients (Butcher et al., 1983). Pritchard and Rosenblatt (1980) found no evidence that the MMPI was racially biased. Giving consideration to socioeconomic level, presenting complaints, diagnoses, and demographic information, Butcher et al. (1983) did a cross-cultural comparison of American Indian, African American, and Caucasian inpatients using the MMPI, and they concluded that any differences were due to symptomatic distinctions. That is, the MMPI did not overpathologize for black patients, and "minority status alone does not account for the obtained differences between black and white psychiatric patients" (p. 593).

There were concerns about the possibility of the MMPI items and standardization being discriminatory and/or outdated (much of the research was done in the 1940s), so the restandardization to develop the MMPI-2 gave particular attention to investigating and remedying these matters. For the MMPI-2, Hathaway and McKinley (1989) report that: items that were "culturally outmoded or psychometrically unsound" (p. 3) were replaced; and ethnic and racial backgrounds, socioeconomic status, and numerous other factors were structured to provide an improved normative sample.

The MMPI-2 is a self-report, that is, the client is asked to read questions and answer them honestly. Here is the problem: Some clients may wish to answer openly and honestly, but their personality leads them to denial or defensiveness or some other quality that produces other than a penetrating revelation of the true characteristics. Hamersma (1972) states: "Self-report inventories are highly susceptible to faking, malingering, and response sets" (p. 102).

There are several types of response bias. Clients may give the socially desirable response (i.e., they say what they think the clinical psychologist wants to hear). Some clients, such as a parent being evaluated in a child custody dispute who wants the clinical psychologist to believe that he or she is the better parent for meeting the best interests of the child, may give only (or predominantly) responses that will make him or her look good. Conversely, some clients, such as one being evaluated for rehabilitation benefits, may give only (or predominantly) responses that will create an appearance of needing services or financial support. There may also be an unrealistic commitment to respond in a certain manner (i.e., positively or negatively); this response set ignores the contents of the item.

The validity scales of the MMPI-2 are helpful for detecting these detriments to clinical assessment, and in fact the MMPI-2 is one of the few self-report inventories that offers any measurement of these biasing factors. A. L. Edwards (1964), the creator of a popular self-report inventory known as the Edwards Personal Preference Schedule (A. L. Edwards, 1954), asserts that a client's responses to an objective personality test, such as the MMPI, should be viewed as only revealing what the client is willing to endorse as acceptable, as opposed to being viewed as a realistic portrayal of the personality. Since penetrating the response bias is a goal of projective personality tests, this leads to the use of the Rorschach Inkblots Method and the Thematic Apperception Test (TAT).

THE PROJECTION HYPOTHESIS

Early on, *projection* was regarded as an ego-defense mechanism associated with paranoia and other disorders (Freud, 1911). While the term still has the ego-defense meaning, its use has been expanded to describe an influence on sense perceptions (Freud, 1919); that is, how the person perceives the outer world may be influenced by the projection of personality features.

The projection principle underlies so-called projective techniques. As Symonds (1946) describes it: "In projective techniques there is the implication that as a person expresses himself in any kind of constructive or interpretive activity he is acting out inner fantasy. If he is telling a story it is believed that he projects into the characters in the story his own impulses, feelings, and thoughts" (p. 515). Or as L. K. Frank (1948) puts it: "The essential feature of a projective technique is that it evokes from the subject what is in various ways expressive of his private world and personality process" (p. 47).

Lindzey (1961) states: "A projective technique is an instrument that is considered especially sensitive to covert or unconscious aspects of behavior, it permits or encourages a wide variety of subject responses, is highly multidimensional, and it evokes unusually rich or profuse response data with a minimum of subject awareness concerning the purpose of the test" (p. 45).

Of importance to the interpretation of projective techniques, the clinical psychologist usually avoids nomothetic ideas, while focusing on idiographic ideas. As Rabin (1968) says: "the task of the examiner-interpreter is complex, for his analysis is holistic-ideographic, and he attributes to the responses that he obtains a multidimensionality necessary for such analysis" (p. 12).

Projective techniques have received strong criticism, particularly because studies reveal that their reliability and validity may not meet current standards. Regardless, projective techniques continue to be heavily relied upon by clinical psychologists, "albeit in more limited and less global ways than in the past" (Wierzbicki, 1993). As for the continued use of an assessment technique, be it projective or otherwise, that has questionable qualities, Hutton, Dubes, and Muir (1992) give the pithy surmise: "Perhaps some psychologists reason that a test with inferior characteristics is better than no test at all" (p. 283). In contradiction to the negativism, there seems reason to believe that, as reflected in the priority given by practicing psychologists, projective techniques do, in fact, provide important substance to clinical assessment, even though traditional psychometric properties are not obtained.

THE RORSCHACH INKBLOTS METHOD

The Rorschach Inkblots Method is derived from studies of perception. It involves a series of ten inkblots (selected from thousands of trial inkblots). The client is told that people see different things in the inkblots, and is asked to tell the clinical psychologist what he or she sees in them.

The Rorschach Inkblots Method was developed by the Swiss psychiatrist Hermann Rorschach. He was born on November 8, 1884, and he died of appendicular peritonitis at the age of 38. Perhaps (in part) because his father was a professor of drawing, Rorschach had a long-term professional interest in the drawings of patients. Pichot (1984) provides a detailed account of Rorschach's life, focusing on how the present-day inkblots came into being. In describing the method, Klopfer and Davidson (1962) state:

> A basic assumption underlying the Rorschach techniques is that there is a relationship between perception and personality. The way in which an individual organizes or "structures" the ink blots in forming his perceptions reflects fundamental aspects of his psychological functioning. Ink blots are suitable as stimuli because they are relatively ambiguous or "unstructured," i.e., they do not elicit particular learned responses, but permit a variety of possible responses [p. 14].

Thus, there are no "correct answers" as such.

As will be discussed shortly, there are certain factors within a client's responses to the Rorschach that lead to an impression of the client's perceptual connection to reality, but the primary interest is in the "distortions" that are unique to the client. Beck (1981) clarifies: "A person's perception, his cognitive functioning, is in instances erratic because he distorts the object. He sees it not as it is, meaning not in accordance with the experienced reality of a normative segment of the population. That is, he sees it not as it is, but as he, the patient, is. Here we enter on the problem of the whole personality as a psychological determinant" (p. 31). Obviously the projective hypothesis is applicable: "His perceptions are selected and organized in terms of his 'projective' needs, experiences, and habitual patterns of response as well as by the physical properties of the blots themselves" (Klopfer and Davidson, 1962, p. 14).

The responses given by the client are scored according to different categories or factors. The original Rorschach approach supported that the responses to inkblots could reveal basic personality tendencies only if the responses were analyzed systematically. This meant having categories that would accommodate precise identification and measurement; that is: "Accordingly, when abstracting from the complex test performance certain components for analysis, he concentrated primarily on formal categories and only secondarily on content categories" (Rickers-Ovsiankina, 1977, p. 4).

There are several alternative systems for scoring and interpreting the Rorschach, such as those by Beck (Beck, Beck, Levitt, and Molish, 1961) and Exner (1974, 1978; Exner and Weiner, 1982). As might be expected, advocates for each system claim superiority. For present purposes, it would be ill-advised to enter into a debate on the merits of the alternative systems. Rather, the Klopfer system will be used as an example. In it, there are five major scoring categories:

1. LOCATION: Where on the card was the concept seen?
2. DETERMINANT: How was the concept seen? What qualities of blot determined it?
3. CONTENT: What was the subject matter of the concept seen?
4. POPULARITY-ORIGINALITY, P-O: How commonly is the concept seen by other subjects? . . . Many responses are neither popular nor original. . . .
5. FORM LEVEL: How accurately is the concept seen? How closely does the concept fit the blot area used? Also, what is the degree of elaboration of the concept? [Klopfer and Davidson, 1962, pp. 48–49].

The use of a scoring system, whichever one may be chosen, is intended to facilitate reliability and validity.

There is more to the analysis of a Rorschach protocol than simply totaling up the scores for a set of categories. As Phillips and Smith (1953) describe it: "Formal scoring represents only a part of the categorization of Rorschach data. The Rorschach test situation elicits far more than the scored perceptual reactions. Such things as the style with which material is developed, elaborations of percepts, and direct responses to the examiner have been shown to be related to significant extra-Rorschach behavior and these reactions too must be categorized" (p. 257). One of the foremost focal points has been the content of and/or the symbolic imagery associated with the responses: "the essential nature of the personality is reflected equally in the content, the quality, and the scoring category of a subject's response" (Miale, 1977, p. 452). This is, however, an area of great controversy, particularly because of dubious reliability and validity. Mindess (1955) asserted: "In the Rorschach literature generally, a visible confusion surrounds the problem of content analysis" (p. 248). Regrettably, the passage of forty years has not eliminated this confusion.

It would be beneficial if there were irrefutable correlations between Rorschach scores and behavior and/or mental processes, but such is not the case. There has, however, been extensive research (more on some systems than on others) that provides guidelines for interpretation that overcome the problems of reliability and validity that plague most, if not all, clinical assessment strategies.

To exemplify how scoring categories are used in clinical interpretation, Ogdon (1982) indicates that a protocol that has a greater than average number of responses involving movement (e.g., a *flying* bat, or two *dancing* women) might support the following: "Introversive, thoughtful, or inhibitory characteristics in normal individuals"; "Above average intelligence and academic achievement at all ages and with many clinical as well as normal populations"; "High creativity, inventiveness or creative potential, especially in linguistic and artistic activities"; "Good ego functioning: the Reality Principle dominates with good planning ability, impulse control and the ability to tolerate frustration, positive and consistent self-orientation, minimal feelings of vulnerability or fragility, and good prognosis in therapy" (p. 23); and other hypotheses as well. Conversely, Ogdon posits that a protocol that has a subnormal number of responses with movement might support the following: "Ego weakness as found in many neurotic conditions associated with a lack of normal flexibility and resistance to change"; "Anxiety, tension or hysteria"; "Low intelligence, low mental age, and possible mental retardation" (p. 24); and other hypotheses as well.

With the number of quite divergent hypotheses that are possible from the same single Rorschach score, it is readily apparent that the interpretation is dependent upon the expertise of the clinical psychologist. That is, while the scoring system can help establish a respectable intrajudge and/or interjudge reliability, the research to date does not assure interpretive validity, even when multiple scores are used: "Direct behavioral parallels may not always exist . . ." (Klopfer and Davidson, 1962, p. 15).

A potential solution may be in the offing. Efforts are underway to create computerized interpretations for the Rorschach Inkblots Method, much like what has been done for the MMPI. It is premature, however, to give one's blessing to this approach.

THE THEMATIC APPERCEPTION TEST (TAT)

The TAT lacks the traditional properties of a psychometric test. Based on the projective hypothesis, the TAT was created by Henry A. Murray (Morgan and Murray, 1935), and was predicated on his translation of psychoanalytically oriented principles into a theory of "personology." This theory is directed at understanding the total functioning of the individual, which necessitates appraisal of the human organism and its placement in an environmental context. Murray focused on the normal personality, as opposed to the disordered one.

The TAT consists of pictures depicting, for the most part, people and scenes. While there are several possible administrative alternatives, the general approach is to ask the client to: "Tell what has led up to the event shown in the picture, describe what is happening at the moment, what the characters are feeling and thinking; and then give the outcome. Speak your thoughts as they come to your mind" (Murray, 1943, p. 3). The contents of the stories are analyzed.

As with the Rorschach, there are several alternative systems for analyzing and interpreting the client's TAT responses. Only a few of the systems provide for quantifying the responses.

To place analysis and interpretation in a nutshell, Murray (1938) supported: "analyzing each successive event in a story into (a) the force or forces emanating from the hero, and (b) the force or forces emanating from the environment" (p. 6). Murray's content analysis dissects the responses for needs (provoked by internal and/or external sources); presses (environmental determinants that facilitate or impede goal-related efforts); thema (the need-press interaction); need integrate (the integration between the need and the environmental object's image-thought); unity-thema (dominant needs formed into an interrelated compound); and regnant processes (mutually dependent processes that constitute dominant configurations in the brain). Intellectual functioning, imaginative processes, family dynamics, inner adjustment, and patterning of overt behavior are just a few of the dimensions that can be obtained from an analysis of the form and content of the client's TAT protocol (Henry, 1956).

It should be noted that there have been numerous thematic apperception strategies; that is, telling stories about pictures. For example, two of the more popular ones are the Children's Apperception Test (CAT) and the Senior Apperception Technique (SAT) (Bellak, 1986); both of these strategies are similar to the TAT in rationale, structure, administration, analysis, and interpretation, but are tailored, respectively, to children and to older adults.

THE RELIABILITY AND VALIDITY OF PROJECTIVE TECHNIQUES

As mentioned, the TAT is not (and has not aspired to be) a psychometric test. This is also basically true for the Rorschach, albeit some scoring systems have confused matters by seeking quantifiable data and developing indices for differential diagnosis (note the complex, quantifiable Rorschach system offered by Exner [1974, 1978] and Exner and Weiner [1982]). Further, all projective techniques are highly dependent on the clinical expertise of the diagnostician.

As a result, there has been much criticism of the reliability and validity of projective techniques: "Little that is encouraging can be said about projective techniques, the literature on which continues to reflect a lack of interest in the generally accepted standards of empirical validation" (Lanyon, 1984, p. 692).

It must be remembered that the interpretation of projective data is for meaning, not for a probability statement (Schwartz and Lazar, 1979). Some defenders of the TAT claim that conventional reliability methods do not have relevance with the TAT (Harrison, 1965).

There are many reasons why psychometric properties are not determinative of the value of projective techniques, such as the TAT. For example: (1) the pictures were not chosen to be paired or to accommodate a split-half analysis; (2) the expectation is that a client receiving a clinical intervention will not remain in a fixed psychological state; (3) clinically, there would be no benefit from gaining an identical second performance on the TAT; and (4) intervening influences are likely to occur over a course of clinical evaluation or treatment (Karon, 1981).

Harrison's (1965) survey of research led him to conclude that intrajudge and interjudge reliabilities are sufficiently positive. Validity also has support (Harrison, 1965; Bellak, 1986), but the importance of the clinical psychologist's expertise is highlighted by the summary statement: "The 'test' is still a test of the tester" (Harrison, 1965, p. 597). A special vulnerability comes from confirmatory bias. Smith and Dumont (1995) assert: "It would seem that therapists tend to find in projectives that they use whatever they are already disposed to find, with greater or lesser accuracy, through other means. They use them to buttress interpretations made on the basis of referral information, intake interviews, and the initial client data elicited through the 'art of conversational inquiry'" (p. 302).

It is necessary to be practical about projective techniques. By its revered scientist–practitioner training model, clinical psychology involves both science and practice; and by public policy, practice is endowed with a duty to rely on "art" within bounds.

The clinical psychologist should recognize that certain assessment strategies, such as (perhaps) projective techniques, do not always attain unimpeachable scientific status. Yet, as was discussed in the preceding chapter, the role that society has assigned to clinical psychologists necessitates the use of certain procedures that are known to be fallible. The important safeguard is, of course, that the clinical psychologist must recognize the strengths and weaknesses of all interventions, be they diagnostic or therapeutic, and must make accommodations accordingly.

PERSONAL CONSIDERATIONS

There are several considerations that are accentuated by being a diagnostician. These include: employability, confidence and competence, creativity, and clinical acumen.

Diagnosis, in general, is understood and endorsed by professionals and laypersons alike. The clinical assessment strategies and their purposes are usually discrete and clear-cut. For example, the evaluation of mental abilities is accomplished by an intelligence test, and the level of intellectual functioning, or the IQ, reflects the person's learning and development patterns—even elementary schoolchildren are aware of intelligence testing and its purpose.

As a result of the foregoing, being a diagnostician means that the clinical psychologist has distinctive and marketable skills. There is usually a good possibility that an employer, such as a mental health clinic, will recognize the need to provide clinical assessment services.

Clinical assessment is a primary service within clinical psychology, and often such functions as the administration of psychological tests or the intake interviewing (e.g., history taking) of clients will be assigned to someone who welcomes a role that is somewhat circumspect. It is rather common for this role, especially if it is technical in nature (e.g., administering psychological tests), to be fulfilled by a fairly junior-level professional, and the job title might be psychometrist or psychometrician instead of psychologist. This does not mean that diagnosis in the complete sense does not require advanced skills. Diagnosis does, in fact, necessitate refined clinical expertise—yet certain functions can be performed well without the sagacity of the senior clinical psychologist.

Confidence is essential to being an effective diagnostician. Obviously this quality cannot be obtained simply by completing university courses in clinical assessment; rather, it is dependent, to a marked degree, on the personality composite of the clinical psychologist.

Why is confidence essential? Because the diagnostician routinely makes judgments that have a far-reaching impact on the lives of many people. For example, when a child's intelligence is assessed to be lower than average, it impacts on the child and his or her entire family, and may shape their lives for years to come. Also, in many jurisdictions, the expert opinions of the clinical psychologist and the psychiatrist are accorded equal authority for a wide variety of legal decisions, such as the involuntary commitment of a person to a mental hospital or for supporting or contradicting a defendant's use of the insanity defense to avoid guilt or responsibility for a crime.

Connected to confidence is competence. In order to function effectively as a diagnostician, there must be a realistic sense of competence. That is, the clinical psychologist must have a substantive knowledge and realistic awareness of the extent and limits of his or her professional abilities.

Competence has critical ethical implications. Most basically, it is unethical to offer any psychological service without adequate competence. There are also legal implications (e.g., avoiding allegations of malpractice by only offering services that are compatible with one's established competence). Much of the decision making about confidence and competence comes from the clinical psychologist's self-regulation on a day-to-day basis.

Being a diagnostician can be boring! If one works all day, every day in psychological assessment, it is likely that the same tests will be used repeatedly, reports following the same format will be produced, and the same phrases will be relied upon. These days it is possible for reports to be generated by computer—that is how repetitive and structured the contents can become. On the other hand, assessment can be a highly creative process. If the services become perfunctory, it is a movement toward being nonprofessional.

There are other pitfalls: One school superintendent insisted that the psychologists "provide IQ numbers, that's what it takes to get reimbursement from the state"; and since he or she had heard that culturally disadvantaged children tended to score lower on the Binet than on the Wechsler, urged the use of the Binet "until we have the special education classrooms full."

Regrettably, it is not uncommon for an employer, particularly one who is not a mental health professional, to have objectives (e.g., gaining state financial reimbursement for handicapped children) that do not honor the objectives of psychodiagnosis (e.g., substituting a minimal testing for a comprehensive clinical assessment). In instances of conflicting objectives, the clinical psychologist may be channeled toward an inappropriate role, such as one in which he or she merely records IQs. Not only is this potentially unprofessional (e.g., it could be unethical to make diagnostic decisions without adequate assessment data), it certainly constricts the clinical psychologist's personal–professional identity, to the potential detriment of all concerned.

Creativity is the hallmark of high-quality diagnostics. From a comprehensive base of assessment data, the clinical psychologist creates idiographic and nomothetic analyses and interpretations that justify the sacrosanct role afforded to clinical psychology by public policy, and honors the best interests of the client. On a personal level, it is creativity that furthers the rewards of being a diagnostician.

Clinical acumen is not easily gained. Confidence, competence, and creativity join with academic knowledge, professional experience, and the clinical psychologist's personality to bring about the sagacity that distinguishes being a diagnostician from other psychological roles and from the opinions of laypersons. Clinical acumen is never fully realized; rather, the quest for it is constant throughout the career of the clinical psychologist.

Chapter 4

Psychotherapy Theories and Strategies

> *Psychotherapy, in its broadest sense, originated with the beginning of mankind—when the first two people formed a relationship, each offering the other solace, comfort and encouragement. . . . The ancient Greeks utilized specific psychotherapeutic techniques in their healing temples, where the ailing person was exposed to music, soothing environments, as well as having the opportunity to express his troubled thoughts and feelings to the priest* [Barron, Fabrikant, and Krasner, 1971, p. 1].

> *What good is psychotherapy? As good as man's faith in his humanity. Men have always believed in their ability to change for the better and to help each other so to change through mutual assistance, love, religion, and art. Conceived in the broadest terms psychotherapy derives from the same faith and, employing of necessity some of the same means, attempts to formulate these more precisely* [Rosenzweig, 1954, p. 303].

As the first quotation suggests, the essence of psychotherapy is a helping relationship in which one human being ministers to another through the healing power of words. As the second quotation suggests, faith in one's ability to change and to help others change is fundamental to the generic meaning of psychotherapy.

As a professional specialty psychotherapy has four defining characteristics (Ford and Urban, 1963): (1) two or more persons engaged in a highly confidential interaction in which one or more is required to be self-revealing; (2) the mode of interaction is usually limited to verbal exchange; (3) the interaction is relatively prolonged; and (4) the agreed-upon purpose is to achieve change; that is, to foster appropriate and realistic thought-feeling-action patterns that are consistent with one's values, and that lead to responsible and satisfying interpersonal relationships. Three critical assumptions are that change is desired, that life circumstances and environment do not rule out change, and that change can be brought about by psychological procedures.

The terms *psychotherapy, counseling, treatment,* and *therapy* are often used interchangeably. However, the term *counseling* ordinarily excludes serious psychopathology; *treatment* is often synonymous with medical interventions; and *therapy* does not differentiate psychological from nonpsychological interventions.

Although *psychotherapy* differs from other therapeutic interventions, such as educational, medical, sociological, environmental, it may be used in conjunction with the latter methods. Although similar in some respects to therapeutically beneficial friendships, psychotherapy differs in having formally designated roles of therapist and client, and in the absence of social consequences that often follow from personal relationships. In both a legal and ethical sense, therapists enter into a fiduciary relationship with their clients (Knapp and VandeCreek, 1994, p. 53).

Psychotherapy can be conducted with one client (child or adult), with a group of unrelated clients, with a couple, or with a family. The length of psychotherapy varies depending upon the goal (e.g., personality restructuring, resolution of specified problems, crisis management); the seriousness of the problem (e.g., mild, moderate, or severe);

the theoretical orientation of the therapist; and the financial resources of the client. Psychotherapy may be long term (usually more than 25 sessions), short-term (generally 10–24 sessions), or brief (less than 10 sessions). Two therapists may work as a cotherapy team, and a client may be in one or more modalities (individual, group, couple, or family) at the same time with the same or different therapists.

At least three stages of psychotherapeutic work can be identified. The first stage is developing a collaborative relationship, specifying problems, and prioritizing goals. The second stage consists of the therapist's application of specific interventions to implement therapeutic goals. The third stage is designed to generalize and maintain therapeutic gains.

More detailed models of change have been offered by various authors. The change model developed by Prochaska and DiClemente (1984) is one example. Change takes place in five stages: precontemplation, contemplation, preparation, action, and maintenance. Change is usually cyclic, and each stage refers both to a period of time and to a set of tasks required for movement to the next stage (Prochaska and Norcross, 1994, pp. 460–470). Almost all current therapy models employ two fundamental change principles: give relevant, timely feedback, and provide opportunities for corrective experiencing (Goldfried, 1980). From the two fundamental change principles, specific change strategies common to most therapy models can be derived and implemented; for example, increasing self-awareness and self-acceptance; learning adaptive coping actions; accessing and reexperiencing heretofore denied feelings; reconciling conflicting states of mind; activating client strengths; utilizing external resources; and developing a new and empowering perspective.

For both clients and therapists the psychotherapy process is sometimes tedious and exhausting, sometimes exciting and energizing, always challenging, and never

quite finished. During the course of psychotherapy a therapist plays many roles: interpersonal model, conceptualizer
of information, change agent, and "professional" friend.

Being a psychotherapist is both a personal as well as
professional undertaking. For those who aspire to be psychotherapists, Strupp (1978) has this to say: "I would place
a good deal of emphasis on the prerequisite of native tal-
ent. Given such endowment, the rest is prolonged hard
work, patience, and extensive experience . . . a fine therapist closely resembles a painter, novelist, or composer.
As is true in all the sciences and the arts, few reach the
summit" (p. 317).

Although the assertion can be debated, psychotherapy
as a unique blend of science and art originated with Freud's
theory of psychoanalysis. Freud formulated a complex
theory and a painstaking method to explore and explicate
a person's past life with the goal of producing an insight-
based catharsis of unconscious conflicts. Although Freud's
psychoanalysis had to make room for inevitable splinter
groups and rival factions, the theory and method maintained a proprietary claim on psychotherapy for nearly half
a century.

The first nonpsychoanalytic theory to mount a serious
and permanent challenge was the client-centered approach
developed by Carl Rogers in the 1940s. Basically, Rogers
(1942) made it intellectually respectable to deal with the
conscious; therapeutically relevant to focus on the present;
professionally permissible for therapists to disclose their
personhood; and scientifically responsible to open both the
process and the outcome of one's psychotherapy sessions to
professional scrutiny.

Following Rogers' lead several learning theorists, notably John Dollard and Neal Miller (1950), demonstrated
that Freudian concepts and principles were not theory-
specific, but could be translated into theoretical language
that allowed greater conceptual clarity and empirical
confirmation or disconfirmation. For example, global

psychoanalytic concepts, such as repression, displacement, conflict, were translated into the specific and empirically derived terms of *drive, cue, response,* and *reward.* Between the midsixties and mideighties there was a mind-boggling proliferation of psychotherapies. Goldfried (1980) cites a figure of 130 different therapeutic approaches, and Corsini (1981) estimates as many as 250 alternative approaches. Even the conservative Civilian Health and Medical Programs of the Uniformed Services (CHAMPUS) includes over 40 different psychotherapeutic procedures in its approved list for reimbursement (APA, 1980). Clearly, *psychotherapy* has become a generic term that subsumes a bewildering array of competing claims to better serve the psychological health needs of the public. For a recent perspective on the history and current status of psychotherapy, including the recent trend to combine and integrate approaches, the reader is referred to Freedheim (1992).

In general, most current psychotherapy systems can be compared and contrasted on six theoretical dimensions: (1) conscious versus unconscious determinants of behavior; (2) insight versus behavior change as the therapeutic goal; (3) a focus on the present–future versus the past; (4) a scientific versus aesthetic attitude; (5) the therapeutic relationship versus the therapist's techniques as a basis for change; and (6) diagnosis versus assessment. As many have noted, what theorists choose to exclude or deemphasize may be as significant personally and professionally as what they choose to include or emphasize in their theories.

CURRENT PSYCHOTHERAPEUTIC ORIENTATIONS

Psychodynamic Orientation

This section presents an overview of Freudian or classical psychoanalytic psychotherapy, Adlerian individual psychotherapy, Jungian analytic psychotherapy, the socio-psychological theories of Karen Horney, Erich Fromm, and Harry Stack Sullivan, the ego analysts, such as Heinz Hartmann, Anna Freud, Erik Erikson, and the object relations theorists, such as Melanie Klein, Heinz Kohut, and Margaret Mahler.

Underlying psychodynamic theories is the fundamental postulate of opposing forces that make painful intrapsychic conflicts inevitable, and that these conflicts, of which the person may or may not be aware, often originate in childhood and have a powerful influence on personality development and the ability to cope with current life stresses (Goldenberg, 1983). Although strongly influenced by Freud's theory of psychoanalysis, the later psychodynamic theorists rejected parts of the theory, modified other aspects, and made significant additions. Other theoretical contributions to the psychoanalytic literature have been Otto Fenichel's theory of neurosis, Otto Rank's will therapy, and Wilhelm Reich's body-oriented theory.

Freudian Psychoanalysis. Although Freud developed a comprehensive theory of personality development, only the traditional psychoanalytic theory of psychotherapy is described. Psychoanalytic psychotherapy is primarily a method of treating neurotic disorders, and usually involves a commitment of two or more years of four to five sessions per week. Over the years variations in the length, procedures, and goals of psychoanalytic psychotherapy have been developed, and are commonly referred to as neo-Freudian or psychodynamic approaches.

Unconscious intrapsychic conflicts are considered to be a major cause of psychological disorder, and to result from unsuccessful mastery of the psychosexual stages of development in infancy and early childhood. The overall goal is: (1) to relieve psychic distress; (2) to strengthen the conscious, adaptive part of the personality (ego) in coping with the pressures of instinctual drives (id), and the demands of conscience (superego); and (3) to improve psychosexual maturity. A key assumption is that current problems of living cannot be successfully resolved without a thorough understanding of the unconscious basis of the early conflictual relationships with parents or parent surrogates. The central focus of the therapy sessions is the interplay between the client's unconscious impulses and unconscious efforts to cope with the impulses by various defense mechanisms. The primary intervention strategy is to resolve unconscious intrapsychic conflicts by gaining insight into the causes and by applying this insight to current behavior. To accomplish this strategy, several techniques are used. Foremost is the technique of free association, which involves free verbal expression of every thought, feeling, or impulse in order to reduce inhibitions, establish meaningful connections between associations, and bring unconscious material into consciousness (Goldenberg, 1983). The analyst remains silent and neutral, except to intercede when the patient is experiencing temporary resistance.

Another technique is dream analysis, in which the client verbalizes the conscious content of a dream, and then free associates to the content so that the analyst can discern the unconscious meaning. Freud postulated that dreams represent a disguised compromise between unconscious wish fulfillment and unconscious fear of wish fulfillment.

Another technique, analysis of transference, is used to identify and resolve clients' "unfinished business" with significant others, by allowing them to react to the analyst as they did (and may still do) to significant persons in their early life (Corey, 1982). The abnormal effect of early parent–child interactions on the client's current interpersonal relationships is counteracted by working through similar problems in the relationship with the analyst (Corey, 1982).

The purpose of resistance is to defend oneself from acute anxiety that would occur if the unconscious suddenly became conscious. In the analysis of resistance, the analyst directs attention to any aspect of the therapeutic relationship that the client is attempting to avoid, as well as to anything that is blocking the process of uncovering unconscious material, so that therapy can progress and the client can begin to understand how resistance interferes with his or her daily life (Corey, 1982). Once clients have overcome resistance, they can then deal directly with the conflicts that underlie the resistance.

Finally, interpretation is an important technique that is combined with the ones outlined above. Interpretation consists of the analyst pointing out, describing, explaining, even teaching clients the meaning of their behavior, as manifested by free associations, dreams, transferential reactions, and resistances (Corey, 1982). Interpretations need to be well timed; that is, made at a point when unconscious material is close to awareness and the client is ready to assimilate painful insights.

The following excerpt shows an analyst's use of analysis of transference, followed by the use of free association.

Client: I don't understand why you're holding back on telling me if this step is the right one for me at this time in my life.

Analyst: This has come up before. You want my approval before taking some action. What seems to be happening here is that one of the conflicts you have with your wife is trying to get her approval of what you have decided you want to do, and that conflict is occurring now between us.

Client: I suppose so. Other people's approval has always been very important to me.

Analyst: Let's stay with that for a few minutes. Would you free associate to that idea of getting approval from others. Just let the associations come spontaneously— don't force them.

The client–analyst relationship can be characterized as very professional and businesslike, the purpose of which is to resolve the client's "there and then" interpersonal problems by working through the problems in the "here and now" interaction with the analyst. The role of the analyst is that of a neutral observer whose task is to encourage, examine, and interpret the meaning of the client's verbalizations. The role of the client is to be a passive participant whose task is to disclose his or her innermost reactions to the therapist.

Three strengths of the psychoanalytic theory are: (1) close attention to the way in which clients replicate in the therapy session the problems experienced outside the session; (2) thorough understanding of unconscious determinants of current behavior; and (3) detailed examination of critical events in the client's past life. Three weakness are: (1) too little attention to the present and immediate future; (2) insufficient emphasis on the client's personal strengths and assets; and (3) preoccupation with hidden or unconscious meanings of a client's in-session behavior.

Although many psychodynamic therapists use psychoanalytic theory to conceptualize problems and therapeutic goals, they may use techniques other than or in addition to the orthodox ones. An extended discussion of Freud's theory can be found in Arlow (1989) and Prochaska and Norcross (1994). The reader is also referred to Freud's (1915–1917) *The Introductory Lectures on Psychoanalysis*.

Adlerian Individual Psychotherapy. Developed by Alfred Adler, a one-time colleague of Freud, this theory, in contrast to Freudian theory, deemphasizes sexuality and emphasizes conscious processes and social determinants of personality.

A major cause of psychological disorder is thought to be self-centered and unrealistic goals that individuals develop early in life to overcome real or imagined inferiorities. The overall goal is to overcome inferiority feelings by setting aside egocentric motivations and values in favor of a socially responsible and individually productive life-style.

A key assumption is that human beings develop a life goal that centers their existence and toward which their life-style is directed, and an individual client can be understood through knowledge of conscious goals and subsequent goal-directed behavior (Goldenberg, 1983). The central focus of therapeutic work is the present and future thrust of the client's conscious memories, needs, values, beliefs, feelings, and actions.

The primary intervention strategy is an examination of early childhood recollections, birth order, family constellation, parental practices, from which the therapist constructs a picture of a client's life-style, shows him or her how the life-style is creating current problems of living, and what positive changes need to be undertaken. The therapist uses the techniques of interpretation, confrontation, and instruction to assist a client to live more productively and responsibly in the present, which then forms a solid foundation for the future. Adlerian therapists may also use Freudian methods, such as dream analysis, transference, and analysis of resistance, but the emphasis is on the present rather than the past.

The following illustrates the method of early memory recollection:

Client: Many times I act as if I believe what someone is telling me, but inwardly I have strong reservations, even mistrust, about believing them.

Therapist: Let's digress for a moment. I'd like for you to identify and describe one of your earliest memories.

Client: Well, I was about 4 or 5. I was standing in my backyard. Two neighborhood kids were there and they were standing over a pail. They asked me to come over and look at what they had in the pail. When I did, they pushed my head into the pail of water. I remember how scared I was—I thought they were going to drown me. I remember them laughing as they did it to me.

The client–therapist relationship is similar to a teacher–student interaction, in which the role of the therapist is to be energetic, directive, and instructive, and the client is expected to be a receptive, motivated learner who seeks to understand and correct in the present, and for the future, the mistakes of the past.

A strength of the Adlerian approach is the perception of problems as an expression of life-style. A limitation is reliance on reeducative methods. For additional information on this approach, the reader is referred to Mosak (1989) and Prochaska and Norcross (1994); for an original source, see Adler's (1929) *Problems of Neurosis: A Book of Case Histories.*

Jungian Analytic Psychotherapy. Developed by Carl Jung, also a one-time colleague of Freud, this theory offers a model of human experiences that is broader than Freud's conception of human beings engaged in an unremitting struggle between instinctual forces and sociocultural taboos.

A major cause of psychological disorder is held to be an unbalanced and opposing relation between conscious and unconscious processes. The overall goal is to assist a client to understand the unconscious, to respect its power, and to utilize its positive, creative elements in order to live a fully developed and evenly balanced life.

A key assumption is that in order to live a life free of disabling symptoms, a client must develop a constructive coupling of conscious and unconscious processes. Jung's concept of the unconscious is more inclusive than Freud's concept insofar as it includes collective–societal elements as well as personal–individual elements, and it is more balanced insofar as it allows for growth-producing as well as growth-inhibiting possibilities.

The central focus of the therapy sessions is the client's inner world of dreams, daydreams, fantasies, and other symbolic expressions. The primary intervention strategy is to achieve a balance between the conscious and unconscious so that the two complement one another rather than be in conflict (Goldenberg, 1983). To this end, the therapist uses interpretation of the unconscious as expressed in a client's waking life. Dream analysis is a major technique which takes into consideration a client's dream history rather than single, isolated dreams (Corey, 1982). Jung believed that dreams were not only a reaction to the past, but also a statement of current life and a portent of the future.

The client–therapist relationship can be likened to that of two persons who join together for a journey into territory unknown to both, in which the therapist as a guide uses his or her training to chart their course.

A strength of the Jungian approach is the conception of the unconscious as a source of growth and creativity; a limitation is its heavy emphasis on the client's inner world of symbolic experiences. For an extended discussion of Jung's theory, the reader is referred to Kaufmann (1989) and Jung's (1956) *Two Essays on Analytical Psychology.*

Social Psychological Theorists. Karen Horney, Erich Fromm, and Harry Stack Sullivan are among the best known of the social psychological theorists, all of whom assigned a major role to social and cultural determinants of normal and abnormal behavior.

The recurrently conflictual relationship between a client and those who transmit the values and beliefs of society (primarily parents and parent surrogates) is considered to be a major cause of psychological disorder. The overall goal is to revise a client's self-image so that it is congruent with potentialities and realistically based goals (Horney), to develop a "productive" orientation to life; that is, to actualize a client's potentials (Fromm); or for a client to understand who he or she is, and could be, in relation to significant others (Sullivan). A key assumption is that there are strong formative influences (positive and negative) beyond those of early childhood, and that psychotherapy has the potential to restore a client's capability to make substantial personality changes. The central focus of the therapy sessions is on past and current relationships with significant others.

The primary intervention strategy is to help clients understand their role and the role of significant others in the development and perpetuation of relationship problems. Horney and Fromm relied on the Freudian techniques of free association and dream analysis, supplemented by whatever techniques seem appropriate at a particular stage of therapy, while Sullivan relied on an interview-based exchange of information.

The client–therapist relationship is one characterized by a genuine respect for the individuality and latent capabilities of the client. Especially for Sullivan, the therapist's sharing of his or her personhood was believed to be therapeutic for the client.

A strength of the social–psychological approach is the interpersonal focus. A limitation is the lack of a systematic strategy for changing behavior. For additional material the reader is referred to Brammer, Shostrom, and Abrego (1989) and Hall and Lindzey (1978).

Ego Analysts. The contribution of the ego analysts, notably Erik Erikson, Heinz Kohut, Heinz Hartmann, and Anna Freud, to psychoanalytic theory is primarily a revised and expanded conceptualization of the structure and functions of the ego.

The unresolved problems of one or more stages of ego development are felt to be a major cause of psychological disorder. The overall goal is to strengthen the autonomous, nonconflictual functions of the ego in order to better organize behavior and to deal constructively with the current personal and social environment. A key assumption of ego analysis is that human beings "are capable of organizing their behavior and directing their activities to deal constructively with their environment" (Goldenberg, 1983, p. 217).

The central focus of therapeutic work is the reactive functions of the ego (i.e., to reduce conflict between the id or instinctual drives and the superego or conscience), and the proactive functions of the ego, which involve nonconflictual, productive interactions with the environment.

The primary intervention strategy is to give the client insight into how the past continues to influence the present, and to develop the client's awareness of what can be done in the present to correct the harmful effects of the past. The usual techniques are interpretation and constructive suggestions, and where applicable, orthodox psychoanalytic methods.

An important focus of Erikson's (1963) developmental theory is the relationship between a client's current developmental problem and success or failure with an earlier developmental problem. For example, a male client in his late twenties was seeking help with difficulties in forming intimate relationships. The therapist soon discovered that the client had never resolved the identity confusion and conflict of adolescence. Before the client could develop and maintain an intimate relationship with another adult, he first had to clarify and gain confidence in his own identity.

The client–therapist relationship is a collaborative one in which the client is an active change agent who makes constructive use of the therapist's shared knowledge of developmental stages and developmental crises.

A strength of this approach is the attention given to the adaptive functions of the ego; a limitation is insufficient emphasis on changing behavior. Erik Erikson (1963) and Blanck and Blanck (1974) provide additional information; see also Prochaska and Norcross (1994).

Object Relations. The primary interest of object relations theorists, such as Otto Kernberg, Melanie Klein, Heinz Kohut, and Margaret Mahler, is how current interpersonal relationships derive from interpersonal relationships with significant persons in infancy and childhood, especially the mother. The object relations model differs from classical psychoanalytic theory in the emphasis placed on a child's early caretakers rather than on the interplay of id, ego, and superego, and on interpersonal rather than intrapsychic stages of development. Since the concept of object relations refers to mental or symbolic representations of self, other, and self–other relations formed early in life through recurring interactions with significant others, a major cause of psychological disorder is a client's lack of a clearly defined, stable identity, as well as unrealistic or inappropriate perceptions, expectations, and affective responses that are acted out in the current interpersonal environment.

The major goal of psychotherapy is twofold: first, to understand and modify a client's mental representations of self, other, and self–other relations, that is, a client's interpersonal relationships that are experienced intrapsychically, and second, to correct the maladaptive perceptions, expectations, affective responses, and actions that characterize a client's current personal and social relationships.

The main intervention strategy is the formation of a healthy attachment between therapist and client within which a therapist utilizes empathy, constructive confrontation, and compassionate instruction to facilitate both internal and external changes. The therapist–client relationship is a collaboration, though not necessarily an egalitarian one, in which the therapist often adopts a surrogate parent role.

Following is a brief excerpt of a therapist–client interaction.

Therapist: I'd like to talk about your silence right now, since it seems to be triggered by my suggestion that we begin to lengthen the interval between our sessions.

Client: I suppose I didn't expect it. Maybe I did expect it . . . that sooner or later you would want to terminate the therapy.

Therapist: I'm hearing that theme of abandonment that we talked about last session, and I'd like to see if we can separate that from what we do in here.

Client: I suppose so, I know I'm not really being abandoned—like I remember as a kid when my Mom wouldn't come home some evenings—and my Dad would be gone trying to find her.

Therapist: I'm not going to abandon you, but I also don't want to make you dependent on me.

Client: I don't feel I'm dependent—or too dependent on you—it's just that I don't feel ready yet to end our sessions.

A strength of the model is the balanced focus between present and past, along with the notion of interpersonally based developmental stages that incorporate the key concepts of attachment, separation, and individuation. A limitation is the relative neglect of postchildhood interpersonal risk and protective factors, as well as the lack of a sociocultural perspective (see Prochaska and Nocross [1994] and St. Clair [1986] for detailed information).

Phenomenological–Humanistic Orientation

This orientation includes person-centered, gestalt, and existential psychotherapies. The phenomenological designation stresses the importance of understanding a client's frame of reference by ascertaining how a client perceives reality and the personal meaning given to reality. The humanistic designation underscores the value placed on freedom and self-determination, and the positive role of life-affirming emotions (love, joy, hope, excitement) in coping with life's problems.

Person-Centered Psychotherapy. The theory, originally titled Client-Centered Therapy, was developed and later modified and expanded by Carl Rogers with important contributions by Eugene Gendlin, Robert Carkhuff, Charles Truax, and Gerard Egan.

A major cause of psychological disorder is failure of the normal growth process. As a result of frustrating interactions in the interpersonal environment, the normal drive to develop oneself fully becomes blocked. Symptoms are manifestations of a discrepancy between one's current level of personal–social functioning and one's capabilities.

The overall goal of person-centered psychotherapy is to assist a client to become more fully the person he or she is capable of becoming. A key assumption is that the relationship which the therapist develops with the client is the primary curative factor. The central focus of the therapy is the conscious experiences of the client in the present, although the therapist assists the client to verbalize implicit or unspoken awarenesses.

The primary intervention strategy is to create a therapeutic relationship by being genuine, by showing unconditional positive regard for the personhood of the client, and by conveying respect for his or her inherent ability to make intelligent and responsible choices about how to live life. Specific techniques are: (1) empathic reflection of explicit and implicit feelings, needs, values, and goals; (2) therapist's self-disclosure of relevant personal and professional experiences, as well as perceptions about the immediate relationship with the client; and (3) nonjudgmental confrontation of discrepancies between clients' self-statements on the one hand, and statements of who they wish to be, their report of what others say about them, or the therapist's perception of them.

Below are three pairs of client and therapist statements. The first pair illustrates empathic reflection, the second, self-disclosure, and the third, confrontation.

Client: I guess I'm feeling bitter right now.
Therapist: You feel bitter because you were misled. I also sense you feel lonely because right now there is no one else to take her place.

Client: I really resent what happened.
Therapist: If that were me, I'd not only feel angry, but also hurt because of having my confidence betrayed.
Client: I suppose I want *them* to do it.
Therapist: Your need to be a follower is strong; yet you have said that you value taking the initiative and asserting yourself.

The client–therapist relationship is an egalitarian, psychologically intimate one, in which the client is viewed as the change agent, and the therapist as a facilitator of and a participant in the client's change process.

A strength of person-centered psychotherapy lies in the importance given to the therapist's interpersonal skills in developing a therapeutic relationship, whereas a limitation is the lack of technical or structured interventions. Rogers (1961) and Raskin and Rogers (1989) provide additional information.

Gestalt Psychotherapy. Fritz Perls is the originator of gestalt psychotherapy with significant contributions by James Simkin, E. Polster, M. Polster, and Walter Kempler.

A client's dissociation of important parts of self from awareness and acceptance is considered to be a major cause of psychological disorder. The overall goal is to assist a client to become aware of and take responsibility for the previously dissociated aspects of self, and to reintegrate into consciousness the disowned parts of self. A key assumption is that a client's psychological resources are sufficient to cope with problems successfully, once the resources can be activated and utilized with conscious purpose. Stated otherwise, increased self-awareness leads to improved self-direction (Goldenberg, 1983). The central focus of each session is on the ongoing, give-and-take interaction between the client's self-awareness and the therapist's awareness of the client.

The primary intervention strategy is to reintegrate into conscious awareness the disowned parts of self. The therapist confronts the discrepancy between what clients say they are doing at the moment, and how the therapist perceives their behavior at that moment. Three commonly used techniques are: (1) two-chair dialogue, in which two chairs represent two sides of a conflict, and the client moves from one chair to the other chair to create a dialogue between conflicting aspects of self; (2) dream analysis, in which the client assumes the role of each element in the dream, and then creates a dialogue between two or more conflictual dream elements (the assumption is that each dream element is either a conscious or a dissociated aspect of self); and (3) awareness exercises, in which the client in a free associative manner reports a sequence of physical and psychological awarenesses, such as sensations, images, thoughts, and memories.

The following is an example of a therapist conducting a two-chair dialogue.

Client: Sometimes I feel it's better just to go along with what they say—other times I want to take a stand.
Therapist: There's a part of you that wants to play it safe, and another part of you that would like to stand up for what you believe is right. Which part are you more in touch with now?
Client: The part of me that wants to go along with others.
Therapist: OK. Then let's put the part of you that wants to take a stand over there in that other chair. Now I'd like for you to have a conversation between these two parts of you. Let's start with the chair you're in, the part of you that wants to play it safe, and let that part express itself. Afterwards, I want you to switch to the other chair and be that part of you that wants to take a stand, and express that part as fully as you can. After you get going with the conversation, I'll just let you decide when you want to switch chairs in order to be the part of you that you're in touch with at the moment.

The client–therapist relationship is one in which the therapist's role is to facilitate clients' awareness of how they use their capabilities ineffectively, and what they do to block self-fulfillment (Goldenberg, 1983). The clients' role is to: (1) center their attention on the here-and-now moment; (2) enter fully into the interventions which the therapist suggests; and (3) be receptive to what the therapist says she or he sees, hears, senses, or intuits. Explanations and interpretations are left to the client. The ultimate goal is for the client to make a commitment to be aware of self *now* rather than *then*, *here* rather than *there*, and to rely on *self* rather than on *others*.

A strength of this approach is belief in a client's "respond-ability," or ability to respond differently. A limitation is the emphasis on immediate and often minute awarenesses. Polster and Polster (1973) and Yontef and Simkin (1989) provide further information.

Existential Psychotherapy. Several psychologists and psychiatrists have contributed to the formulation and applications of existential psychotherapy, notably Rollo May, Irvin Yalom, Viktor Frankl, and James Bugental. Rather than being a theory of psychotherapy with a repertoire of interventions, existential psychotherapy is a set of values and attitudes (i.e., a philosophical position), which a psychotherapist applies to self and clients.

The failure to be aware of, accept, and act on one's personal freedom and responsibility is regarded as being a major cause of psychological disorder; the failure is expressed symptomatically in anxiety, guilt, alienation from important aspects of self and others, and despair over the lack of meaning, purpose, and direction in life. In the existential view, clients have problems of living rather than mental illness or psychopathology.

The overall goal of psychotherapy is to help clients expand self-awareness, recognize the freedom they have, accept responsibility for setting the direction of their life, and actualize their potential to make critical life choices

(Corey, 1982). A key assumption is that the therapeutic relationship is both a stimulus for and an ongoing response to therapeutic changes. The central focus in existential psychotherapy sessions is on a client's choices, decisions, values, and personal meanings in the context of the present and the immediate future. The therapist's communication of an empathic and compassionate understanding of the client's present subjective world is the primary intervention strategy. By sharing her or his personhood with passion and conviction, the therapist creates an interpersonal environment in which clients confront who they have been and are now in relation to the person they might become, and reclaim the freedom and responsibility to make decisions that validate their self-chosen values. Although techniques are secondary to the therapeutic use of the relationship, therapists may choose specific techniques from other theories to facilitate particular changes (Corey, 1982).

Below is a brief excerpt of an existential therapist responding to a client statement.

Client: I know it's probably the right thing for me to do, but somehow I don't feel right when I do it.

Therapist: My hunch is that you're trying to live up to someone else's values, and in doing so, you're not living up to your values. It doesn't feel right because you're being untrue to yourself.

The client–therapist relationship is an egalitarian, I–thou, interpersonal encounter in which the therapist's growth and the client's growth are mutually facilitative. The role of the therapist is to: (1) stimulate the client's self-confrontation; (2) support the client's letting go of unauthentic aspects of self; and (3) encourage the client to make choices, however painful they may be, and to take responsibility for their choices, however fearful that responsibility may be.

A strength of this approach is the view that negative emotions are natural responses to one's existential problems rather than symptoms to be eliminated. A limitation is reliance on an I–thou encounter as the primary basis for therapeutic change. Bugental (1978) and May and Yalom (1989) offer extended discussions of existential psychotherapy.

Cognitive and Behavioral Orientations

These two orientations are grouped together because of (1) an emphasis on the present and near future; (2) a problem-solving orientation that focuses on changing cognitions and/or overt behavior; and (3) attention to conscious rather than to unconscious determinants of behavior. In addition, both orientations view a therapist as an active change agent who applies his or her professional knowledge and procedures to assist a client to cope more effectively with current problems in living. Included within the cognitive orientation are rational–emotive therapy, transactional analysis, and cognitive therapy; the behavioral orientation includes behavioral psychotherapy and cognitive–behavioral therapy. Behavior modification, applied behavior analysis, and radical behavioristic approaches are not included.

Rational-Emotive Psychotherapy. This theory, developed by Albert Ellis and taught, practiced, and researched by countless others, is a cognitive–philosophical one insofar as the client is helped to develop a realistic and pragmatic philosophy of living.

Irrational thinking that leads to emotional distress, self-defeating actions, and an attitude of blaming self and others for lack of self-fulfillment is considered to be a major cause of psychological disorder. Although clients have been conditioned by their interpersonal environment to think irrationally, they are responsible for maintaining and perpetuating unrealistic beliefs that underlie irrational thinking. The overall goal of this form of psychotherapy is to deemphasize emotionality and to eliminate self-defeating behavior by adopting rational, realistic, and tolerant beliefs about self and others. A key assumption is that clients can change their actions and feelings through rational thought processes based on realistic beliefs and values. The central focus of the sessions is primarily on thoughts, attitudes, and beliefs, and secondarily on feelings and actions.

The primary intervention strategy is one in which clients are taught that it is not the problem situation (interpersonal or otherwise) that causes emotional and behavioral problems; instead it is the incorrect way they interpret the problem situation—their interpretation, in turn, is the result of one or more irrational beliefs. Next, the therapist teaches clients how to dispute and challenge their beliefs, and to think about problem situations in a manner that facilitates appropriate feelings and constructive actions. Finally, the therapist must monitor and evaluate the client's thinking, feeling, and acting so that the client can maintain and perpetuate the new beliefs, just as they maintained and perpetuated the irrational ones.

A therapist may use a variety of therapeutic techniques, including explanation, confrontation, activity oriented assignments, and selected behavioral techniques. Central to the practice of rational-emotive therapy is the A-B-C-D paradigm. A refers to the stressful event or person; C is the emotional reaction to the event or person; B is the client's interpretation of or belief about A that causes the negative emotional reaction at C; and D means to dispute the belief or interpretation that occurs at point B. To change the negative emotional reaction, the client, assisted by the therapist, challenges and corrects the interpretation or belief that causes the negative emotional reaction. Consider this exchange between a therapist and client.

Client: Every time my boss corrects me at work, I feel enraged.

Therapist: Okay, this is a good place to try out the *A-B-C-D* method I explained at our last session. *A* is the situation, your boss correcting you. *C* is your feeling of rage. Now *A* cannot directly cause *C*. You have to be saying something to yourself about that situation that causes you to feel rage, and what you're saying to yourself is the point we call *B*.

Client: Like no one should ever criticize me? Like I think I have to be perfect?

Therapist: You could be making one or both of those statements. Now I'd like for you to take a different approach and see if you can challenge the validity of those statements—point out the flaws in each one. Afterwards, we'll look at some alternative ways for you to interpret the boss's criticism.

The client–therapist relationship is not considered the primary therapeutic ingredient. It can be likened to a mentor–mentee relationship based on mutual respect. The role of a client is similar to that of a student; a client learns how to apply rationality to the problems of living and how to exercise reasonable tolerance for human nature. As mentor, a therapist explains, challenges, confronts, models, and persuades a client, all for the purpose of stimulating the client to formulate a more realistic, and eventually more satisfying set of beliefs for conducting his or her life.

A strength of rational–emotive psychotherapy is the clearly formulated procedure for restructuring self-defeating beliefs; a limitation is the secondary role assigned to emotions. Ellis (1989) and Ellis and Grieger (1986) are useful references for this approach.

Transactional Analysis. Originated by Eric Berne with contributions by Thomas Harris, Robert and Mary Goulding, Muriel James, Dorothy Jongeward, and John and Katherine Dusay, transactional analyses can be classified as cognitive–decisional insofar as it is designed to replace old life-negating decisions with new, life-affirming ones.

A major cause of psychological disorder is considered to be recurring, dysfunctional behavior patterns that are based on decisions that a person made at a time of life when he or she was dependent and easily influenced by significant others. The overall goal of psychotherapy is to replace anachronistic decisions about what to expect of self and others with appropriate and realistic decisions about how to think, feel, and act. A key assumption is that at an early age human beings make important and enduring decisions about how to cope with life; yet they can overcome the past by redeciding how they will live their life.

The central focus of therapeutic work is the identification of current thoughts, feelings, and actions that are derived from earlier, and now anachronistic, decisions about how to cope with conflicts and threats. The primary intervention strategy is to assist a client to develop more effective thought-feeling-action patterns based on current knowledge and experience. Commonly used techniques are: (1) structural analysis, in which clients identify their ego states (critical parent, nurturant parent, adult, adapted child, and natural child), and correct faulty interaction between the ego states; (2) analysis of transactions, in which clients identify and correct self-defeating interactions between their ego states and the ego states of significant others; (3) multiple chair technique, in which each chair represents an ego state of the client, and the client moves back and forth between the chairs in creating a dialogue to resolve interpersonal conflict; (4) script analysis, in which the client's life plan is examined in terms of parent ego state messages that led to decisions about how to think and feel about oneself, and how to feel and act toward authority figures and peers; and (5) selected gestalt and behavioral techniques to overcome therapeutic impasses within and between sessions.

In the following excerpt, a therapist uses analysis of ego states to intervene in a client's procrastination.

Client: And I keep going round and round on what I should do first.

Therapist: Okay. Let me hear how you go round and round with the decision.

Client: Well, I know that this is the time to send in the applications for grad school . . . but then you should take care of term papers first because . . . well, I just can't do everything at once. I'm afraid I won't get anything done the way I'm going.

Therapist: That's an instance of what I meant by getting bogged down in a conflict between your different ego states. Your *adult* ego state says something pretty straight: I know this is the time to send in the applications. But then your *critical parent* ego state comes up with the stopper: you should take care of these other things. Then your *adapted child* ego state expresses a fear of the consequences of not doing anything. So let's start again with your *adult* ego state.

Client: I know this is the time to take care of the applications.

Therapist: What does your *natural child* ego state want?

Client: I want to go to grad school.

Therapist: From your *adult* ego state, tell me what you will do, and what you won't do.

Client: I will set aside the next three Sunday afternoons to work on the applications. And I will set aside the next three Saturday mornings to work on the term papers. And I won't spend those times hassling myself about it.

The client–therapist relationship is a partnership based on a mutually agreed-upon contract between therapist and client that spells out joint responsibilities for achieving the client's specific goals. The role of the client is to identify specific goals, prioritize them, and implement them, by experimenting with new ways to behave within and between therapy sessions. The role of the therapist is to restore the client's belief in self-change; that is, to make more appropriate decisions now as opposed to living by archaic decisions of the past (Corey, 1982). A strength of this approach is the conviction that clients have the power to redecide the course of their lives. A limitation is the undue emphasis on decisions as the cause and solution of problems. Dusay and Dusay (1989) and Goulding and Goulding (1979) offer additional information on transactional analysis, though the theory has lost much of its former luster and has a much smaller following.

Beck's Cognitive Therapy. Aaron Beck began the development of his cognitive therapy model in the 1970s; that is, it is a more recent model than those previously discussed models. By 1980 the model was attracting a large following of psychotherapy practitioners, researchers, and theorists (Michael Mahoney and Arthur Freeman to mention two better known names), who have continued to make significant contributions to theory development, comparative outcome research, and innovations in practice.

The primary cause of psychological disorders is habitual or recurrent cognitive deficits and distortions, which are manifested in perceptual errors, biased selection and acceptance of information, and several types of reasoning errors. Furthermore, each disorder has its characteristic cognitive deficits-distortions or profile of dysfunctional information processing.

The purpose of therapy, ordinarily completed within 12 to 15 sessions, is to correct faulty information processing and to assist clients in modifying assumptions or core beliefs that maintain the dysfunctional thinking, feeling, and actions. A realist, Beck recognizes that for some clients symptom relief measures must be taken before the overall goal is addressed.

As Beck and Weishaar (1989) state, the key postulate is: "the primacy of cognition in promoting and maintaining therapeutic change" (p. 300); that is, modifying or eliminating maladaptive cognitions and developing realistic ones will result in adaptive changes in feeling and action. The central focus of therapy sessions is to change a client's cognitive processing as it is manifested directly or indirectly at three levels of thinking: voluntary, conscious thoughts; automatic, less conscious thoughts; and underlying assumptions or core beliefs (sometimes referred to as schemas).

The primary intervention strategy is an educative one. A therapist teaches a client didactically and experientially how to: identify and monitor negative automatic thoughts; examine, challenge, and disconfirm faulty or unrealistic automatic thoughts/conclusions; develop and maintain accurate information processing; and ultimately recognize and alter the core beliefs or assumptions that are expressed in both automatic, nonconscious thinking and conscious, voluntary thinking. Both cognitive and behavioral techniques are utilized. The former are techniques, for instance guided imagery and role-playing to elicit recall of automatic thoughts, and verbal analysis to discern recurring themes present in automatic thoughts in order to identify core beliefs; the latter are techniques, for example, detailed homework assignments, exposure trials, and behavior rehearsal–skill training. The client–therapist relationship is a complementary one inasmuch as each supplies something important to the other, and they collaborate to develop an effective, problem-solving course of therapy.

Following is a brief therapist–client exchange.

Therapist: By the look on your face, I guess the job performance review went badly.
Client: You're right! Well, that's not quite right. I mean this seems to happen a lot. Actually, I guess I received a very favorable review, but it felt like a poor one.

Therapist: Well, go through the conversation between you and your supervisor. Replay it for me so I-we can see how you reached that conclusion.
Client: Well, let me see. She actually said several complimentary things. In retrospect, I'd have to say most of her feedback was positive—but the one piece about my time management needing some improvement— it was like that's all I could hear or concentrate on.
Therapist: Okay. So that sounds like one of those reasoning errors that you seem to be very susceptible to— we call it selective abstraction. In other words, you framed the whole situation, that interaction between the two of you, on the basis of one comment taken out of context. So let's work on that today.

A strength of Beck's model is the commitment to an active, clearly defined sequence of interventions which are amenable to empirical evaluation; a limitation is the preemptive focus on rational thinking and information processing.

Beck and Weishaar (1989) and Freeman, Simon, Beutler, and Arkowitz (1989) offer up-to-date, well-informed explanations of the cognitive therapy model. Also, Prochaska and Norcross's (1994) chapter on cognitive therapies facilitates a comparison between the Ellis and Beck models.

Behavioral Psychotherapy. Although several major learning theorists have made significant contributions to the formulation of behavioral psychotherapy, the pioneering work was conducted by first-generation behavioral psychotherapists, notably Joseph Wolpe, Arnold Lazarus, Leonard Krasner, Hans Eysenck, and Albert Bandura. Behavioral psychotherapy can be characterized as an action-oriented, directive, time-limited, structured approach to correct overt dysfunctional behavior.

Learned maladaptive behavior is considered to be a major cause of psychological disorder. The problem is defined as the overt behavior rather than assuming the behavior is a manifestation of an underlying disorder or illness. The overall goal of psychotherapy is for the therapist, in collaboration with the client, to develop a plan to replace maladaptive behavior patterns with adaptive behavior patterns (Goldenberg, 1983). A key assumption is that abnormal behavior, having been learned in the same way as normal behavior, can be unlearned and replaced by new learned patterns (i.e., eliminate the abnormal behavior and the client's disorder is eliminated [Goldenberg, 1983]). The central focus of the sessions is how the client and the client's interpersonal environment maintain the maladaptive behavior, and what the client can do to change behavior. The primary intervention strategy is to stop reinforcement of undesired behavior and to begin reinforcement of alternative behaviors. The following are widely used techniques.

Systematic desensitization is designed to diminish or eliminate negative emotional responses that are inhibiting adaptive responses to currently stressful situations. To counteract negative emotional responses, a client uses deep muscle relaxation (often in conjunction with positive imagery) in response to visualization of a stressful situation, beginning with the least stressful and proceeding to the most stressful aspect. Once a client can imagine the problem situation without negative emotional reactions, he or she then visualizes how to cope with the situation in an adaptive manner. At this point the client moves from imaginal desensitization to an in vivo desensitization by practicing the new learning in the actual problem situation. A variation, implosion or flooding, is used to extinguish negative emotional reactions by prolonged imaginal exposure without the counteracting effect of relaxation and positive imagery.

Another technique is behavior rehearsal in which a therapist first instructs a client in adaptive actions to take in a problem situation, then models the adaptive actions, followed by the client rehearsing and practicing the actions, and finally by planning how to transfer the adaptive actions to the actual problem situation.

Still another technique is based on aversion procedures that are used to eliminate maladaptive behaviors, such as substance abuse or sexual deviation, by associating the undesirable behavior with actual unpleasant consequences (e.g., electric shock) or imagined unpleasant consequences (e.g., aversive images).

Contingency management or contracting within and between sessions is a frequently used technique in which a client receives a specific reward if he or she performs the mutually agreed-upon behaviors, and a specific penalty if the behaviors are not performed.

A therapist may use a client's statement of a problem as a cue to introduce an intervention, such as behavior rehearsal.

Client: I plan ahead just how I'm going to ask a girl for a date, but I think there's something wrong with the way I approach it.

Therapist: Perhaps you're saying all the right things, but it's how you're saying it. I think it would be helpful if you and I role-play it. I'll be the girl, and you say what you typically say. Then, I'll react as I think she might. Afterwards, we can rehearse some different ways of broaching the subject of a date.

The client–therapist relationship is basically an educative one in which the role of therapist is to teach clients how to replace maladaptive with adaptive behaviors, as well as to model adaptive behaviors within the therapy session for clients to acquire by imitation. The client's role is to be actively involved by cooperating with the interventions suggested by the therapist, and by making a genuine effort to transfer and generalize the learning acquired within the sessions to problem situations outside the sessions (Corey, 1982). Mutual respect and interpersonal compatibility between therapist and client are important in order to strengthen and sustain a client's motivation to relinquish familiar behavior patterns and to experiment with new ones.

A strength of behavioral psychotherapy lies in the notion of learning by doing; a limitation is the failure to utilize the therapeutic relationship to help resolve clients' interpersonal problems (an exception is Kohlenberg and Tsai's [1991] Functional Analytic Psychotherapy). Additional information on the behavioral model can be found in O'Leary and Wilson (1987), Wilson (1989), and Wolpe (1990).

Cognitive–Behavioral Psychotherapy

This approach, a variation of behavioral psychotherapy and a significant overlap with cognitive therapy, places primary emphasis on cognitions instead of overt behavior.

A major cause of psychological disorder is negative thinking about oneself, unrealistic or inaccurate expectations about self and others, and misinterpretation of life events, which result in both emotional distress and ineffective or inappropriate behavior. The overall goal is twofold: to assist a client to identify and correct inaccuracies in thinking about oneself and one's life situation, and second, to teach a client to replace maladaptive behaviors with adaptive behaviors.

A key assumption is that reorganizing and improving self-statements and internal dialogue will lead to improved emotional and behavioral responses. Therefore, the central focus of therapy sessions is to identify and eliminate the dysfunctional elements in self-talk which are associated with emotional distress and disordered behavior.

The primary intervention strategy is cognitive restructuring, in which clients are first trained to listen to their subvocal talk, both what they say to themselves and how they say it, and then to examine how subvocal talk can evoke unwanted feelings, activate maladaptive responses, and inhibit adaptive responses. Next, the therapist assists clients to make specific changes in their self-talk and to practice these changes until a connection is formed to positive feelings, sensation, images, and adaptive actions. A cognitive–behavioral psychotherapist may also employ traditional behavioral techniques (e.g., behavior rehearsal, contingency contracting, modeling) to supplement cognitive restructuring. The client–therapist relationship is similar to that of cognitive and behavioral psychotherapies but is an integration of the two.

A strength of cognitive–behavioral psychotherapy is underscoring the importance of a client's self-dialogue; a limitation is insufficient attention to emotional processes. Detailed discussions of the therapy can be found in Goldfried and Davison (1976) and Meichenbaum (1977, 1986).

Integrative or Eclectic Orientation

Since the early 1980s, the field of psychotherapy has witnessed an increasing rapprochement between competing therapy models and a robust development of eclectic or integrative models of practice. A frequently quoted definition of *eclectic* psychotherapy is the "process of selecting concepts, methods, and strategies from a variety of current theories which work" (Brammer, Shostrom, and Abrego, 1982, p. 11). A more recent term, psychotherapy *integration* as defined by Arkowitz (1992), "includes various attempts to look beyond the confines of single-school approaches in order to see what can be learned from other perspectives. It is characterized by an openness to various ways of integrating diverse theories and techniques" (p. 262). To clarify the distinction between eclectic and integrative, Prochaska and Norcross (1994) offer this culinary metaphor: "the eclectic selects among several dishes to constitute a meal; the integrationist creates new dishes by combining different ingredients" (p. 432). In our judgment, there is a growing consensus that the broad-based trend toward convergence and synthesis of current therapy models is better served by the term *integration*; not only does it denote more conceptual breadth than *eclecticism*, but it also possesses a neutral connotation. It is likely that in the future the term *eclecticism* will be used in a narrower sense to refer to an atheoretical, pragmatically based combination of specific interventions.

The distinction between the two terms, however, is less significant than the trend to shift from a single model of practice to one that incorporates concepts and interventions from two or more therapy models. The trend reflects several key developments cited by Norcross and Newman (1992): insufficiency of any single model across the spectrum of psychosocial disorders; inconsistency of differential effectiveness among traditional therapy models; an expanding network of therapists, researchers, and practitioners identified with contributions to the development of psychotherapy integration; and factors common to differing therapies that account for a significant portion of therapeutic change. In short, by the end of the 1980s many practitioners, researchers, and theorists concluded that no current system possessed the conceptual breadth and depth to address the range and complexity of psychosocial disorders, nor the flexibility to accommodate the diversity of client personalities (Robertson, 1995, chapter 1). New approaches began to be constructed by thoughtfully combining, blending, or distilling the best that the field had to offer, as gleaned from the literature, informal exchanges, and cumulative results of clinical experience.

Aside from an eclectic bent among many practitioners noted in surveys as early as the 1960s, an integrative trend, or at least a significant cross-fertilization, has long been present within and between major psychotherapy orientations. Within the cognitive and behavioral orientation, cognitive therapy early on incorporated behavioral concepts and techniques (Ellis now designates his theory as Rational-Emotive-Behavior Therapy). Later, behavioral therapy found room for cognitive processes. In fact, Meichenbaum's (1977) *Cognitive-Behavior Modification: An Integrative Approach*, is one of the earliest examples of integrating two therapies that can be subsumed under the same psychotherapeutic orientation. For many years, concepts and change strategies of transactional analysis have been informally blended with gestalt techniques by leading exponents like Mary and Robert Goulding. And as Lebow (1987) concludes, family therapists of whatever theoretical orientation have routinely been integrative both in theory and in practice. More recently, the psychodynamic orientation has incorporated a strong interpersonal emphasis, and the cognitive therapy concept of core belief or schema has found its way into psychodynamic discourse. Currently, the triad of cognitive, behavioral, and cognitive–behavioral therapies have begun to accord a prominent place to concepts and procedures associated with emotional processing, which traditionally has been present in both psychodynamic and humanistic orientations.

With the proviso that classifications always have debatable and arbitrary features, current forms of integrative psychotherapy could be classified as follows. *Theoretical integration* in which two or more theories are combined according to major tasks such as conceptualizing the dynamics of a disorder and the treatment goals (e.g., Psychodynamic), developing and managing the therapeutic alliance (e.g., Person-Centered), selecting and implementing specific interventions (e.g., Cognitive-Behavioral). One of the earliest and best known exemplars of theoretical integration is Wachtel's (1977) *Psychoanalysis and Behavior Therapy: Toward an Integration*. *Technical integration* is based on a single theoretical framework (e.g., social learning) and incorporates from other models specific intervention strategies and techniques which are conceptually congruent with the theoretical framework and which have demonstrated empirical effectiveness with specific disorders.

Two of the earliest and best known exemplars of technical eclecticism or integration are Lazarus (1981, 1989), *The Practice of Multimodel Therapy,* and Beutler (1983) *Eclectic Psychotherapy. Common factors integration* blends change strategies and accompanying therapist behaviors that are present in many single-theory approaches and which have been consistently associated with positive outcome. Again, one of the earliest and well regarded forms of common factors integration is Garfield's (1980) *Psychotherapy: An Eclectic Approach.* The defining quality of the fourth group, which might be described as emergent or transtheoretical, is that theoretical concepts, change processes, and specific interventions from a number of current therapies are woven together to form a new conceptual structure. One of the most widely known models is Prochaska and DiClemente's (1984) *Transtheoretical Approach* (see also Prochaska and Norcross [1994, pp. 457–484]).

The following two paragraphs are consistent with an integrative orientation, though not every statement applies to each integrative approach.

The major cause of psychological disorder is recurring maladaptive patterns of thinking-feeling-behaving, which result from faulty socialization experiences and create intrapersonal distress, dysfunctional marital-family and social relationships, and impaired educational and occupational adjustment. The overall goal of integrative psychotherapy is similar to that of other approaches (i.e., relief of personal distress, improved interpersonal relationships, and increased ability to cope with problems of the living). A key assumption is that theoretical concepts and postulates, basic change strategies, and specific interventions can be drawn from different models and integrated in a form that is theoretically and empirically defensible. The central focus of the sessions is a client's perceptual, cognitive, emotional, and behavioral interactions with his or her interpersonal environment.

The primary intervention strategy consists of change processes which are common to most psychotherapy theories, and from which specific interventions of known effectiveness are utilized to implement agreed-upon therapeutic goals. The client–therapist relationship is a collaborative partnership. With input and feedback from a client, a therapist develops and implements a treatment plan that is relevant to a client's goals, realistic in terms of a client's psychosocial adjustment and environmental resources, and ethically responsible with respect to the welfare of a client and society at large.

A well-known form of technical integration-eclecticism is *multimodal therapy* developed by Lazarus (1981, 1989) who earlier coined the term *technical eclecticism*. Multimodal therapy employs an array of specific intervention procedures within a framework of social learning theory supplemented by systems theory and communications theory. Client problems, such as anxiety, depression, interpersonal conflict, intrapersonal conflict, are assessed and conceptualized in terms of planned changes in seven modalities: (1) behavior; (2) affect; (3) sensation; (4) imagery; (5) cognition; (6) interpersonal relationships; (7) biology, which includes substance use and abuse, prescription medicine, sleep, diet, exercise. Specific interventions are selected for the problem(s) in each modality, and the modalities addressed within a particular therapy session depend upon a client's receptiveness and a therapist's level of intervention skill and clinical experience. Below is an abridged therapist–client exchange followed by a hypothetical multimodal profile. For each modality and the problem(s), a therapist would plan one or more intervention procedures to promote positive change, and then determine an optimal sequence for implementing the positive changes. According to Lazarus, the *affect* modality can only be changed indirectly through changes in other modalities (Prochaska and Norcross, 1994, p. 441).

Client: When I think about my situation, I get really overwhelmed about where to start and if counseling can actually help.

Therapist: When you start to tick off each problem, you begin to feel helpless about how to cope with it, and even hopeless about what we can do in our sessions.

Client: Well, that *is* how I'm feeling, not all the time of course, but much of the time lately.

Therapist: I sense you need some kind of plan or strategy that would help you feel hopeful again and even empowered. Let me see if I can organize what you have told me and then decide about where and what we can do. You've described several recurring problem scenarios, and in each one your reaction to those modalities I told you about earlier is similar. Let me draw up a profile here and see if it fits you. When you go into a situation where there are women you're attracted to [interpersonal relationships], you start getting images [imagery] about being rejected—you start to get excitable and tense [sensation] and then try very hard [behavior] to please—if they act disinterested, you feel rejected [affect] and begin to pull away [behavior] and tell yourself [cognition] you'll never be attractive or lovable enough, and that often has effects later on when you can't get to sleep and you medicate the sleep problem with alcohol [biology].

Client: That's pretty much it, but I'm not sure what to tackle first.

Therapist: Well, let's start early in that sequence with the sensations you experience and the images—and then we can work on the interpersonal part and also what you typically tell yourself. Following that, we can focus on your avoiding and withdrawing—after we've made some progress, I think you'll notice the feeling of rejection starting to lessen. Also, I'd like to find an alternative to the alcohol to get to sleep.

Behavior: withdrawal and trying very hard. *Intervention:* role reversal training.

Affect: feeling rejected. *Intervention:* (change expected with successful implementation of change in one or more of the other modalities).

Sensation: tense/excitable. *Intervention:* relaxation exercises.

Imagery: fantasizing about future rejections. *Intervention:* develop positive emotive images.

Cognition: self-statements about being unlovable. *Intervention:* cognitive restructuring.

Interpersonal Relationships: interacting with the opposite sex. *Intervention:* assertive training.

Biology: using alcohol to overcome sleep difficulties. *Intervention:* substitute for the alcohol some constructive activity, e.g. get out of bed and read in a standing position until ready to fall asleep.

One strength of the integrative orientation is the collaboration among theorists, researchers, and practitioners in seeking what works best for clients; another strength is that integrative therapies select from a broad theoretical base, choose from a wide-ranging armamentarium of treatment strategies and problem-specific interventions, and can be adapted to a diversity of therapist personal styles (Lebow, 1987, p. 588). One limitation is a paucity of education and training opportunities to acquire competence in more than one therapy model; another limitation is the lack of research that compares integrative therapies with single-theory approaches. Additional information on the integrative orientation can be found in Norcross and Goldfried's (1992) *Handbook of Psychotherapy*, Prochaska and Norcross's (1994, chapter 13) *Systems of Psychotherapy*, Robertson's (1995) *Psychotherapy Education and Training: An Integrative Perspective*, and the

Journal of Psychotherapy Integration published quarterly by Plenum Press.

Comparative Analysis

With respect to the six dimensions listed earlier (see p. 161), the four psychotherapy orientations can be characterized as follows. First, unconscious determinants of psychological disorder are emphasized in the psychodynamic orientation; minimized in the humanistic orientation; and acknowledged in the cognitive and behavioral orientation, and in the integrative orientation, but preferably as nonconscious (instead of unconscious) determinants.

Second, psychodynamic therapists view insight into unconscious conflicts as a prerequisite for change; humanistic therapists value present-centered awareness, with the emphasis on what one does and how one does it rather than why one does it; for that reason they prefer the term *self-awareness* to the term *insight*. Behavioral therapists are likely to view overt behavior change as a way to change thoughts and feelings, and may even consider overt behavior change as a prerequisite for insight or self-awareness. Cognitive therapists stress insight into or awareness of self-statements as a basis for changing thoughts, feelings, and actions. Integrative therapists support all of the above perspectives, but with somewhat more emphasis on conscious and nonconscious change processes.

Third, with respect to the time dimension, psychodynamic therapists emphasize the past. Humanistic therapists stress the present, even the present moment, and to some degree the immediate future. Cognitive and behavioral therapists focus on the current context of the client's life with some attention to the past and future, as do many integrative therapists.

Fourth, in the humanistic orientation, the client–therapist relationship has a primary role in facilitating therapeutic change. In the cognitive and behavioral orientation the relationship traditionally has had an adjunctive role; that is, it facilitates a positive response to the interventions. In the psychodynamic orientation, both formal interventions and analysis of the transferential relationship are potent factors in fostering therapeutic change. The integrative orientation stresses the importance of the therapeutic relationship both as a means to motivate a client to respond productively to interventions and as a source of information about a client's relationships outside therapy.

Fifth, in the psychodynamic orientations, diagnostic evaluation of a client's problems is crucial and usually precedes psychotherapy. In the behavioral and cognitive orientation, assessment of the ways in which both the client and his or her interpersonal environment maintain the problems provides the basis for planning the therapy sessions. In the humanistic orientation, formal diagnosis is considered intrusive and unnecessary; assessment and change are interactive processes in psychotherapy. The integrative orientation is closer to the cognitive and behavioral orientation.

Sixth, in the psychodynamic orientation the practice of psychotherapy is viewed as both art and science. An aesthetic rather than scientific attitude characterizes the practice of the humanistic orientation. In the cognitive and behavioral orientation, the practice of psychotherapy involves the application of scientific principles to problems of living, and most therapists with an integrative orientation would concur.

THEORIES AND METHODS
FOR PRACTICE

Conclusion

The purpose of the chapter has been to give an introduction to the state-of-the-art, or the state-of-the-science, of psychotherapy, together with an overview of current psychotherapy orientations. It has often been said that the choice of and commitment to a psychotherapy orientation is a significant decision in the process of becoming a therapist. A theory may be chosen for professional or personal reasons; for example, sustained contact with the theory of a professional mentor, selective exposure to research favoring a specific theory, compatibility with one's cognitive style, closeness to one's philosophical values, or a positive experience as a client with a particular orientation and theory of practice.

It should be acknowledged that the foregoing presentation of psychotherapy orientations and their respective theories is not exhaustive, and the reader may wonder about certain omissions. Some of the omissions and the reasons for them are commented on below.

A psychotherapy orientation that was omitted from the preceding discussion is a systems orientation. A systemic perspective represents a nontraditional way of conceptualizing the development and treatment of psychological disorder. In short, psychological disorder is an interpersonal, not an intrapersonal-intrapsychic phenomenon; an individual's problem is a manifestation of a problem within an important system to which an individual belongs; therefore, the primary focus of psychotherapy must be the system (e.g., family, work group, religious community); and to change or heal a member of the system, one must change or heal the system first. For the most part, systemically oriented psychotherapy theories (e.g., strategic, structural) have been developed to treat couples and families; for that reason, the theories will be presented in the next chapter under alternative therapy modalities.

A psychodynamically oriented theory which has shown considerable promise is interpersonal therapy; the omission is due to its recentness and lack of a body of literature on its application to disorders other than depression. The model does have its roots in the interpersonal school of psychoanalysis founded by Harry Stack Sullivan and Adolph Meyer. Like Beck's cognitive model, interpersonal therapy is a short-term (12–15 sessions), present-centered, manual guided treatment for depression (Klerman, Weissman, Rounsville, and Chevron, 1984). While Beck's cognitive model has expanded well beyond its original focus on depression, interpersonal therapy, developed about a decade later, is still officially a treatment for depression. Problem conceptualization relies primarily on the impact of developmentally early relational experiences on later interpersonal adjustment. Problem resolution, on the other hand, is directed at overcoming *current* interpersonal maladaptations and improving relationship skills. Unlike more traditional psychodynamic approaches, client–therapist relationship dynamics are addressed only if they become a barrier to progress. To become informed about current application of the model to disorders other than depression, consult Klerman and Weissman (1993).

Omitted also are several approaches sometimes classified as emotional flooding therapies, which had a high profile in the 1960s and 1970s but have not lived up to their early promise (though not an emotional flooding therapy, the same might be said of reality therapy). An exception, perhaps, is implosive therapy which began as a loose merger of psychoanalytic concepts and learning theory principles and methods. It has reattracted interest largely because of the potential for treating some of the anxiety disorders that are closely linked to severe traumas (refer to Prochaska and Norcross, 1994, chapter 8).

Finally, the promising developments in brief psychodynamic therapies will be taken up in the next chapter under the brief/crisis therapy modality.

Chapter 5

Psychotherapy Effectiveness, Special Modalities, Time-Limited Therapies, and Futuristic Issues

Over the past half-century the breadth and depth of changes in psychotherapy have been truly impressive. Psychotherapy has expanded from the single dominant psychoanalytic orientation to a total of five well-established orientations that comprise at least two dozen currently practiced models; from exclusive reliance on the traditional dyadic modality to utilization of group, marital, and family modalities and combinations thereof; from conventional long-term duration to short-term, brief, even single session duration; and finally, from anecdotal reports of its effectiveness to experimentally and quantitatively sophisticated outcome process research.

EFFECTIVENESS OF PSYCHOTHERAPY

Outcome Research

This section of the chapter is divided into *outcome* research and *process* research. In actuality, outcome and process occur together; in fact, researchers and theorists increasingly refer to process-outcome relations; and terms, such as goals, intervention, alliance, between session assignments, may be conceptualized as both outcome and process.

Some forty years ago belief in psychotherapy's effectiveness, which was absolutely critical for the profession's raison d'etre, was shaken by Eysenck's (1952) controversial report of nonsignificant effects. What followed was more than a quarter of a century of research efforts to establish an unequivocal rebuttal to Eysenck's conclusion. The next challenge, to discover what makes psychotherapy work, has proved to be just as formidable. Stiles, Shapiro, and Elliott (1986) put it quite simply: "Although we know that psychotherapy works, we do not clearly understand how it works" (p. 175). Part of the problem, following VandenBos's (1986) reasoning, is that demonstrating both an outcome effect (i.e., the phenomenon exists) and differential outcome effects among competing therapy models has preempted the attention of researchers. Only since the mid-1980s has a sustained effort been made to elucidate the fundamental processes that underlie therapeutic effectiveness.

Progress has been slow, due in large measure to conceptual and methodological obstacles. Persistent research limitations include: small sample size as well as large within group variability; questionable measurement techniques; lack of relevant, clearly defined, multidimensional outcome measures; insufficient attention to the timing of outcome assessment along with a neglect of long-term evaluation of outcome; lack of individualized treatment plans that incorporate both diagnostic and nondiagnostic variables; vague specification of in-session therapist behaviors, client behaviors, and the interaction of the two; and inadequate control of variability of therapist competence and therapist adherence to a treatment protocol (Kazdin, 1986; Stiles et al., 1986; Beutler, 1991a; Persons, 1991).

For meaningful comparisons among a large number of outcome studies and for a measure of control over reviewer biases, quantitative reviews based on meta-analysis, a form of statistical analysis, are beginning to replace the traditional qualitative reviews. Meta-analysis consists of a group of statistical methods that enable reviewers to combine and interpret many dissimilar studies more expeditiously and objectively. Despite its current popularity as a research tool, meta-analysis is not without its critics. For a brief, nontechnical discussion, see Sue et al. (1994, p. 563), and for the quantitatively sophisticated reader, see Brown (1987).

Turning now to outcome results, there is a strong consensus that psychotherapy can be expected to benefit the majority of consumers (i.e., typically 65 to 75 percent), as evidenced by diverse outcome measures, such as reports of clients, therapists, significant others, professional observers, or psychological test results. For major reviews over the past 15 years, refer to Smith, Glass, and Miller (1980), Landman and Dawes (1982), Imber, Pilkonis, and Glanz (1983), Lambert, Shapiro, and Bergin (1986), Lambert and Bergin (1992); for children and adolescents only, Kazdin (1993b) and Lipsey and Wilson (1993). More specifically, the magnitude of positive change is roughly equivalent to one standard deviation; for the most part the therapeutic gains occur in the first few months of weekly or biweekly sessions; and at least at short-term follow-up, that is, less than one year, the changes are more likely to be stable than unstable. Long-term retention (more than one year) of therapeutic gains is another matter. With the passage of time, especially the impact of negative life events over time, some attrition of positive changes and disorder relapse can be expected (Goldstein, Lopez, and Greenleaf, 1979; Imber et al., 1983; and for couple therapy, Jacobson and Addis, 1993, p. 86). Long-term stability of clinical improvement does not occur automatically; in addition to the impact of negative life circumstances, long-term stability reflects the quality of the psychotherapy given, a client's commitment to self-growth following treatment termination, and the nature of the disorder (for instance, improvement is neither very robust nor very durable in substance use and personality disorders).

From another perspective, those who are likely to benefit from but do not receive psychotherapy, or receive a placebo procedure, do not improve as much or as soon as those who remain beyond a few sessions (Smith et al., 1980; Landman and Dawes, 1982). The reported rates of spontaneous symptom remission vary according to the type and severity of a disorder, and the figure of one-third is a reasonable overall estimate (Garfield, 1981). On the other hand, even the staunchest supporters of psychotherapy effectiveness concede that some clients become worse during or shortly after psychotherapy (Lambert and Bergin, 1983). Reported deterioration rates typically vary between 3 and 10 percent. Actually, deterioration or worsening of a client's condition is only one subset of what has been designated as "failed psychotherapy"; for a significant minority of clients, psychotherapy is unhelpful rather than harmful (see Giles, 1993, cited in Giles and Marafiote, 1994, for related discussion).

Reviews of outcome studies that compare different psychotherapy models (sometimes dubbed the proverbial horse race) report no or minimal evidence for differential effectiveness of competing models for a large majority of psychosocial disorders (Smith et al., 1980; Landman and Dawes, 1982; Lambert et al., 1986; Lambert and Bergin, 1992; Whiston and Sexton, 1993). The highly publicized, methodologically sound National Institute of Mental Health collaborative research study on depression treatments concluded that both cognitive therapy and interpersonal therapy were effective, but not differentially so (Elkin, Shea, Watkins, Imber, Sotsky, Collins, Glass, Pilkonis, Leber, Docherty, Feister, and Parloff, 1989).

In response to the above findings, the research focus has shifted from what model is most effective overall to what model is most effective for what disorder or group of disorders. Lambert and Bergin (1992) and Giles (1993, cited in Giles and Marafiote, 1994) conclude that the more directive, prescriptive, cognitive and behavioral models are more efficacious than other models for specifically targeted, circumscribed disorders, for instance, some forms of anxiety, certain compulsions, selected communication and social skills deficits, and particular types of sexual dysfunction. Kazdin (1986), Stiles et al. (1986), and Beutler (1991a) offer closely reasoned and balanced analyses of whether diverse therapy models are, in fact, equivalent in their outcomes, as the literature sometimes suggests. One factor that complicates comparison of different models is that some approaches may take longer to be effective, particularly if they are designed to intervene in more complex and change-resistant behavior patterns. Furthermore, if one applies the clinically relevant but more stringent criterion of clinical significance, then in comparison to the traditional criterion of pre- to posttreatment improvement, psychotherapy by whatever model falls short of conventional markers of effectiveness (Jacobson and Truax, 1991).

Before leaving the topic of outcome effectiveness, two caveats are in order. First, researchers' theoretical orientation may be pertinent to their evaluation of therapy models (Smith et al., 1980; Jacobson and Addis, 1993); second, "a treatment has to be around for a while and tested repeatedly before its effects can be evaluated with confidence" (Jacobson and Addis, 1993, p. 86). Finally, other than anecdotal reports and a few empirically based exploratory studies, the literature does not offer definitive guidelines for predicting which clients will and which will not improve in psychotherapy.

Process Research

What follows is an overview of four process factors: therapist characteristics, client characteristics, therapeutic relationship or alliance, and treatment duration. The overview draws from both traditional process research, typically based on distal relations between global process measures and equally global indexes of clinical recovery, and recent process research, based on proximal relations between specific process measures and equally specific and multifaceted indexes of recovery that are examined across successive phases of treatment. A highly regarded example of the second type of process research strategy is the "events paradigm," in which an event is defined by Greenberg (1986) as the relation between the occurrence in a session of a client problem marker, a therapist intervention response to the marker, followed by a client response to the intervention, and then the reported in-session outcome.

Turning to the first factor (with the proviso that in practice the four factors are interactive and interrelated), therapist skill proficiency which includes both interpersonal and technical skills, has consistently been cited as a critical variable in positive outcome (Lambert and Bergin, 1983; Lambert et al., 1986; Orlinsky and Howard, 1986; McConnaughy, 1987; Lambert, 1989; Goldfried, Greenberg, and Marmar, 1990). Interpersonal skill incorporates basic therapeutic communication skills and positive interpersonal attitudes (Robertson, 1995, chapter 3). Technical skill refers to proficiency in the selection, timing, and execution of specific interventions, in addition to adherence to the prescribed treatment protocol (Robertson, 1995, chapter 4). As periodically noted in the literature (e.g., Strupp, 1989; Herman, 1993), competence depends much less on theoretical orientation and length of clinical experience, and much more on the personhood of the therapist and his or her effective utilization of the research literature.

The second factor, client characteristics, has also consistently been cited as a significant contributor to therapy outcome, perhaps even more so than therapist characteristics (see reviews by Lambert et al., 1986; Stiles et al., 1986; Goldfried et al., 1990; and for discussion of related

material, Robertson, 1995, chapter 4). Client characteristics include the nature, severity, and type of onset of the
disorder(s), in addition to preexisting interpersonal traits.
Other significant characteristics are: motivational readi-
ness for change, available external support systems, realistic versus unrealistic expectations of psychotherapy,
perseverance, and key in-session behaviors including
openness versus defensiveness, proactive versus reactive
responding, and depth of inner exploration and experiencing. For whatever reason, the client process factor has
been researched much less than the other three factors.

The third factor is the therapeutic relationship or
alliance. Except for occasional negative or inconsistent
findings, reviews of the literature clearly support a positive association across diverse therapy approaches between alliance as assessed by therapists, trained judges
or clients, and various outcome measures (refer to
Greenberg, 1983; Orlinsky and Howard, 1986; Gaston,
1990; Horvath and Symonds, 1991; Horvath and Luborsky,
1993). Of the three types of assessment, alliance ratings
by clients and by trained judges are more likely than ratings by therapists to correlate significantly with outcome
measures; in fact, client ratings appear to be the best
predictor of outcome. Though the early phase of psychotherapy is the optimal time to develop an alliance, both
early- and late-phase alliance ratings are predictive of
outcome. Typically, mid-phase alliance ratings have a weak
association with positive outcome, most likely reflecting
the relational stress and strain that so often characterizes
the middle stage of treatment (Horvath and Luborsky,
1993; see Robertson, 1995, chapter 5 for additional discussion of the mid-phase alliance). To cap the issue of outcome,
a strong, stable alliance is a necessary, albeit insufficient,
condition for clinically significant improvement.

Conceptually and experientially, the concept of
therapeutic alliance has three dimensions (Robertson,
1995, chapter 5). First is a structural dimension which

encompasses Bordin's (1979) threefold definition of (1) shared goals of therapist and client; (2) their agreed-upon and mutually performed in-session tasks; and (3) their relational bond (mutual positive attachment). Second is a developmental dimension, what Bordin refers to as the continuing interaction of the therapist–client relational bond, and their collaboration on therapy goals and tasks. Third is a transactional dimension, that is, the interaction of therapist interpersonal skills, technical skills, and client perception of and response to both. It is the continuing transactions between therapist and client that contribute to the formation of a relational bond, agreement on goals, collaborative participation in therapy tasks, and that also reflect developmental changes in the alliance.

As often noted in the literature, the essence of a therapeutic alliance is the respective contributions of the therapist and client, and the reciprocal effect of each on the other. The argument is sometimes made that the alliance concept is a convenient umbrella for clinically relevant therapist and client characteristics. The argument fails, however, to take into account the ongoing interaction of therapist and client characteristics and the changing configuration of the interaction in response to the unfolding course of therapy. An important implication of the alliance concept is that a therapist's interpersonal and technical skills, and a client's response to both, though conceptually distinct, in practice are inseparable, interactive components of change that shape and are shaped by the quality of the alliance (Robertson, 1995, chapter 5). Another important implication is that insofar as therapist competency is defined by the interpersonal and technical skills to which clients respond differentially, therapeutic competence is variable rather than fixed.

The fourth factor is the psychotherapy duration and its relation to outcome effectiveness. In their review of process-outcome literature, Orlinsky and Howard (1986) examined 114 estimates of the relationship between amount of treatment and therapy outcome, of which 110 of the 114 estimates supported a positive association between duration of treatment and extent of client improvement. The authors and their associates then followed with a landmark study (Howard, Kopta, Krause, and Orlinsky, 1986) of the relationship between the "dosage" of treatment (number of sessions) and clinical improvement. They calculated the cumulative percentage of approximately 2400 clients (drawn from several types of outpatient treatment centers) who were reported to be measurably improved at higher dosages of treatment. The authors report that 10 to 18 percent showed some improvement *before* the first session, presumably due to the beneficial effects of hope engendered by anticipation of imminent professional help; 48 to 58 percent improved measurably by the eighth session; 75 percent by the end of six months of weekly sessions; and 85 percent by the end of 12 months of weekly sessions. Not surprisingly, the authors confirmed an axiom of the field, to wit, the more chronic and pervasive the disorder, the greater the treatment dosage or number of sessions a client needs to demonstrate measurable improvement. Consistent with the findings reported above under outcome research, improvement tends to occur in the earlier rather than later stages, except for clients with more severe disorders.

In reviewing the Howard et al. (1986) study, Herron, Eisenstadt, Javier, Primavera, and Schultz (1994) conclude that both the kind of change shown and the required session dosage are significantly influenced by the type and severity of the disorder. Herron et al. also take note of several limitations of the Howard et al. study, including lack of specific, well-defined improvement criteria, relying primarily on therapist judgments of improvement, and therapy limited to psychodynamic and interpersonal models. Herron et al. also offer the caveat that: "The amount of psychotherapy used is not automatically equivalent to the most effective amount. A more accurate measure would be the amount generally shown to be effective" (p. 279).

To conclude, a widely quoted set of outcome percentages from a frequently cited literature review (Lambert et al., 1986) is the following: 40 percent of outcome variance attributed to the positive characteristics of a client and his or her interpersonal environment; 30 percent due to treatment factors common to most therapy models; and the remaining 30 percent divided evenly between model-specific interventions and placebo effects. Of the four process factors summarized above, client characteristics would be equivalent to what Lambert et al. include in the 40 percent category; therapeutic alliance, therapy–dose effect, and therapist characteristics (specifically therapeutic competency) correspond closely to the authors' common factors category.

GROUP PSYCHOTHERAPY

Overview

The proliferation of psychotherapy approaches between the midsixties and midseventies was accompanied by a rising interest in group therapy. Diverse forms of group work were developed and include: group therapy, group counseling, T-groups/sensitivity training, encounter groups, and self-help/consciousness-raising groups. The main focus of this section, however, is group therapy which overlaps with group counseling, though the latter ordinarily excludes clients with severe psychosocial disorders (see Hansen, Warner, and Smith, 1980, for historical and descriptive information on group approaches).

Group therapy came into prominence after World War II in response to a shortage of trained therapists. By means of a group format, the skills of a limited number of therapists could be extended to a growing number of clients and patients. The group format was a cost-effective method of assisting people to achieve more satisfying interpersonal relationships and to lead more productive lives. Regrettably, group therapy sometimes became a dumping ground for those who were considered unsuitable for individual therapy because of limited verbal skills, weak motivation, or problems that were refractory to insight-based psychotherapy. As the use of groups expanded, however, practitioners realized that in addition to efficiency, the group modality was also an effective method of treating a wide range of psychological disorders. Currently, group therapy is valued both as an efficient and effective modality in its own right, and as a complement to individual therapy. In short, group therapy has a strong presence as evidenced by its widespread application in both the public and private sectors.

In response to external pressures from client-consumers, consumer-advocate groups, and third-party payers, the practice of group therapy has become more pragmatic and less constrained by theoretical considerations. With this shift, many practitioners have sought to devise an optimal combination of individual and group therapy for their clients. Although some clients are unsuited to individual therapy and others to group therapy, the large majority are likely to benefit from individual therapy's emphasis on intrapersonal learning and group therapy's complementary emphasis on interpersonal learning. Many of the interventions in group therapy are also utilized in individual therapy.

The length of group therapy varies according to the therapist's theoretical orientation, the number and diversity of goals, and the adjustment level of the clients. Long-term groups, typically 25 or more sessions, can give equal attention to intrapersonal and interpersonal problems; in short-term groups, typically 10 to 25 sessions, interpersonal learning is primary and intrapersonal learning is secondary; brief or crisis groups, less than 10 sessions, are primarily supportive in nature; that is, they assist a

client to partially recover a level of psychosocial functioning that has been impaired by a developmental or situational crisis. Generally the shorter the duration of the
group the more the members must have a common purpose or goal, because there is insufficient time to attend
to differing goals; in long-term groups there is time to
reconcile differences among the members in their purpose
for being there (Levine, 1979).

Overall, the principal advantages of group therapy
over individual therapy are (1) experiential learning of
interpersonal skills; (2) closer approximation of the group
to the "real world"; (3) vicarious learning from other members' coping efforts; (4) the advantage for the therapist
of observing a client's interpersonal problems instead of
having to rely on a client's self-report; and (5) peer-centered
corrective feedback and support for making difficult
changes. Three limitations are (1) group therapy cannot
provide a client with the sustained attention and depth
of therapeutic work that individual therapy provides;
(2) rapid exposure of one's problems to other group members is too threatening to some clients; and (3) there is a
greater likelihood of breaches of confidentiality; so far
laws have been slow to grant the therapist's privileged
communication to nonprofessional members of a group.
As an aside, in comparison to marital and family therapy,
group therapy is a less frequently practiced modality.
Norcross, Prochaska, and Gallagher (1989) found that
one-half or more of surveyed clinicians were routinely
practicing marital and family therapy, though less than
one-half were practicing group therapy. There are notable
exceptions, of course, because in substance abuse treatment centers group therapy is invariably the treatment
of choice. The high profile which marital and family therapy
has had in the literature and in continuing education programs, together with an increased demand for treatment
of relationship disorders, may account for its greater recognition, especially in the private sector and in graduate

training programs. On the other hand, Dies (1992) cites several factors likely to create more emphasis on group treatment, for instance, mounting pressure from the managed care sector for more efficient and cost-effective therapies, heightened appreciation of group therapy's strong suit of fostering "here and now" interpersonal learning, and greater availability of user friendly manuals to facilitate the practice of group therapy, particularly for the early-career practitioner.

Group Theory and Group Dynamics

Most group therapy today represents an extension and/or modification of theories of individual psychotherapy. Current group therapy models include: psychoanalytic, Adlerian, person-centered, existential, transactional analysis, gestalt, cognitive, behavioral, and psychodrama. These models are presented in the preceding chapter (with the exception of psychodrama) and the reader is referred to Corey (1990, 1995) for discussion of their application (including psychodrama) to groups.

As in individual psychotherapy, many group therapists employ an integrative or eclectic model of practice, though the authors are unaware of an integrative or eclectic model of practice that has been constructed solely for group treatment and is widely practiced; there is Lazarus' (1981, 1989) multimodal therapy adapted to a group context, and Corey's (1990, 1995, chapter 17) description of his eclectic group model. Basically, an eclectic–integrative group practitioner develops a rationale for blending concepts from various models, change strategies commonly employed in different group approaches, and specific interventions which have demonstrated utility for particular kinds of groups.

A distinction is made between *group outcome* and *group dynamics. Outcome* refers to changes made by group members and the stability of changes following termination. The term *group dynamics* refers to group-as-a-whole phenomena. Group dynamics is sometimes subdivided into group development, or the developmental phases which a group moves through and the salient themes of each phase, and group process, or the interaction between members and between members and therapist. Group development and group process are linked by the tasks within each developmental phase that reflect the salient themes of a specific phase. There are at least four phases of group development: the initial/joining/testing-the-waters phase; the early/transitional/struggle phase; the middle/cohesive/working phase; and the late/consolidation/termination phase. The number of sessions for each developmental phase varies from group to group; more often than not the phases overlap; and groups differ in the ease with which they move from one developmental phase to the next. Finally, in practice there is no clean separation between group outcome and group dynamics; their purposes are inextricably interwoven and their effects are synergistic.

Outcome Effectiveness

Dies (1992) contends that group therapy is like a microcosm of a client's interpersonal environment; the problems for which a client seeks treatment are very likely to be activated or replicated spontaneously in the group sessions; and the parallel between interpersonal interactions in the group and those outside the group facilitates generalization of in-session changes to relationships outside the group. On the other hand, it must be said that research support for the efficacy of group therapy is not quite as solid as it is for individual therapy.

Admittedly, the problems of demonstrating outcome effectiveness are formidable and include: difficulty in sorting out individual client goals from group-as-a-whole goals; number and diversity of personalities and adjustment levels within a single group; confounding of treatment effects due to the concurrent use of another therapy modality (e.g., individual, marital); lack of a clear description of what type of group is being conducted; absence of comparable treatment groups or a control group for comparison purposes; vague specification of improvement criteria and insufficient evidence of maintenance and generalization of client improvement.

Despite methodological problems, there is a consensus that for a majority of clients group therapy does have a salubrious effect (for reviews, see Smith et al., 1980; Kaul and Bednar, 1986; Orlinsky and Howard, 1986; and Tillitski, 1990, cited in Dies, 1992). Both therapists and clients are more likely to report improvement than no improvement or harmful outcome (deterioration rates are slightly higher than in individual psychotherapy), although improvement may not be discerned or reported by other interested parties. Differential effectiveness of individual therapy and group therapy, though more often favoring individual therapy, is considered minimal. Consistent evidence for the superiority of one group model over another has not been forthcoming; an exception is cognitive–behavioral group therapy which has proved to be a potent and cost-effective approach to social skills training (Rose, Tolman, and Tallent, 1985).

Dies (1992) sums up the appraisal of group therapy: "Despite the rather optimistic appraisal of group therapy outcome, the general consensus among experts is that our knowledge of specific treatment effects is modest at best" (p. 61). To maximize positive outcome, practitioners are well advised to heed Ferber and Rantz's (1972) counsel to make a thorough assessment of group members in order to set "reachable goals" and provide "workable tasks." Finally, as in individual therapy a continuing challenge for group therapy research and practice is to specify what type of group and therapist style are effective for what type of client with what type of disorder.

MARITAL–FAMILY THERAPY

Overview

As was true for other modalities, the aftermath of World War II created a strong impetus for the development of marital therapy. The impetus was sustained during the fifties as a result of the high value placed on the preservation of marriage and "couple togetherness" (Barker, 1984). Ordinarily, the terms *marital counseling* and *marital therapy* are used interchangeably, as are the more recent designations, *couple counseling* and *couple therapy*. Although the goal of individual psychotherapy is sometimes the amelioration of marital–family dysfunction, marital–couple therapy is conjoint; both partners are seen together.

Consequently, the basic premise of conjoint couple therapy is that the couple is the client and the therapist treats the relationship. In shifting the focus from therapist-client to therapist-couple, marital therapy became a forerunner of conjoint family therapy (Goldenberg, 1983, chapter 12). Family therapy, which grew out of efforts to treat schizophrenics by involving their families in treatment, was at first an adjunct to individual and marital therapy. Since 1960, family therapy has become a treatment modality in its own right; and marital therapy with its variations of sex therapy, remarriage therapy, couples group therapy, may be considered a specialty within family therapy or a separate therapy modality. In this section, marital–couple therapy is sometimes referred to as a separate modality and at other times as an integral component of family therapy.

In response to the current trend of adapting treatment to the needs of clients, family therapy may include individual therapy for one or more members, parent skill training, couple sex therapy, couples group therapy, children's group therapy, in order to achieve a broad-based treatment strategy. Although family therapy is a type of group therapy, its composition of persons who have a history and (expect to have) a future together sets it apart from regular group therapy.

At least three stages of marital–family therapy can be delineated. In the first stage, clients are provided with a rationale for being seen together, rapport is established, problems are identified, and goals set. The second stage is the application of interventions to improve the functioning of each client and the client unit as a whole. A major focus is to foster interactions that reduce conflict and increase cohesion, and that assist each one to improve communication and to better manage negative emotions. The third stage is to prepare for termination by decreasing dependence on the therapist and by assisting a couple or family to transfer positive in-session changes to the home environment. In the past, the presence of the entire family was considered the sine qua non for doing family therapy; today, the essential ingredient is a sustained focus on family relationships and interactions irrespective of the number of members present in a session. As in group therapy, a therapist must set "reachable goals" and give "workable tasks" (Ferber and Rantz, 1972).

Marital–Family Models

With the exception of psychodynamic, humanistic–experiential, and behavioral theories which have been adapted to a couple–family format, current theories are infused with systems thinking. The notion of treating the couple or family system instead of one member has long been the cornerstone of most couple–family approaches. In particular, the family as a system derives from several theoretical propositions advanced by numerous writers: the locus of an individual problem or symptom is in the interactions with others; causation is reciprocal, that is, a member's problem is both a stimulus for and a response to the behavior of other members; the system which is composed of subsystems has an explicit hierarchical structure based on power, control, or knowledge; a change in one member creates change in one or more other members; the couple or family seeks stability, that is, maintenance and preservation of its structure and function, even (and often) at the expense of one member, usually the one labeled as the problem. What follows is a summary of six widely practiced family therapy models; the reader is referred to Goldenberg and Goldenberg (1991) and Nichols and Schwartz (1991) for comprehensive coverage.

Psychodynamic Model. Some of the better-known proponents are Nathan Ackerman, James Framo, and Ivan Borszormenyi-Nagy. While there is more than one etiological perspective, it can be said that current family problems stem from parents/partners' unresolved conflicts with their family of origin (Goldenberg and Goldenberg, 1991). Relationship problems in the family of origin are introjected and then projected onto the spouse and one or more children. A goal of therapy is for a couple to transfer their unresolved conflicts with their parents to the therapist, and in so doing give the therapist a direct and immediate opportunity to intervene and help them resolve the conflictual issues. Although the emphasis is on past intrapersonal issues of the parents, therapists do address current interactions of family members during a session. The assumption is that as spouses perceive and react to their own parents as real people instead of fantasized figures, they will begin to perceive and react to each other and to their children as individuals instead of fantasized figures. One strength of the psychodynamic model is imparting the knowledge of how one's conflictual relationships with one's family of origin contribute to current relational problems with a spouse and children. One limitation is insufficient emphasis on the reciprocal interactions of current family members.

Bowen Model. Founded by Murray Bowen, the model postulates that a dysfunctional family system is a response to long-standing negative emotions which have been displaced from the couple's families of origin to the marital and parental relationships. Two major concepts are triangulation and self-differentiation. Triangulation occurs when parents use a child's problem to avoid facing their marital problem. A therapist inserts herself or himself in the triangle in place of the child and redirects the parents' attention to their relational issues. Self-differentiation is the developmental process of growing out of a child role and into an adult role with one's parents. A therapist works with each spouse alone and with both together in order to help them achieve a clear and stable self-differentiation. One strength of the Bowen model is the concept of intergenerational connections and transmission of problems (Nichols and Schwartz, 1991). One limitation is that much of the therapeutic work involves only the spouses, singly or together, instead of the family as a whole.

Structural Model. Originated by Salvador Minuchin and several collaborators who went on to achieve fame in their own right, the structure of the family system is considered to be the basis for adaptive or maladaptive functioning. The family structure is defined by its subsystems (e.g., marital, parental, parent-child, sibling), and by its specific boundaries, that is, rules that define how subsystems are expected (or required) to relate to each other and how members within a subsystem are expected to interact. For example, rigid boundaries or rules create distance between family members, and weak boundaries or rules cause enmeshment of one or more family members. The goal of the structural family therapist is to change the family structure, first by accepting and aligning with it, next by assessing and challenging it, and then by introducing systems based interventions to change the structure (Nichols and Schwartz, 1991). One strength of the model is a careful delineation of the structure of the family system as a basis for determining when, where, and how to intervene. One limitation is an overemphasis on the family as a whole and a relative neglect of the personal growth of individual family members.

Humanistic–Experiential Model. Leading exponents have been Walter Kempler, Virginia Satir, and Carl Whitaker. Like the psychodynamic model, the humanistic– experiential model is an adaptation of the model used in individual psychotherapy; and whatever systemic characteristics may be present are due to the individual practitioner. The primary goal is to stimulate self-understanding and self-expression rather than interpersonal change; the assumption is that relationships will improve with improved intrapersonal functioning. Consequently, the approach emphasizes personal growth and self-fulfillment of each family member in contrast to the emphasis in many approaches on improved family problem solving (Nichols and Schwartz, 1991).

In therapy sessions, a therapist adopts the role of a catalyst; that is, a therapist utilizes personal self-disclosure and his or her interpersonal strengths to free family members from the fears, conflicts, and defensive maneuvers that interfere with the natural human thrust toward growth. A strength of the model is its respect for and attention to the personhood of each family member; a limitation is the secondary role assigned to interpersonal learning and interactional changes.

Behavioral and Cognitive Model. This model encompasses many variants; well-known exemplars are Gerald Patterson, Richard Stuart, Robert Liberman, Neil Jacobson, to mention just a few. Although not a systems based model, cognitive and behavioral family therapists do view each family member as both a stimulus for, and a response to, the behavior of other family members. As the designation of the model implies, behavioral family therapists have for some time now incorporated cognitions (e.g., critical beliefs, expectations, perceptions) as important mediating variables in the reciprocal responses family members make to one another (Goldenberg and Goldenberg, 1991).

Basically, marital–family problems result from maladaptive learning in which inappropriate cognitions and actions of one or more members are reinforced, perpetuated, and generalized. The task of the therapist is to train family members to identify and reinforce positive cognitions and actions, and to eliminate or modify negative ones. In recognition of the hierarchical component in family systems (e.g., power, control), a therapist concentrates on changing the parents' cognitive–behavioral patterns in order to effect changes in the children. Evaluation of interventions and posttherapy follow-up contacts are integral components of the treatment plan. A strength of the model is the value placed on targeting specific cognitions and behaviors for intervention work. One limitation is insufficient attention to emotional aspects of marital–family relationships.

Strategic Model. The strategic approach includes at least three well-known variants: the Milan school, the Jay Haley and Cloe Madanes camp, and the MRI (Mental Research Institute); well-known theorists closely associated with strategic family therapy include Don Jackson, Jay Haley, Cloe Madanes, and Paul Watzlawic. Fundamental to all three variants is a problem-centered, pragmatic goal of changing interactional patterns by relying on therapist-presented paradoxical or nonparadoxical reframes and directives instead of therapist-engendered insight and understanding (Nichols and Schwartz, 1991). Paradoxical reframes and directives are prototypical of strategic interventions. A paradox is a therapist message to a family not to change, but the message is part of a context that has a strong expectation of change (Goldenberg and Goldenberg, 1991). Thus, prescribing a symptom is a message not to eliminate the symptom, yet the normal expectation is to eliminate a distressing symptom.

The focus of sessions is clearly and emphatically on current family life; the goal of sessions is to resolve the problem(s) as defined by a couple or family; and sessions are connected by prescribed assignments. One strength of the model is the development of methods to circumvent or overcome resistance to change. A limitation is the deemphasis on forming an egalitarian, collaborative relationship between therapist and family members.

As is true of individual and group therapy modalities, there is a strong eclectic trend among couple–family practitioners. In short, practitioners are inclined to search for commonalities among different models and incorporate the best features of each model. Lebow (1987) argues that the family therapy field has always been eclectic/integrative in as much as (1) many first-generation models (e.g., Bowen model) had an integrative quality; (2) there has been a proliferation of recently developed integrative models (e.g., psychoanalysis-systems-behaviorism, structural-strategic, gestalt-systems), and (3) a significant percentage of marital–family practitioners have developed their own form of integrative therapy. Grebstein (1986) notes that marital–family therapy has developed to the point where integrative therapies are being published as well as practiced. For three examples of published eclectic–integrative therapies, refer to chapters 7, 9 and 14 in Norcross (1987).

Effectiveness of Marital–Family Therapy

In comparing marital and family therapy with no formal treatment, approximately 65 to 75 percent of clients improve (see reviews by Gurman and Kniskern, 1981; Gurman, Kniskern, and Pinsof, 1986; Hazelbrigg, Cooper, and Borduin, 1987; Jacobson and Addis, 1993; Shadish, Montgomery, Wilson, P., Wilson, M., Bright, and Okwumabua, 1993). More specifically, findings from the above reviews indicate that with the exception of the humanistic–experiential model, other models are more effective than a control or placebo condition; differential effectiveness of various models is minimal; the behavioral–cognitive, structural, and strategic approaches appear to have the best track record, though strategic therapy has a much smaller research base than the other two. No marital therapy model has shown consistent superiority; however, most of the well-designed empirical studies have been conducted only on behavioral couple therapy. Both marital and family therapy are superior to individual therapy for marital and family centered problems. Structural family therapy has been especially effective for substance abuse and psychosomatic problems thought to be related to dysfunctional family interactions, while behavioral family therapy is better suited than other models to problems of aggression, opposition, and noncompliance in children. For couples with sexual dysfunction and no serious long-standing relational problems, behaviorally oriented sex therapy is the treatment of choice.

Most of the above findings hold for both posttreatment evaluation and short-term follow-up. Outcome evaluation beyond one year is seldom reported; Jacobson and Addis (1993) do report significant attrition of positive changes for couples after two years. If the more stringent criterion of clinical significance is applied, outcome effectiveness of marital–family therapies (like the individual and group therapies) would be noticeably less; for instance, Jacobson and Addis (1993) estimate only a 50 percent improvement rate for couple therapy.

On an optimistic note, Parkinson (1983) concludes: family therapy is more effective than no therapy and is superior to other modalities for adolescent psychosomatic problems and substance abuse; deterioration rates are uniformly low (fluctuating around 5 percent); inclusion of the father is a critical factor in a family's attendance and in treatment outcome; a therapist's interpersonal skill is a strong contributing factor to successful outcome; and with the exception of structural and behavioral models, there is a paucity of well-designed, competently executed outcome research. As in other modalities, a lack of conceptual clarity and methodological rigor makes for cautious interpretation and tentative conclusions. Inasmuch as no one approach has been singled out as consistently superior to all others, the challenge, as always, is to discover what theories and treatment procedures are most efficacious for what types of couples-families with what types of dysfunctions.

TIME-LIMITED PSYCHOTHERAPY

Early Status

Time-limited psychotherapy, in particular crisis intervention, has been a part of the history of psychotherapy since the 1940s. The systematic development of theory, research, and practice, however, was in response to the philosophy and policies of the community mental health movement of the 1960s. Crisis intervention and brief psychotherapy were part of the zeitgeist of the community mental health movement that emphasized preventive intervention before problems become serious and chronic, round-the-clock assistance for psychiatric emergencies, and the availability of time-limited psychotherapy to a large segment of the client population who did not require (or even ask for) long-term psychotherapy. Stated otherwise, the goal of getting people on their feet so they could better manage their problems, even if they might need to return later for additional assistance, was perceived to be a more efficient and effective mental health policy than protracted, dependency-fostering psychotherapy.

Relatedly, the rise of the human potential movement that championed personal growth over psychopathology, together with the advent of behavioral psychotherapy which promoted time-limited, symptom-directed treatment, gave an additional impetus for psychotherapy that would be prescriptive, structured, solution focused, and quickly and conveniently accessible to clients who would be proactive participants in their own recovery. Since then, virtually all current models have developed a time-limited treatment format for individual, group, marital, and family therapy.

Current Status

Time-limited therapy is an umbrella designation that covers crisis, brief, and short-term therapy, all of which have overlapping features. For simplicity, the three types are differentiated as follows. *Crisis therapy* is ordinarily completed in one to three sessions; it is designed to intervene in immediate life disruptions that are due to developmental crises (e.g., life stage transitions, developmental task failures), or to situational crises (e.g., loss of a loved one, job burn-out), where external or precipitating factors are believed to be more critical than internal or predisposing factors. Typical interventions are: imparting relevant and timely information, empathic listening and responding, assessing personal strengths, utilizing community agencies and the support of close friends and family, and where indicated, prescriptive suggestions for practical decision making. The primary goal is to return clients to their pre-crisis level of functioning. Should a client's condition fail to improve or worsen, referral is made to longer-term therapy that may include more intensive treatment contact such as an intensive outpatient program or inpatient/residential facility.

Brief therapy is generally concluded by the tenth or twelfth session; the goal is almost always to improve a client's efforts to cope with one or two related, relatively circumscribed problems of recent onset which both client and therapist consider to be of high priority. Brief therapy is (1) characterized by rapid problem assessment and treatment planning; (2) contractually based in terms of session agenda and intersession assignments; and (3) present-centered and collaboratively implemented with specific and limited goals. Commonly used interventions are those that foster the practice of more adaptive coping thoughts and actions, accessing and reexperiencing previously denied emotions, reconciling conflicting states of mind, the development of an empowering perspective on one's problems and efforts to cope, activation of client strengths, and utilization of community resources

Best suited to brief therapy are clients who present relatively localized and sharply defined, nonchronic problems of mild to moderate severity; and who have some problem-solving skills as well as the capability to form a collaborative relationship with a therapist within one to three sessions. The fact that a client may have a long-standing, pervasive interpersonal or personality disorder makes it highly unlikely that brief therapy will be "length-appropriate" because of the time needed to form a therapeutic relationship. Also best suited to conducting brief therapy are therapists who engage clients rapidly, know how to individualize treatment plans and treatment sessions, have good time management skills, are willing to delegate therapeutic initiative and tasks to clients, and are results oriented. *Short-term therapy* has an upper limit of approximately 24 sessions, and is conducted as a slower paced, extended form of brief therapy.

Crisis therapy is conducted in varied settings from outpatient offices, suicide prevention centers, domestic assault and rape facilities, to walk-in clinics for alcohol and drug related crises. It is implemented by means of telephone hotlines, face-to-face contact, or mobile crisis teams; and it is provided by clinicians or paraprofessionals with backup support from experienced professionals. In recent years crisis and suicide prevention programs have been developed for educational and commercial institutions not only to prevent a potential (sometimes lethal) crisis, but also to provide immediate mental health services to secondary victims who have been in close proximity to the crisis and/or have a significant relationship with the primary crisis victim. As expected, brief and short-term psychotherapy are conducted by trained psychotherapists in conventional treatment settings.

It can be said that out of the community mental health movement came the philosophy and policy guidelines for time-limited psychotherapy. Subsequent impetus for the development of time-limited therapy came from published accounts that indicated: (1) much of the time consumer expectation and preference are for brief, even very brief psychotherapy (it is estimated that in the public sector 70 percent of the clients do not return after the fifth or sixth session, with an average length of four to six sessions [Phillips, 1988], cited in Herron et al. [1994]); and (2) time-limited therapy is as effective as time-unlimited therapy, which Bloom (1992b) states "is not only the most consistent finding in the psychotherapy literature, it is also the most affirmative" (p. 162). Not long after, a powerful, albeit controversial, impetus came from third-party payers who began to impose limits on the number of reimbursable sessions within a calendar year; later, further constraints on benefit limits were added as the managed care policymakers (pointing to the outcome studies on time-limited therapy) hailed brief/short-term therapy as cost- and quality-effective.

The irony is that the justification for time-limited therapy had already been made philosophically and scientifically before the pressures and mandates of "psychoeconomics" were applied to practitioners. Another irony is that a de facto brief therapy was already in place for a large number of public sector clients who for reasons of financial constraints due to very limited or no mental health insurance coverage, dissatisfaction with progress, satisfaction with a modicum of improvement (e.g., ebbing of the crisis), a fortuitous change in life circumstances, or incompatibility with a therapist's interpersonal style or theoretical orientation, terminate after a half a dozen or so sessions. One can only speculate that in spite of the first irony (perhaps due to professional inertia or habit), and because of the second irony (perhaps due to economic threat), many practitioners were resistant to letting go of a long-term therapy format and embracing the time-limited therapy format. Be that as it may, most assuredly the advent of therapy manuals and manual-guided treatment has made the teaching and learning of brief/short-term therapies more efficient and efficacious than the traditional teaching and learning of time-unlimited therapies.

Effectiveness of Time-Limited Psychotherapy

Very little is known about either short-term or long-term benefits of crisis therapy because evaluation studies have been hampered by the fact that clients frequently remain anonymous, sessions are often telephone-conducted, and therapeutic contact is uncertain, very brief, and seldom planned. The few published survey studies on suicide prevention centers yield variable results (Sue et al., 1994, pp. 410–412; see also Swenson and Hartsough [1983] for an evaluation of crisis intervention in general). Reviews of studies that have evaluated the efficacy of brief/short-term therapy conclude that on balance it is as beneficial as long-term therapy for a broad range of problems, irrespective of theoretical orientation (Butcher and Koss, 1978; Strupp and Binder, 1984; Koss and Butcher, 1986; Bloom, 1992a,b; Steenbarger, 1994). Similar findings have been reported for time-limited marital and family therapy (Gurman, Kniskern, and Pinsof, 1986) and for group therapy (Budman, Demby, Feldstein, and Gold, 1984). Furthermore, the widely known forms of time-limited therapy (e.g., psychodynamic, cognitive,

cognitive-behavioral, interpersonal, strategic) are considered equally beneficial.

The consistent lack of significant association between duration and outcome is not surprising if one remembers that for outcome research in general, most of the positive changes occur early on and diminish with time. A notable exception is the Howard et al. (1986) study, which evaluated improvement within studies (rather than the usual between-study comparisons) and found significant improvement between the 8th and 25th sessions. Moreover, Howard and his colleagues report that clients with more severe and chronic disorders do not begin to show recognizable clinical improvement until they reach short-term therapy's upper limit of 25 sessions. And not to be forgotten is the observation made by several authors (e.g., Herron et al., 1994) that psychotherapies of differing durations yield effective but different (instead of equivalent) outcomes.

As both recent and current literature has made abundantly clear, time limited psychotherapy is congruent with health care's preemptive goal to make treatment cost effective. And almost 20 years ago, Cummings (1977) made his prophetic pronouncement that brief therapy makes it economically feasible to offer long-term therapy to the 10 to 15 percent of clients for whom it is clinically and ethically indicated. For the interested reader, additional coverage of crisis therapy models can be found in Aguilera and Messick (1982); of brief/short-term therapy in Budman and Gurman (1983, 1988), Bloom (1992a), and the *International Journal of Short-Term Psychotherapy*.

PROFESSIONAL AND PERSONAL GROWTH

Stresses and Satisfactions

In their survey of psychotherapists' satisfactions and stresses, Farber and Heifetz (1981) comment: "Psychotherapy is a difficult, albeit fulfilling career, one that may generate personal as well as professional strains" (p. 629). Frequently mentioned satisfactions are promoting growth and change in self and clients, having an intimate involvement in clients' lives, and achieving professional status and respect. Stresses include feeling personally depleted after long hours of therapy, balancing objectivity and compassion in the therapeutic relationship, and coping with severe psychopathological symptoms and resistant behaviors. Noteworthy is the finding that therapists' experience level was not a significant variable; not surprisingly, institutionally based therapists reported higher stress levels than did private practitioners.

As expected, the literature has much more to say about the stress and strain than about the satisfaction and fulfillment of psychotherapy practice. It is probably an example of the saw that "bad news makes good copy." In any case, regardless of experience level, work setting, or type of therapy modality, therapists must cope with a variety of stresses and strains. LaPerriere (1979) poignantly describes a commonly occurring stress in family therapy practice: "some families present us with problems so alien, with world views so unacceptable, that we cannot find access to the common humanity we need to ply our trade because we are busy denying that we feel angry, or scared, or repelled" (p. 883). To be sure, a private practice setting may protect a therapist from bureaucratic frustrations indigenous to institutional settings; yet the rapidly increasing number of private practice therapists has created intense competition for clients. And both private and public sector therapists must face continual pressure to meet client care monitoring standards, declining levels of revenue-reimbursement, and an escalating tension between the cost and quality of psychological treatment, one familiar example of which is obtaining preauthorization to begin or continue therapy sessions.

The ratio of stresses to satisfactions is always critical, and when there is a continuing imbalance of job stresses
over satisfactions, therapists are susceptible to burnout
(Farber and Heifetz, 1982). Burnout has been described
as a syndrome of emotional exhaustion, energy depletion,
pessimism-cynicism, and psychophysiological symptoms
common in the helping professions based in the public
sector (Raquepaw and Miller, 1989). The authors also found
that rather than the actual size of the caseload, it was a
therapist's *perception* of the size of their caseload and their
satisfaction or dissatisfaction with it that were associated
with burnout. Not to be overlooked is the fact that burnout, debilitating as it may well be to therapists, also
lowers, sometimes considerably, the quality of the psychotherapy rendered.

Deutsch's (1985) survey of psychotherapists found
that over half had experienced relationship dysfunction,
depression, and other personal problems; and over half
had sought psychotherapeutic assistance for the problems,
with women more likely than men to avail themselves of
psychotherapy and psychotropic medication. In a laudable
move, the American Psychological Association, through its
Committee on Distressed Psychologists, has offered a
network of professional assistance for practitioners suffering from mental health or substance abuse problems.
One organization, Psychologists for Helping Psychologists,
is a self-help group for psychologists with substance use
disorders (Thoreson, Nathan, Skorina, and Kilburg, 1983).
It is quite common in large urban areas for practitioners
to organize informal support or peer consultation groups
in which participants receive as well as give assistance
(Greenburg, Lewis, and Johnson, 1985). Overall, the profession has made notable strides in offering opportunities
for professional growth through an impressive array of
continuing education programs, and in providing assistance to therapists with psychological problems stemming
from their work or personal life.

Training

Psychotherapy training has received mixed reviews in the past, but more recently significant progress has been made as a result of greater emphasis on skill-based coursework, more time devoted to supervised practica, and utilization of competency-based criteria (see Robertson, 1995, chapter 2). To establish competency-based criteria, Bootzin and Ruggill (1988) underscore the following objectives: clear, operational definition of therapy skills to be acquired; specification of measurable goals for each training component; determination of trainee baseline skill levels; and application of quantitative evaluation measures.

Two types of therapy skills for which competency-based criteria must be established are: (1) communication–relationship skills (e.g., accurate listening, empathic responding, constructive confrontation, relevant and timely therapist self-disclosure); and (2) technical–intervention skills (e.g., interpretation, imaginal and in vivo exposure procedures; cognitive restructuring; behavioral rehearsal). Both types of skills are taught through a combination of didactic instruction (defining, describing, explaining) and experiential learning (roleplay format to practice skills as a therapist and to experience skills as a client). The advent of therapy manuals, developed originally for psychotherapy outcome research, hold considerable promise for improving skill training (Robertson, 1995, chapters 2 and 4). A manual-guided training format can specify what skills are to be learned, provide instruction on how and when to apply particular skills, and establish clearly defined, acceptable levels of skill proficiency.

Supervision is a critical link between didactic learning in coursework and experiential learning in practica and internship. Supervision, conducted in a one-to-one and/or small group format, offers trainees individualized and personalized learning of relationship skills, intervention skills, and ethical sensitivity. Like any teaching tool, supervision must be adjusted to the experience and skill level of a supervisee; and a supervisee's rate of progress is a function of his or her relationship and intervention skill level, and a supervisor's interpersonal and technical competence (Robertson, 1995, chapter 2). Guest and Beutler (1988) recommend that early-stage supervision emphasize learning relationship skills, with a supervisor in a quasitherapeutic role; middle-stage supervision should concentrate on teaching intervention skills, with a supervisor in a more formal training role; and advanced supervision should be conducted with a supervisor adopting a consultative role to ensure that a supervisee integrate previously acquired relationship and intervention skills in the context of a therapeutic relationship. The authors' recommendations are congruent with supervisees' expectations as reported in the literature; namely, less experienced supervisees value formal learning of basic therapy skills from their supervisors, and more experienced supervisees desire assistance in managing relationship dynamics, particularly with interpersonally difficult clients.

With few exceptions the literature recommends that supervision offer a professional growth experience instead of personal therapy for supervisees. Yet professional growth shades into personal therapy inasmuch as supervisors must assist supervisees to better manage personal reactions that may vitiate objective listening, empathic responding, and the ability to intervene in a timely and suitable manner. It can be argued that experience in a client role gives a trainee an important perspective on a therapeutic relationship that cannot be learned in a therapist role. Relatedly, a sizable number of practitioners obtain personal therapy during their postgraduate years, and in retrospect state that it ought to be part of one's training as a clinician (Norcross and Prochaska, 1982). To conclude, a clear mandate for psychotherapy education is to design training experiences that blend personal and professional growth, so that trainees learn how to combine relationship-building skills that foster trust, hope, and self-efficacy in clients with technical skills to match interventions to clients' personalities, problems, and environmental resources (Robertson, 1995, chapter 2).

TRENDS, CHALLENGES, AND NEW DIRECTIONS

Trends

The four trends identified by Woody and Robertson (1988) are continuing, namely, psychotherapy integration, differential therapeutics, expanding networks of continuing education, and broadening the application of psychotherapy to the medical/health-care sector. As expected, additional trends have appeared. Over the past half-dozen years, psychotherapy manuals have been utilized regularly to improve outcome research and are now required or strongly recommended for most funded psychotherapy research and for publication of results in refereed journals. In psychotherapy research (which invariably utilizes short-term or brief models), manuals ensure that all research therapists are (1) conducting the same form of a therapy model being examined; (2) adhering to the model throughout the duration of treatment; and (3) performing the model at a predetermined level of competence. In addition, efforts have been under way to make psychotherapy manuals an integral component in psychotherapy training programs, which eventually should lead to a sharp increase in their utilization by practicing psychotherapists (see Lambert and Ogles, 1988; Beutler, 1988).

Another quite noticeable trend is that an interpersonal emphasis has infused most current therapies. Examples are psychodynamic (e.g., object relations and self psychology forms as well as the psychodynamically derived, time-limited interpersonal psychotherapy), gestalt, cognitive, cognitive-behavioral, and radical behavioral (functional analytic psychotherapy) forms, a few integrative therapies; and of course an interpersonal orientation has always characterized the systems based marital–family approaches. An interpersonal emphasis is also evident in the recent theoretical and empirical attention given to the therapeutic alliance (Robertson, 1995, chapter 5). A recent, albeit daunting, trend is *differential therapeutics* or prescriptive treatment, which sets out to match interventions to particular disorders and specified client characteristics (Beutler and Clarkin, 1990; Beutler, 1991b; Clarkin, Frances, and Perry, 1992). The ultimate goal is to devise and prescribe the "right" therapy for the "right" disorder (or disorder subtype), for the "right" client personality, and the "right" therapist (meaning the "right" combination of interpersonal and intervention skills). So far, progress has been gradual with respect to accurate predictions of optimal client-treatment matching.

Still another trend, which is causing ambivalent reactions, is the formation of large, efficiently managed private practice groups. Such groups seek to deliver prompt, diversified, and cost-effective therapies (often referred to as "one-stop shopping") in order to become approved providers for the growing number of managed care companies and industry sponsored employee assistance programs that are increasingly exerting proprietary control over referrals, benefit authorizations, and reimbursements.

Challenges

At least three challenges can be discerned. The first is related to the trend of differential therapeutics. Though considerable progress has been made in evaluating outcome effectiveness of different forms of psychotherapy and in identifying and assessing the contribution of key variables to outcome effectiveness, we still cannot predict whether a particular client will or will not benefit (or get worse) from psychotherapy. For instance, we cannot accurately estimate what is the "length appropriate" therapy to produce an optimal effect for a particular client. Predicting a client's response to therapy involves assessing several key factors that operate individually and interactively: (1) important characteristics of clients and their disorders (e.g., severity and chronicity of a disorder, cognitive deficiencies, behavioral deficits–social incompetence, emotional dysregulation, available support systems, coping attitudes and abilities, type of motivation and expectations; (2) a therapist's interpersonal skills and attitudes, as well as disorder-specific intervention skills; and (3) what goes on in a client's life during psychotherapy.

A second challenge is to make psychotherapy more "user friendly." As psychotherapy has traditionally been conceptualized and practiced, it has been partial to educated, middle and upper socioeconomic, heterosexual, white males, and underutilized by others (except white females who nevertheless have had to contend with a male bias). Over the past 10 to 15 years, a concerted effort has been mounted to make psychotherapy theory and practice more helpful to, and in accord with the needs, beliefs-values, and goals of special populations such as the cultural–ethnic, sexual, developmentally disabled/handicapped, aged (elderly), economically disadvantaged minorities. Dahlquist and Fay (1983) identify several areas of potential (and actual) class, cultural, age, and sex bias. The authors strongly recommend employing a cross-cultural model that is based on general, panhuman characteristics of adaptive functioning, yet allows for differences that include, but are not limited to, gender, socioeconomic class, age, and cultural background. The interested reader can consult Sue and Sue (1990) or peruse a few recent issues of the *Journal of Multicultural Counseling and Development* or the *Journal of Gay and Lesbian Psychotherapy*.

A third challenge that has led to a never-ending series of published articles, newsletter reports, and books is coping with managed care philosophy and policies. For the practicing psychotherapist, the central issue is quality effectiveness versus cost effectiveness. On the one hand, psychotherapists have an ethical mandate to provide adequate and effective psychotherapy; yet, as Giles and Marafiote (1994) conclude, "it has become increasingly more difficult to provide adequate and effective treatment due to restrictions placed on providers by managed care companies" (p. 241). From an admittedly biased perspective, managed care policy seems to assume that psychotherapy lacks practical effectiveness, and that both clients and therapists cannot be relied on to terminate treatment when the treatment has served its stated purpose or goal. Psychotherapists, on the other hand, contend that research has established favorable effectiveness rates for most psychotherapy models and differential effectiveness for certain types of dysfunctions; moreover, there is evidence that psychotherapy also results in reduced medical care services (VandenBos and Deleon, 1988).

In response to what is perceived by many of us as managed care's major complaint, it can be pointed out that most psychotherapy is very short-term anyway, at least for a large segment of outpatient clients; the large majority of clients do seem to terminate when they experience sufficient improvement, and those who desire longer term therapy likely do so because they have not experienced enough improvement. While it is the case that many therapists still resist time-limited therapy for reasons of inertia, lack of training in time-limited forms, or economic threat, most clients will terminate when they see fit. Furthermore, professional peer-review boards could monitor the need for and efficacious use of long-term therapy, and could determine at what point therapists and/or clients are guilty of unnecessary utilization; Herron et al. (1994) propose a marker of 25 sessions for an initial progress review and decision about treatment continuance. Stern (1993) argues persuasively that the managed care policy of restricting utilization of therapeutic services is skewed in the direction of preventing unnecessary treatment while increasing the risk of denying treatment to those genuinely in need of a lengthier course of psychotherapy. Stern echoes the sentiments of many others when he concludes that "when patients leave therapy with their problems unsolved they simply generate new and greater social costs of one form or another later on" (p. 172). In a very similar vein, Herron et al. (1994) caution managed care against cost containment based on maximum dosage usage instead of the more realistic and humane criterion of maximum dosage effectiveness. A wide range of articles on the topic is available in Wiggins and Welch (1988).

New Directions

A prediction from Rubenstein's (1985) report on future projections of the psychotherapy marketplace is that psychologists will become identified as family practice therapists. Consistent with the opposition to continuous psychotherapy, they will provide a full-range of brief or short-term psychotherapeutic services (individual, group, marital, family) on an intermittent basis as new or cyclical crises arise during the life span of clients and their family members.

In response to cost containment and the restrictions placed on psychotherapy utilization, a realistic prediction would be for (1) much greater use of high quality, professionally developed self-help approaches in manual or cassette form with minimal, periodic therapist contact (see Gould and Clum, 1993); and (2) computer-assisted therapy programs developed from the more structured, directive, and prescriptive models, again with minimal, periodic therapist contact (refer to Bloom, 1992c).

Another prediction, admittedly a gloomy one based on a worst case scenario resulting from rigidly applied managed care policies, is that instead of medication being primarily an adjunct to psychotherapy, the latter will become an adjunct to medication treatment; if psychologists' efforts to secure approval for limited prescription privileges fail, nonmedical therapists will have an adjunctive role in relation to psychiatric physicians instead of the near-parity role they have struggled long and hard to achieve. The onus for the above prediction, however, cannot be placed entirely on managed care. Outcome research shows that while medication treatment and psychotherapy have similar improvement rates, on the average the former takes two and one-half months to be effective and the latter six months to be effective (Smith et al., 1980). The time differential translates into lower costs and more rapid relief from symptomatic distress. Therefore, psychotherapy must base its justification on the fact that it produces more substantive and durable improvement with lower relapse rates and fewer and less serious iatrogenic effects (and there are indications that justification is developing). To continue to build justification for psychotherapy as a cost effective and quality effective treatment for psychological problems, professional psychology must become more disciplined scientifically and insist that where possible only empirically validated or empirically promising psychological treatments be taught and practiced (for related discussion, see APA, September, 1993; also Sanderson, 1994).

Chapter 6

Afterword: The Future of Clinical Psychology

In Woody and Robertson's (1988) publication, the authors underscored the following key developments for the future of clinical psychology practice: the federal government's shifting fiscal responsibility to the states, third-party payers' imposing practice restrictions, and increasing competition among mental health service providers. The authors stated that these developments would necessitate creating alternative work roles, practice settings, sources of income, and training models. In general, these ideas have become reality, but in a much more dramatic fashion than was envisioned. Moreover, a major theme set forth in the authors' companion volume (Woody and Robertson, 1996) and acknowledged in this volume's chapter 5 is that all health care providers are, in the 1990s, facing increased governmental (both federal and state) regulations, fiscal conservatism, and demands for accountability that would have not been predicted in the late 1980s.

Woody and Robertson (1988) also highlighted six emerging trends that were expected to lead clinical psychology into the future. They were: mass communication media; the practitioner training model; computerization;

shifts in professional roles; psychotherapy integration; and systemic conceptualizations. With the exception of the first two, the other four, along with psychological assessment, are addressed below.

TREND 1: COMPUTERIZATION

Computers have paved the way for developments in assessment and diagnosis. Computerized testing with microcomputers is already altering the way clinical psychologists administer, score, and interpret tests. Test scores are available within minutes instead of days or weeks. Psychologists are relieved of the time consuming features of traditional assessment and can redirect their energies into other clinical areas. Besides, many clients prefer the anonymity of the computer based test administration.

Use of computers in psychotherapy has been slower to develop; many applications remain in an experimental stage and others have a provisional status. However, as noted in the previous chapter cost containment, notably restrictions placed on psychotherapy utilization, have spurred the design of computer-assisted programs for the more structured and prescriptive therapy models, such as cognitive and behavioral therapies.

Computerization also plays a significant role in automating a host of support functions for practitioners: accounting and billing, and more recently electronic billing; claims processing; quality assurance, for instance, to record, organize, and analyze data on treatment outcomes in order to satisfy managed care requests for documentation of efficient and effective treatments. The cost of setting up and later trading up office automation is more than offset by the savings achieved through significant reduction of support staff costs. In addition, automation of support services means the freeing up of time to devote to client care and to marketing activities to expand the client referral base, as well as providing electronic communication networks to easily and quickly interact with other providers and provider health care systems.

TREND 2: SYSTEMIC CONCEPTUALIZATION

Systemic conceptualizations in both psychological assessment and treatment will benefit from advances in computer technology. An overarching systemic perspective that has drawn a strong consensus over the past decade is a biopsychosocial model of normality and abnormality. In short, competent assessment and treatment must be grounded not only in an understanding of biopsychological determinants, but in knowledge about the individual's family, the individual's social network, and the community organizations and institutions as well.

The systemic ideas implicit in the exciting work that is going on in the neurosciences cannot help but further our understanding of the causes, treatment, and rehabilitation of the more serious and costly mental disorders, most notably the seriously mentally ill with coexisting polysubstance disorders.

A systemic perspective is becoming more evident in the number of psychologists who are blending their education as a clinical psychologist with training in neurobiology, psychopharmacology, law, education, public policy, or business.

Finally, the systemic orientation that has infused the marital-family therapies over the past 20 years is firmly in place and is still considered the sine qua non for treating relationship problems.

TREND 3: OUTLOOK FOR PSYCHOLOGICAL ASSESSMENT

Psychological assessment is still an integral part of the training and practice of the clinical psychologist, though

much of the hands-on assessment activities have shifted
to the subdoctoral practitioner.

If recent reviews are accurate, the expectation is
that established psychological tests will continue to be
much like they are today in both structure and usage
(Matarazzo, 1992; Watkins, Campbell, Nieberding, and
Hallmark, 1995). These authors find that the current
practice of psychological assessment is surprisingly similar to what it was 25 to 30 years ago. Watkins et al. point
to the addition of the Millon inventories to current assessment and diagnosis of psychopathology and express
confidence in the future of projective techniques.
Matarazzo expects further implementation of biological
tests of intelligence and cognitive processes, in addition
to the increased status of neuropsychological evaluation.
And both cite the advances in computerized assessment
and diagnosis over the past 10 to 15 years. Certainly,
every effort has been made to make psychological assessment user friendly for the busy practitioner; besides computerized administration, scoring, and interpretation of
widely used assessment procedures, complete reports
detailing multiaxial diagnosis, prognosis, and treatment
plan are available from several companies for a reasonable fee.

Even more than psychotherapy, psychological assessment has been curtailed in the name of health care
cost containment. By and large, the business side of health
care has not been persuaded that psychological assessment is cost effective or even quality effective. So it is
incumbent upon practitioners who intend to invest significant time in assessment practice to demonstrate con-
vincingly that psychological assessment does benefit the
consumer, i.e., the client-patient and the insurers.
If conducted competently as an integral part of treatment, assessment procedures can make a valuable contribution to ongoing treatment planning and treatment
evaluation.

A daunting development in the 1990s is the unexpectedly large increase in the number of clients suffering from dual (sometimes multiple) disorders for whom safe, effective, and timely treatment is a major challenge for those who work in the public sector facilities. Accurate and efficient psychological assessment would assist practitioners to identify and prioritize dual or multiple disorders with respect to treatment planning and implementation.

Finally, whether or not psychologists attain limited prescription privileges, the current trend to medicalize psychological disorders and the concomitant rise in medication intervention offer psychologists who specialize in assessment an opportunity to make a useful contribution through determining optimal personality–medication interactions. This assumes a knowledge of both assessment tools and psychopharmacology, and is reflective of the rising importance of biopsychology in the training of clinical psychologists.

TREND 4: CHANGES IN PSYCHOTHERAPY

If psychotherapy is destined to become more standardized, prescriptive, and time-limited, then the training of psychotherapists must become more structured and manual-guided with a strong emphasis on short-term approaches. If the "gold standard" of treatment is to be the proficient use of an empirically validated psychotherapy, then trainees must be trained in the competent practice of those psychotherapies that have met the stringent criteria for empirical effectiveness.

We are reasonably sure that some degree of theoretical diversity will be maintained, and the current forms of psychodynamic, cognitive, behavioral, cognitive–behavioral, interpersonal, structural, and strategic therapies will remain viable alternatives. Their viability, however, will depend on whether there is objective evidence that the treatments are safe, effective, and efficient.

Conceivably, the emerging trend both to practice and to train psychologists in psychotherapies that have been empirically validated for specific disorders could deliver the long-awaited answer to Gordon Paul's (1967) oft quoted or paraphrased question: "*What* treatment, by *whom*, is most effective for *this* individual with *that* specific problem under *which* set of circumstances?" (p. 111).

In all likelihood, the psychotherapy integration movement described in chapter 4 will gain further visibility and recognition as a therapy orientation in its own right. Like the better known single theory approaches mentioned above, integrating differing therapies or interventions from diverse therapy models will have to conform to empirical findings on what therapy or set of interventions is most efficacious for which phase of treatment or for which type of disorder.

Furthermore, the four traditional modalities (individual, group, couple, and family) will be utilized, as they are now, either concurrently or sequentially. The deployment of the various modalities will one hopes be conducted more thoughtfully and with greater regard for optimal timing and outcome efficacy. Finally, it is hoped that psychotherapy will become a complement, not an adjunct, to medication, and that the integration of particular psychological treatments and current medications will be based on the empirically determined strengths of each type of treatment, instead of reliance on arbitrary criteria, subjective preference, or force of habit. Moreover, in standing up for the efficacy of psychotherapeutic interventions, clinical psychologists can draw confidence from Barlow's (1994) conclusion: "But the point that is often missed is that psychological interventions have demonstrable, substantial, and long-lasting effects on neurobiological processes and even genetic expression" (p. 110).

TREND 5: SHIFTS IN PROFESSIONAL ROLES

Several changes in professional practice anticipated in the late 1980s (Woody and Robertson, 1988) have evolved during the 1990s. For the most part, the changes reflect an ongoing conflict of priorities, for example, between practice oriented and science oriented clinical psychologists, between subdoctoral and doctoral level practitioners, between psychiatrists and psychologists, between the values of the practice sector of health care and the values of the business sector.

One response to the conflicting priorities is to reexamine the profession's traditional mission statement articulated by Korchin (1976), to wit, a unique blend of teaching, research, and practice roles. Clearly, it is the practice role that continues to be challenged and to be the focus of reexamination. One reconceptualization that has garnered consistent support is to define clinical psychology as a generic discipline that includes school psychology, counseling psychology, behavioral medicine, and any other specialty areas that meet the criteria of a health care specialty.

Another reconceptualization, albeit more complicated and probably more controversial, is to consider professional psychology as synonymous with a human services profession that is not limited to the health care field. Professional psychology would then have generic standards and training requirements that would be applicable to the entire spectrum of psychological practice. Criteria would be drawn up to differentiate within professional psychology the *specialties* (e.g., clinical psychology) from its *subspecialties* (e.g., behavioral medicine, neuropsychology) and from its specific *proficiencies* (e.g., biofeedback, hypnotherapy).

On a more practical level, an ongoing change that seriously affects the role of psychological practice is the sharp

curtailment of private practice opportunities resulting
from managed care policies, such as restricting referrals
of insured clients to providers in large private practice
groups; limiting the number of authorized therapy sessions primarily for financial rather than therapeutic considerations; and setting provider reimbursement fees
lower, sometimes substantially lower, than provider-
competitive rates. These cost-driven policies threaten the
very livelihood of practitioners whose primary source of
income is full-time private practice. The response has
been varied with some practitioners deciding to work for
much less; others have taken positions in a public sector
facility; some have left the profession to enter a different occupation; and the more fortunate have joined large,
well-established group practices or have succeeded in
merging with other solo practitioners.

In addition to changes already in progress, longer
term trends are starting to emerge. Large private practice groups are poised to merge with one another to form
regional practice groups that serve larger geographical
areas and consumer populations (Cummings, 1995). Taking their cue from the private sector, public sector treatment facilities are experimenting with mergers to form
regional community treatment centers, at the same time
they are contemplating limited mergers or at least affili-
ations with treatment centers in the private sector (M. J.
Sullivan, 1995).

Faced with a decline in third-party reimbursements,
private sector practitioners are exploring ways to diver-
sify their consumer base. Under consideration is the development of a range of services that are requested by
clients who are self-pay by choice, or by necessity because
third-party reimbursement has been used up or is not
authorized for certain types of services (e.g., parent training, assertiveness training, conflict resolution training).
On the other hand, Cummings (1995) contends that new
payment methods, such as capitation and prospective

reimbursement, are expected to do away with some of the obstacles resulting from older payment plans.

Other viable possibilities are: midsize corporations that do not have in-house employee assistance programs or that need assistance in developing and enhancing employee morale and productivity; school systems that wish to design prevention programs for a multitude of student problems; long-term care facilities that seek psychological consultation in order to better meet the needs and address the problems of an increasing number of elderly residents; and finally a wide range of self-help groups that rely on experienced group therapists for direction and troubleshooting skills.

For now and the foreseeable future, the psychological practitioner must shift from the traditional independent, fee-for-service style of practice to an unfamiliar role of working productively within a large human service or health care organization, providing a greater diversity of services to a larger volume of clients for shorter periods of time. Moreover, the role expectation includes: knowing when to utilize an illness model and when to employ a human effectiveness or competency model; investing significant resources in a continuing education program that will provide additional certificates of clinical proficiency; and being willing to monitor, disclose, and improve the effectiveness of services provided. Some in the profession are even calling for a "back to fundamentals" approach in which the training and practice of clinical psychology would put more emphasis on the original functions of education and research.

To conclude, it is evident that clinical psychology is much more complex and demanding today than at any other point in its evolution, even since the authors' (1988) appraisal. The threats and impediments to the future development of the profession notwithstanding, there is as much or more potential for further expansion of the profession than at any other time. Setting aside the doomsayers' projections that have become so prevalent in practitioner newsletters, this eve of the twenty-first century is a most opportune time to enter or continue in the field of clinical psychology, accepting that professional success and personal fulfillment come only through dedication to excellence in knowledge and skill acquisition and through commitment to the highest professional and scientific standards.

References

Abeles, N. (1990), Rediscovering psychological assessment. *Clin. Psycholog.*, 10:3–4.

Adamovich, B. B., Henderson, J. A., & Auerbach, S. (1985), *Cognitive Rehabilitation of Closed Head Injured Patients: A Dynamic Approach.* San Diego, CA: College-Hill Press.

Adler, A. (1929), *Problems of Neurosis: A Book of Case-Histories.* New York: Harper Torchbooks, 1964.

Aguilera, D. C., & Messick, J. M. (1982), *Crisis Intervention: Theory and Methodology*, 4th ed. St. Louis, MO: Mosby.

Aiken, L. R. (1988), *Psychological Testing and Assessment*, 6th ed. Boston: Allyn & Bacon.

—— (1989), *Assessment of Personality.* Boston: Allyn & Bacon.

Allard, G., Butler, J., Faust, D., & Shea, M. T. (1995), Errors in hand scoring objective personality tests: The case of the Personality Diagnostic Questionnaire-Revised (PDQ-R). *Prof. Psychology*, 26:304–308.

Allport, G. W. (1942), *The Use of Personal Documents in Psychological Science.* New York: Social Science Research Council.

American Educational Research Association/American Psychological Association/National Council on Measurement in Education (1985), *Standards for Educational and Psychological Testing.* Washington, DC: American Psychological Association.

American Psychiatric Association (1952), *Diagnostic and Statistical Manual of Mental Disorders.* Washington, DC: American Psychiatric Association.

—— (1968), *Diagnostic and Statistical Manual of Mental Disorders*, 2nd ed. (DSM-II). Washington, DC: American Psychiatric Press.

252   References

(1994), *Diagnostic and Statistical Manual of Mental Disorders*, 4th ed. (DSM-IV). Washington, DC: American Psychiatric Press.
American Psychological Association (1980), *APA/CHAMPUS Outpatient Psychological Providers Manual*. Washington, DC: American Psychological Association.
————— (1989), In U.S., mental disorders affect 15 percent of adults. *APA Monitor*, 20:16.
————— (1992), Ethical principles of psychologists and code of conduct. *Amer. Psycholog.*, 47:1597–1611.
————— (1993), Promotion and dissemination of psychological procedures. *Clinical Psychology Task Force Report*, 1–23, 4.55–4.63.
Arbuckle, D. S. (1965), *Counseling: Philosophy, Theory, and Practice*. Boston: Allyn & Bacon.
Archer, R. P., Maruish, M., Imhof, E. A., & Piotrowski, C. (1991), Psychological test usage with adolescent clients: 1990 survey findings. *Prof. Psychol.*, 22:247–252.
Arkowitz, H. (1992), Integrative theories of therapy. In: *The History of Psychotherapy: A Century of Change*, ed. D. Freedheim. Washington, DC: American Psychological Association.
Arlow, J. A. (1989), Psychoanalysis. In: *Current Psychotherapies*, 4th ed., ed. R. J. Corsini & D. Wedding. Itasca, IL: F. E. Peacock, pp. 19–62.
Asher, S. R., & Wheeler, V. A. (1985), Children's loneliness: A comparison of rejected and neglected peer status. *J. Consult. & Clin. Psychol.*, 53:500–505.
Bachrach, L. L. (1988), Defining chronic mental illness: A concept paper. *Hosp. & Commun. Psychiatry*, 39:383–388.
Bak, F. S., & Greene, R. L. (1980), Changes in neuropsychological functioning in an aging population. *J. Consult. & Clin. Psychol.*, 48:395–399.
Bales, R. F. (1950), *Interaction Process Analysis*. Reading, MA: Addison-Wesley.
Ball, J. D., Archer, R. P., & Imhof, E. A. (1994), Time requirements of psychological testing: A survey of practitioners. *J. Personal. Assess.*, 63:239–249.
Barker, R. L. (1984), *Treating Couples in Crisis*. New York: Free Press.
Barlow, D. H. (1994), Psychological interventions in the era of managed care competition. *Clin. Psychol.*, 1:109–122.
Barron, J., Fabrikant, B., & Krasner, J. D. (1971), *Psychotherapy: A Psychological Perspective*. New York: Selected Academic Readings/ Simon & Schuster.
Bartol, C. R., & Bartol, A. M. (1994), *Psychology and Law: Research and Application*, 2nd ed. Pacific Grove, CA: Brooks/Cole.
Beck, A. T., & Weishaar, M. E. (1989), Cognitive therapy. In: *Current Psychotherapies*, 4th ed., ed. R. J. Corsini & D. Wedding. Itasca, IL: F. E. Peacock, pp. 285–320.

Beck, S. J. (1981), Reality, Rorschach, and perceptual theory. In: *Assessment with Projective Techniques: A Concise Introduction*, ed. I. Rabin. New York: Springer Publishing, pp. 23–46.

—— Beck, A. G., Levitt, E. E., & Molish, H. B. (1961), *Rorschach's Test: I. Basic Processes*, 3rd ed. New York: Grune & Stratton.

Beckman, L., & Dokecki, P. R. (1989), Public and private responsibility for mental health services. *Amer. Psycholog.*, 44:133–137.

Bellack, A. S. (1986), Schizophrenia: Behavior therapy's forgotten child. *Behav. Ther.*, 17:199–214.

Bellak, L. (1986), *The Thematic Apperception Test, the Children's Apperception Test, and the Senior Apperception Technique in Clinical Use*, 4th ed. Larchmont, NY: Grune & Stratton.

Beller, E. K. (1962), *Clinical Process: The Assessment of Data in Childhood Personality Disorders*. New York: Free Press.

Bender, L. (1938), *A Visual Motor Gestalt Test and Its Clinical Use*. New York: American Orthopsychiatric Association.

Beutler, L. (1983), *Eclectic Psychotherapy: A Systematic Approach*. New York: Pergamon.

—— (Series Editor) (1988), A special series: Training to competency in psychotherapy. *J. Consult. & Clin. Psychol.*, 56:651–709.

—— (1991a), Have all won and must all have prizes? Revisiting Luborsky et al.'s verdict. *J. Consult. & Clin. Psychol.*, 59:226–232.

—— (1991b), Selective treatment matching: Systematic eclectic psychotherapy. *Psychotherapy*, 28:457–462.

—— Clarkin, J. F. (1990), *Systematic Treatment Selection: Toward Targeted Therapeutic Interventions*. New York: Brunner/Mazel.

Bigler, E. D., & Ehrfurth, J. W. (1981), The continued inappropriate singular use of the Bender visual motor gestalt test. *Prof. Psychology*, 12:562–659.

Binet, A., & Simon, T. (1905), Methodes nouvelle pour le diagnostic du niveau intellectuel des anormaux. *L'Annee Psychologique*, 11:191–244.

Blanck, G., & Blanck, R. (1974), *Ego Psychology: Theory and Practice*. New York: Columbia University Press.

Bleuler, E. (1912), *The Theory of Schizophrenic Negativism*, tr. W. A. White. Washington, DC: Nervous & Mental Disorders.

Bloom, B. L. (1992a), *Planned Short-Term Psychotherapy: A Clinical Handbook*. Boston: Allyn & Bacon.

—— (1992b), Planned short-term psychotherapy: Current status and future challenges. *Appl. & Prevent. Psychol.*, 1:157–164.

—— (1992c), Computer-assisted psychological intervention: A review and commentary. *Clin. Psychol. Rev.*, 12:169–197.

Bootzin, R. R., & Ruggill, J. S. (1988), Training issues in behavior therapy. *J. Consult. Clin. Psychol.*, 56:703–709.

Bordin, E. S. (1979), The generalizability of the psychoanalytic concept of the working alliance. *Psychotherapy*, 16:252–269.

Brammer, L. M., Shostrom, E. L., & Abrego, P. J. (1989), *Therapeutic Psychology: Fundamentals of Counseling and Psychology*, 5th ed. Englewood Cliffs, NJ: Prentice-Hall.

Brint, S. (1994), *In an Age of Experts: The Changing Role of Professionals in Politics and Public Life*. Princeton, NJ: Princeton University Press.

Brodzinsky, D. M. (1993), On the use and misuse of psychological testing in child custody evaluations. *Prof. Psychology*, 24:213–219.

Bromberg, W. (1975), *From Shaman to Psychotherapist: A History of the Treatment of Mental Illness*. Chicago: Henry Regnery.

Brown, J. (1987), A review of meta-analyses conducted on psychotherapy outcome research. *Clin. Psychol. Rev.*, 7:1–23.

Brown, V. B., Ridgely, M. S., Pepper, B., Levine, I. S., & Ryglewicz, H. (1989), The dual crisis: Mental health and substance abuse. *Amer. Psycholog.*, 44:565–569.

Bryant, E. T., Scott, M. L., Golden, C. J., & Tori, C. D. (1984), Neuropsychological deficits, learning disability, and violent behavior. *J. Consult. & Clin. Psychol.*, 52:323–324.

Budman, S. H., & Gurman, A. S. (1983), The practice of brief therapy. *Prof. Psychology*, 14:277–292.

———— ———— (1988), *Theory and Practice of Brief Therapy*. New York: Guilford Press.

———— Demby, A., Feldstein, M., & Gold, M. (1984), The effects of time-limited group psychotherapy: A controlled study. *Internat. J. Group Psychother.*, 34:587–604.

Bugental, J. F. T. (1978), *Psychotherapy and Process: The Fundamentals for an Existential-Humanistic Approach*. Menlo Park, CA: Addison-Wesley.

Buss, A. H., & Plomin, R. (1975), *A Temperament Theory of Personality Development*. New York: John Wiley.

Butcher, J. N. (1990), *The MMPI-2 in Psychological Treatment*. New York: Oxford University Press.

———— Braswell, L., & Raney, D. (1983), A cross-cultural comparison of American indian, black, and white inpatients on the MMPI and presenting symptoms. *J. Consult. & Clin. Psychol.*, 51:587–594.

———— Kendall, P. C., & Hoffman, N. (1980), MMPI short forms: Caution. *J. Consult. & Clin. Psychol.*, 48:275–278.

———— Koss, M. P. (1978), Research on brief and crisis-oriented therapies. In: *Handbook of Psychotherapy and Behavior Change: An Empirical Analysis*, 2nd ed., ed. S. L. Garfield & A. E. Bergin. New York: John Wiley.

Camara, W. J., & Schneider, D. L. (1994), Integrity tests: Facts and unresolved issues. *Amer. Psycholog.*, 49:112–119.

Canter, A. (1985), The Bender-Gestalt Test. In: *Major Psychological Assessment Instruments*, ed. C. S. Meumark. Boston: Allyn & Bacon, pp. 217–248.

Carpignano, J. (1987), Problems in the practice of responsible school psychology. *School Psychologist*, 41:1–4.

Cichetti, D. V. (1994), Guidelines, criteria, and rules of thumb for evaluating normed and standardized assessment instruments in psychology. *Psychological Assessment*, 6:284–290.

——— Toth, S., & Bush, M. (1988), Developmental psychopathology and incompetence in childhood. In: *Advances in Child Psychology*, Vol. 11, ed. B. B. Lahey & A. E. Kazdin. New York: Plenum Press, pp. 125–158.

Clarkin, J. F., Frances, A., & Perry, S. (1992), Differential therapeutics: Macro and micro levels of treatment. In: *Handbook of Psychotherapy Integration*, ed. J. C. Norcross & M. R. Goldfried. New York: Basic Books.

Cohen, D. B. (1974), On the etiology of neurosis. *J. Abnorm. Psychol.*, 83:473–479.

Coleman, J. C. (1956), *Abnormal Psychology and Modern Life*, 2nd ed. Chicago: Scott, Foresman.

Corey, G. (1982), *Theory and Practice of Counseling and Psychotherapy*, 2nd ed. Monterey, CA: Brooks/Cole.

——— (1990), *Theory and Practice of Group Counseling*, 3rd ed. Pacific Grove, CA: Brooks/Cole.

——— (1995), *Theory and Practice of Group Counseling*, 4th ed. Pacific Grove, CA: Brooks/Cole.

Corsini, R. J., Ed. (1981), *Handbook of Innovative Psychotherapies*. New York: John Wiley.

Cummings, N. A. (1977), Prolonged (ideal) versus short-term (realistic) psychotherapy. *Prof. Psychology*, 8:491–501.

——— (1995), Impact of managed care on employment and training: A primer for survival. *Prof. Psychology*, 26:10–15.

Dahlquist, L. M., & Fay, A. S. (1983), Cultural issues in psychotherapy. In: *The Handbook of Clinical Psychology: Theory, Research, and Practice*, Vol. 2, ed. C. E. Walker. Homewood, IL: Dow Jones-Irwin, pp. 1219–1255.

Dahlstrom, W. G., Welsh, G. S., & Dahlstrom, L. I. (1972), *An MMPI Handbook*, Vol. 1, *Clinical Interpretation*. Minneapolis: University of Minnesota Press.

——— ——— ——— (1975), *An MMPI Handbook*, Vol. 2, *Research Applications*. Minneapolis: University of Minnesota Press.

Delano Clinic (1989), Did you know? *Mind Matters: A Special Report*, 2:1–4.

DeLeon, G., Freudenberger, H. J., & Wexler, H. K. (1993), Foreword to the special issue: Psychotherapy for the addictions. *Psychotherapy*, 30:185–186.

Deutsch, C. J. (1985), A survey of therapists' personal problems and treatment. *Prof. Psychology*, 16:305–315.

Dies, R. R. (1992), The future of group therapy. *Psychotherapy*, 29:58–64.

Doane, J. A. (1978), Family interaction and communication deviance in disturbed and normal families: A review of research. *Fam. Proc.*, 17:357–376.

Dohrenwend, B., & Dohrenwend, B. (1969), *Social Status and Psychological Disorder.* New York: John Wiley.

Dollard, J., & Miller, N. (1950), *Personality and Psychotherapy.* New York: McGraw-Hill.

Draguns, J. G. (1985), Psychological disorders across cultures. In: *Handbook of Cross-Cultural Counseling and Psychotherapy,* ed. P. Pederson. Westport, CT: Greenwood Press.

Dunleavy, R. A., & Baade, L. E. (1980), Neuropsychological correlates of severe asthma in children 9–14 years old. *J. Consult. & Clin. Psychol.*, 48:214–219.

Dusay, J. M., & Dusay, K. M. (1989), Transactional analysis. In: *Current Psychotherapies,* 4th ed., ed. R. J. Corsini & D. Wedding. Itasca, IL: F. E. Peacock, pp. 405–453.

Eccles, J. S., Midgley, C., Wigfield, A., Buchanan, C. M., Reuman, D., Flanagan, C., & MacIver, D. (1993), Development during adolescence: The impact of state-environment fit on young adolescents' experiences in schools and families. *Amer. Psycholog.*, 48:90–101.

Edwards, A. L. (1954), *Manual: Edwards Personal Preference Schedule.* New York: Psychological Corporation.

———— (1964), Social desirability and performance on the MMPI. *Psychometrika,* 29:295–308.

———— (1971), *Individual Mental Testing, Part I: History and Theories.* Scranton, PA: Intext Educational.

———— (1972), *Individual Mental Testing, Part II: Measurement.* Scranton, PA: Intext Educational.

———— (1975), *Individual Mental Testing, Part III: Research and Interpretation.* New York: Intext Educational.

Einstein, A. (1936), Some thoughts concerning education. Proceedings of the Seventy-Second Convocation of the University of the State of New York. *Univ. State New York Bull.*, 1100:43–47.

Elkin, I., Shea, M. T., Watkins, J. T., Imber, S. D., Sotsky, S. M., Collins, J. F., Glass, D. R., Pilkonis, P. A., Leber, W. R., Docherty, J. P., Feister, S. J., & Parloff, M. B. (1989), National Institute of Mental Health treatment of depression collaborative research program: General effectiveness of treatments. *Arch. Gen. Psychiatry,* 46:971–972.

Ellis, A. (1989), Rational-emotive therapy. In: *Current Psychotherapies,* 4th ed., ed. R. J. Corsini & D. Wedding. Itasca, IL: F. E. Peacock, pp. 197–238.

———— Grieger, R., Eds. (1986), *Handbook of Rational-Emotive Therapy,* Vols. 1 & 2. New York: Springer.

Erikson, E. H. (1963), *Childhood and Society,* 2nd ed. New York: W. W. Norton.

Exner, J. E. (1974), *The Rorschach: A Comprehensive System,* Vol. 1. New York: John Wiley.

References 257

——— (1978), *The Rorschach: A Comprehensive System*, Vol. 2, *Current Research and Advanced Interpretation*. New York: John Wiley.

——— Weiner, I. B. (1982), *The Rorschach: A Comprehensive System*, Vol. 3, *Assessment of Children and Adolescents*. New York: John Wiley.

Eysenck, H. J. (1952), The effects of psychotherapy: An evaluation. *J. Consult. Psychol.*, 16:319–324.

Farber, B. A., & Heifetz, L. J. (1981), The satisfaction and stresses of psychotherapeutic work: A factor analytic study. *Prof. Psychology*, 12:621–630.

——— ——— (1982), The process and dimensions of burnout in psychotherapists. *Prof. Psychology*, 13:293–301.

Fassinger, R. E. (1991), Counseling lesbian women and gay men. *Counseling Psycholog.*, 19:156–176.

Ferber, A., & Rantz, J. (1972), How to succeed in family therapy: Set reachable goals—give workable tasks. In: *The Book of Family Therapy*, ed. A. Ferber. New York: Science House.

Florida Board of Psychological Examiners (1995), *Laws and Rules*. Tallahassee, FL: Agency for Health Care Administration.

Ford, D. H., & Urban, H. B. (1963), *Systems of Psychotherapy*. New York: John Wiley.

Foxman, P. N. (1980), Tolerance for ambiguity: Implications for mental health. In: *Encyclopedia of Clinical Assessment*, Vol. 1, ed. R. H. Woody. San Francisco, CA: Jossey-Bass.

Frank, G. (1975), *Psychiatric Diagnosis: A Review of Research*. New York: Pergamon.

Frank, L. K. (1948), *Projective Methods*. Springfield, IL: Charles C Thomas.

Freedheim, D. K., Ed. (1992), *History of Psychotherapy: A Century of Change*. Washington, DC: American Psychological Association.

Freeman, A., Simon, K. M., Beutler, L. E., & Arkowitz, H., Eds. (1989), *Comprehensive Handbook of Cognitive Therapy*. New York: Plenum.

Freud, S. (1911), Psycho-analytic notes upon an autobiographical account of a case of paranoia (dementia paranoides). *Collected Papers*, Vol. 3. London: Hogarth Press, 1949.

——— (1915–1917), Introductory Lectures on Psychoanalysis. *Standard Edition*, 15 & 6. London: Hogarth Press, 1961.

——— (1919), Totem and Taboo. *Standard Edition*, 13:1–161. London: Hogarth Press, 1955.

Garfield, S. L. (1980), *Psychotherapy: An Eclectic Approach*. New York: John Wiley.

——— (1981), Critical issues in the effectiveness of psychotherapy. In: *Clinical Practice of Psychology*, ed. C. E. Walker. New York: Pergamon, pp. 161–188.

——— (1982), The emergence of the scientist-practitioner model: Background and rationale. *Clin. Psycholog.*, 36(1):4–6.

Gaston, L. (1990), The concept of the alliance and its role in psychotherapy: Theoretical and empirical considerations. *Psychotherapy*,
27:143–153.

Genthner, R. W. (1980), Personal responsibility. In: *Encyclopedia of
Clinical Assessment*, Vol. 1, ed. R. H. Woody. San Francisco, CA:
Jossey-Bass.

Gilberstadt, H., & Duker, J. (1965), *A Handbook for Clinical and
Actuarial MMPI Interpretation*. Philadelphia, PA: Saunders.

Gilbert, L. A. (1981), Toward mental health: The benefits of psychological androgeny. *Prof. Psychology*, 12:29–38.

Giles, T. R. (1993), *Handbook of Effective Psychotherapy*. New York:
Plenum.

——— Marafiote, R. A. (1994), Managed care and psychotherapy
outcome: Has the pendulum swung too far? *Behav. Therapist*,
17:239–244.

Golden, C. J., Hammeke, T. A., & Purisch, A. D. (1980), *The Luria–
Nebraska Neuropsychological Battery: Manual*. Los Angeles, CA:
Western Psychological Services.

——— Kuperman, S. K. (1980a), Graduate training on clinical
neuropsychology. *Prof. Psychology*, 11:55–63.

——— ——— (1980b), Training opportunities in neuropsychology
at APA-approved internship settings. *Prof. Psychology*, 11:907–918.

Goldenberg, H. (1983), *Contemporary Clinical Psychology*, 2nd ed.
Monterey, CA: Brooks/Cole.

Goldenberg, I., & Goldenberg, H. (1991), *Family Therapy: An Overview*, 3rd ed. Pacific Grove, CA: Brooks/Cole.

Goldfried, M. R. (1980), Toward the delineation of therapeutic change
principles. *Amer. Psycholog.*, 35:991–999.

——— Davison, G. C. (1976), *Clinical Behavior Therapy*. New York:
Holt, Rinehart & Winston.

——— Greenberg, L. S., & Marmar, C. (1990), Individual psychotherapy: Process and outcome. *Ann. Rev. Psychology*, 41:659–688.

Goldstein, A. P., Lopez, M., & Greenleaf, D. O. (1979), Introduction.
In: *Maximizing Treatment Gains: Transfer Enhancement in Psychotherapy*, ed. A. P. Goldstein & F. H. Kanfer. New York: Academic Press, pp. 1–22.

Goldstein, M. J., Baker, B. L., & Jamison, K. R. (1980), *Abnormal
Psychology*. Boston, MA: Little, Brown.

Goodwin, D. W., & Guze, S. B. (1989), *Psychiatric Diagnosis*, 4th ed.
New York: Oxford University Press.

Gould, R. A., & Clum, G. A. (1993), A meta-analysis of self-help treatment approaches. *Clin. Psychol. Rev.*, 13:169–186.

Goulding, R., & Goulding, M. (1979), *Changing Lives through Rede-
cision Therapy*. New York: Brunner/Mazel.

Graham, J. R. (1977), *The MMPI: A Practical Guide*. New York: Oxford University Press.

——— (1993), *MMPI-2: Assessing Personality and Psychopathology*,
2nd ed. New York: Oxford University Press.

References 259

Grebstein, L. D. (1986), Eclectic family therapy. In: *Handbook of Eclectic Psychotherapy*, ed. J. C. Norcross. New York: Brunner/Mazel, pp. 282–319.

Greenberg, L. S. (1983), Psychotherapy process research. In: *The Handbook of Clinical Psychology: Theory, Research, and Practice*, Vol. 1, ed. C. E. Walker. Homewood, IL: Dow Jones-Irwin.

——— (1986), Change process research. *J. Consult. & Clin. Psychol.*, 54:4–9.

Greenburg, S. L., Lewis, G. J., & Johnson, M. (1985), Peer consultation groups for private practitioners. *Prof. Psychology*, 16:437–447.

Greenspoon, J., & Gersten, C. D. (1967), A new look at psychological testing: Psychological testing from the standpoint of a behaviorist. *Amer. Psycholog.*, 22:848–853.

Guest, P. D., & Beutler, L. E. (1988), Impact on psychotherapy supervision on therapist orientation and values. *J. Consult. & Clin. Psychol.*, 56:653–658.

Gurman, A. S., & Kniskern, D. P. (1981), Family therapy outcome research: Knowns and unknowns. In: *Handbook of Family Therapy*, ed. A. S. Gurman & D. P. Kniskern. New York: Brunner/Mazel, pp. 742–776.

——— ——— Pinsof, W. (1986), Research in the process and outcome of marital and family therapy. In: *Handbook of Psychotherapy and Behavior Change*, 3rd ed., ed. S. Garfield & A. Bergin. New York: John Wiley.

Gurucharri, C., Phelps, E., & Selman, R. (1984), Development of interpersonal understanding: A longitudinal and comparative study of normal and disturbed youths. *J. Consult. & Clin. Psychol.*, 52:26–36.

Hall, C. S., & Lindzey, G. (1957), *Theories of Personality*. New York: John Wiley.

——— ——— (1978), *Theories of Personality*, 3rd ed. New York: John Wiley.

Halstead, W. C. (1947), *Brain and Intelligence*. Chicago: University of Chicago Press.

Hamersma, R. J. (1972), *Educational and Psychological Tests and Measures*. Dubuque, IA: Kendall/Hunt.

Hammond, W. R., & Yung, B. (1993), Minority recruitment and retention practices among schools of professional psychology: A national survey and analysis. *Prof. Psychology*, 24:3–12.

Hansen, J. C., & Himes, B. S. (1980), Normality. In: *Encyclopedia of Clinical Assessment*, Vol. 1, ed. R. H. Woody. San Francisco, CA: Jossey-Bass.

——— Warner, R. W., & Smith, E. J. (1980), *Group Counseling: Theory and Process*, 2nd ed. Chicago, IL: Rand McNally.

Hanson, F. A. (1993), *Testing Testing: Social Consequences of the Examined Life*. Berkeley, CA: University of California Press.

Harrison, R. (1965), Thematic apperceptive methods. In: *Handbook of Clinical Psychology*, ed. B. B. Wolman. New York: McGraw-Hill, pp. 562–620.

Hartup, W. W. (1989), Social relationships and their developmental significance. *Amer. Psycholog.*, 44:120–126.

Hathaway, S. R., & McKinley, J. C. (1967), *The Minnesota Multiphasic Personality Inventory Manual.* New York: Psychological Corporation.

―――― ―――― (1989), *Manual for Administration and Scoring: MMPI-2.* Minneapolis: University of Minnesota Press.

Havighurst, R. J. (1972), *Developmental Tasks and Education*, 3rd ed. New York: Mckay.

Haynes, S. N. (1993), Treatment implications of psychological assessment. *Psycholog. Assess.*, 5:251–253.

Hazelrigg, M. D., Cooper, H. M., & Borduin, C. M. (1987), Evaluating the effectiveness of family therapies: An integrative review and analysis. *Psycholog. Bull.*, 101:428–442.

Helmes, E., & McLaughlin, J. D. (1983), A comparison of three MMPI short forms: Limited clinical utility in classification. *J. Consult. & Clin. Psychol.*, 52:786–787.

Henderson, N. B., Butler, B. V., & Goffeney, B. (1969), Effectiveness of the WISC and Bender-Gestalt Test in predicting arithmetic and reading achievement for white and nonwhite children. *J. Clin. Psychol.*, 25:268–271.

Henry, W. E. (1956), *The Analysis of Fantasy: The Thematic Apperception Technique in the Study of Personality.* New York: Robert E. Krieger, 1973.

Herman, K. C. (1993), Reassessing prediction of therapist competence. *J. Counsel. & Devel.*, 72:24–32.

Herron, W. G., Eisenstadt, E. N., Javier, R. A., Primavera, L. H., & Schultz, C. L. (1994), Session effects, comparability, and managed care in psychotherapies. *Psychotherapy*, 31:279–285.

Highlen, P. S. (1994), Racial/ethnic diversity in doctoral programs of psychology: Challenges for the twenty-first century. *Appl. & Prevent. Psychol.*, 3:91–108.

Horvath, A. O., & Luborsky, L. (1993), The role of the therapeutic alliance in psychotherapy. *J. Consult. & Clin. Psychol.*, 61:561–573.

―――― Symonds, B. D. (1991), Relation between working alliance and outcome in psychotherapy: A meta-analysis. *J. Consult. & Clin. Psychol.*, 38:139–149.

Houck, J. E., & Hansen, J. C. (1972), Diagnostic interviewing. In: *Clinical Assessment in Counseling and Psychotherapy*, ed. R. H. Woody & J. D. Woody. New York: Appleton-Century-Crofts, pp. 119–186.

Howard, K. I., Kopta, S. M., Krause, M. S., & Orlinsky, D. E. (1986), The dose-effect relationship in psychotherapy. *Amer. Psycholog.*, 41:159–164.

Hoy, C., & Gregg, N. (1994), *Assessment: The Special Educator's Role.* Pacific Grove, CA: Brooks/Cole.

Hutt, M. L. (1980), Adience–abience. In: *The Encyclopedia of Clinical Assessment*, Vol. 2, ed. R. H. Woody. San Francisco: Jossey-Bass, pp. 902–910.

—— Briskin, G. J. (1960), *The Clinical Use of the Revised Bender-Gestalt Test*. New York: Grune & Stratton.

Hutton, J. B., Dubes, R., & Muir, S. (1992), Assessment practices of school psychologists: Ten years later. *School Psychol. Rev.*, 21:271–284.

Imber, S. D., Pilkonis, P. A., & Glanz, L. (1983), Outcome studies in psychotherapy. In: *The Handbook of Clinical Psychology: Theory, Research, and Practice*, Vol. 1, ed. C. E. Walker. Homewood, IL: Dow Jones-Irwin.

Jacobson, N. S., & Addis, M. E. (1993), Research on couples and couple therapy: What do we know? Where are we going? *J. Consult. & Clin. Psychol.*, 61:85–93.

—— Truax, P. (1991), Clinical significance: A statistical approach to defining meaningful change in psychotherapy research. *J. Consult. & Clin. Psychol.*, 59:12–19.

Jahoda, M. (1958), *Current Concepts of Positive Mental Health*. New York: Basic Books.

Johnson, D. L. (1989), Schizophrenia as a brain disease. *Amer. Psycholog.*, 44:553–555.

Jung, C. G. (1956), *Two Essays on Analytical Psychology*. New York: Meridian Books.

Kalish, R. A., & Knudtson, F. W. (1976), Attachment versus disengagement: A life-span conceptualization. *Hum. Develop.*, 19:171–181.

Kamphaus, R. W. (1993), *Clinical Assessment of Children's Intelligence*. Boston: Allyn & Bacon.

Kaplan, M. S. (1980), Parenting assessment. In: *Encyclopedia of Clinical Assessment*, Vol. 1, ed. R. H. Woody. San Francisco, CA: Jossey-Bass.

Karenken, D. A., & Williams, J. M. (1994), Human judgment and estimation of premorbid intellectual function. *Psycholog. Assess.*, 6:83–91.

Karon, B. P. (1981), The Thematic Apperception Test (TAT). In: *Assessment With Projective Techniques*, ed. A. I. Rabin. New York: Springer, pp. 85–120.

Kaufman, A. S., & Kaufman, N. L. (1993), *Manual: Kaufman Assessment Battery for Children (K-ABC)*. Circle Pines, MN: American Guidance Service.

Kaufmann, Y. (1989), Analytical psychotherapy. In: *Current Psychotherapies*, 4th ed., ed. R. J. Corsini & D. Wedding. Itasca, IL: F. E. Peacock, pp. 119–152.

Kaul, T. J., & Bednar, R. L. (1986), Experiential group research: Results, questions, and suggestions. In: *Handbook of Psychotherapy and Behavior Change*, 3rd ed., ed. S. L. Garfield & A. E. Bergin. New York: John Wiley.

Kazdin, A. E. (1980), *Behavior Modification in Applied Settings*, rev. ed. Homewood, IL: Dorsey Press.

—— (1986), Comparative outcome studies of psychotherapy: Methodological issues and strategies. *J. Consult. & Clin. Psychol.*, 54:95–105.

—— (1989), Developmental psychopathology. *Amer. Psycholog.*, 44:180–187.

—— (1993a), Adolescent mental health: Prevention and treatment programs. *Amer. Psycholog.*, 48:127–141.

—— (1993b), Psychotherapy for children and adolescents. *Amer. Psycholog.*, 48:644–657.

Kiesler, C. A. (1993), Mental health policy and the psychiatric inpatient care of children. *Appl. & Prevent. Psychol.*, 2:91–100.

Kleinmuntz, B. (1982), *Personality and Psychological Assessment.* New York: St. Martin's Press.

Klerman, G. L., & Weissman, M. M., Eds. (1993), *New Applications of Interpersonal Psychotherapy.* Washington, DC: American Psychiatric Press.

—— —— Rounsville, B. J., & Chevron, E. S. (1984), *Interpersonal Psychotherapy of Depression.* New York: Basic Books.

Klopfer, B., & Davidson, H. H. (1962), *The Rorschach Technique: An Introductory Manual.* New York: Harcourt Brace Jovanovich.

Knapp, S., & VandeCreek, L. (1994), Unavoidable multiple relationships. *Psychother. Bull.*, 29:53–55.

Kohlenberg, R. J., & Tsai, M. (1991), *Functional Analytic Psychotherapy: Creating Intense and Curative Therapeutic Relationships.* New York: Plenum.

Koppitz, E. M. (1963), *The Bender Gestalt Test for Young Children.* New York: Grune & Stratton.

Korchin, S. (1976), *Modern Clinical Psychology.* New York: Basic Books.

Koss, M. P., & Butcher, J. N. (1986), Research on brief psychotherapy. In: *Handbook of Psychotherapy and Behavior Change: An Empirical Analysis*, 3rd ed., ed. S. L. Garfield & A. E. Bergin. New York: John Wiley.

Kovacs, M. (1989), Affective disorders in children and adults. *Amer. Psycholog.*, 44:209–215.

Kraepelin, E. (1907), *Clinical Psychiatry*, tr. A. R. Diefendorf. New York: Macmillan.

Kramer, J. H. (1993), Interpretation of individual subtest scores on the WISC-III. *Psycholog. Assess.*, 5:193–196.

L'Abate, L., & Goodrich, M. E. (1980), Marital adjustment. In: *Encyclopedia of Clinical Assessment*, Vol. 1, ed. R. H. Woody. San Francisco, CA: Jossey-Bass.

Lachar, D. (1974), *The MMPI: Clinical Assessment and Automated Interpretation.* Los Angeles, CA: Western Psychological Services.

Lambert, M. J. (1989), The individual therapist's contribution to psychotherapy process and outcome. *Clin. Psychol. Rev.*, 9:469–486.

—— Bergin, A. E. (1983), Therapist characteristics and their contribution to psychotherapy outcome. In: *The Handbook of Clinical Psychology: Theory, Research, and Practice*, Vol. 1, ed. C. E. Walker. Homewood, IL: Dow Jones-Irwin.

—— —— (1992), Achievements and limitations of psychotherapy research. In: *History of Psychotherapy: A Century of Change*, ed.

D. K. Freedheim. Washington, DC: American Psychological Association.

—— Ogles, B. M. (1988), Treatment manuals: Problems and promise. *J. Integr. & Eclect. Psychother.*, 7:187–204.

—— Shapiro, D. A., & Bergin, A. E. (1986), The effectiveness of psychotherapy. In: *Handbook of Psychotherapy and Behavior Change*, 3rd. ed., ed. S. L. Garfield & A. E. Bergin. New York: John Wiley.

Landman, J. T., & Dawes, R. M. (1982), Smith and Glass' conclusions stand up under scrutiny. *Amer. Psychology*, 37:504–516.

Lanyon, R. I. (1984), Personality assessment. *Ann. Rev. Psychol.*, 35:667–701.

LaPerriere, K. (1979), Toward the training of broad-range family therapy. *Prof. Psychology*, 10:880–883.

Larry v. Riles (1972), 343 F. Supp. 1306, N. D. Cal.

LaVoie, J. C. (1980), Adult development. In: *Encyclopedia of Clinical Assessment*, Vol. 1, ed. R. H. Woody. San Francisco, CA: Jossey-Bass, pp. 17–45.

Lazarus, A. A. (1981), *The Practice of Multimodal Therapy*. New York: McGraw-Hill.

—— (1989), *The Practice of Multimodal Therapy*, rev. ed. Baltimore: John Hopkins University Press.

Lebow, J. L. (1987), Family therapy: An overview of major issues. *Psychotherapy*, 24:584–594.

Levine, B. (1979), *Group Psychotherapy: Practice and Development*. Englewood Cliffs, NJ: Prentice-Hall.

Levinson, D. J. (1977), The mid-life transition: A period in adult psychosocial development. *Psychiatry*, 40:99–112.

Lezak, M. D. (1983), *Neuropsychological Assessment*, 2nd ed. New York: Oxford University Press.

Liberman, R. P., Kopelowicz, A., & Young, A. S. (1994), Biobehavioral treatment and rehabilitation of schizophrenia. *Behav. Ther.*, 25:89–107.

Lindzey, G. (1961), *Projective Techniques and Cross-Cultural Research*. New York: Appleton-Century-Crofts.

Lipsey, M. W., & Wilson, D. B. (1993), The efficacy of psychological, educational, and behavioral treatment. *Amer. Psycholog.*, 48:1181–1209.

Lipsitz, J. D., Dworkin, R. H., & Erlenmeyer-Kimling, L. (1993), Wechsler comprehension and picture arrangement subtests and social adjustment. *Psycholog. Assess.*, 5:430–437.

Lubin, B., Larsen, R. M., & Matarazzo, J. D. (1984), Patterns of psychological test usage in the United States: 1935–1982. *Amer. Psycholog.*, 39:451–454.

Luria, A. R. (1970), The functional organization of the brain. *Sci. Amer.*, 222:66–78.

Lykken, D. T. (1993), Predicting violence in the violent society. *Appl. & Prevent. Psychol.*, 2:13–20.

Lyman, H. B. (1963), *Test Scores and What They Mean*. Englewood Cliffs, NJ: Prentice-Hall.

―――― (1991), *Test Scores and What They Mean*, 5th ed. Boston: Allyn & Bacon.

Maddi, S. R. (1980), *Personality Theories: A Comparative Analysis*, 4th ed. Homewood, IL: Dorsey Press.

Magnussen, M. G. (1980), Child and adolescent development. In: *Encyclopedia of Clinical Assessment*, Vol. 1, ed. R. H. Woody. San Francisco, CA: Jossey-Bass.

Maloney, M. P., & Ward, M. P. (1976), *Psychological Assessment: A Conceptual Approach*. New York: Oxford University Press.

Matarazzo, J. D. (1990), Psychological assessment versus psychological testing: Validation from Binet to school, clinic, and courtroom. *Amer. Psycholog.*, 5:999–1017.

―――― (1992), Psychological testing and assessment in the 21st century. *Amer. Psycholog.*, 47:1007–1018.

May, R., & Yalom, I. (1989), Existential psychotherapy. In: *Current Psychotherapies*, 4th ed., ed. R. J. Corsini & D. Wedding. Itasca, IL: F. E. Peacock, pp. 363–402.

McConnaughy, E. A. (1987), The person of the therapist in psychotherapeutic practice. *Psychotherapy*, 24:303–314.

Meehl, P. E. (1954), *Clinical Versus Statistical Prediction: A Theoretical Analysis and a Review of the Evidence*. Minneapolis, MN: University of Minneapolis Press.

―――― (1956), Wanted—A good cookbook. *Amer. Psycholog.*, 11:263–272.

Mehrens, W. A., & Lehmann, I. J. (1991), *Measurement and Evaluation in Education and Psychology*, 4th ed. Orlando, FL: Harcourt Brace Jovanovich.

Meichenbaum, D. (1977), *Cognitive Behavior Modification: An Integrative Approach*. New York: Plenum.

―――― (1986), Cognitive-behavior modification. In: *Helping People Change*, 3rd ed., ed. F. H. Kanfer & A. P. Goldstein. New York: Pergamon, pp. 346–380.

Menninger, R. W. (1944), The history of psychiatry. *Dis. Nerv. System*, 5:52–55.

Menninger, W. C. (1948), Psychiatry and psychology. *Amer. J. Psychiatry*, 105:389–390.

Miale, F. R. (1977), Symbolic imagery in Rorschach material. In: *Rorschach Psychology*, ed. M. A. Rickers-Ovsiankina. Huntington, NY: Robert E. Krieger, pp. 421–454.

Miller, L. S., Bergstrom, D. A., Cross, H. J., & Grube, J. W. (1981), Opinions and use of the DSM system by practicing psychologists. *Prof. Psychology*, 12:385–390.

Millon, T. (1981), *Disorders of Personality DSM: Axis II*. New York: John Wiley.

Mindess, H. (1955), Analytical psychology and the Rorschach Test. *J. Project. Technique*, 19:243–252.

Monahan, J. (1992), Mental disorder and violent behavior: Perceptions and evidence. *Amer. Psycholog.*, 47:511–521.

Moreland, K. L., & Dahlstrom, W. G. (1983), Professional training with and use of the MMPI. *Prof. Psychology*, 14:218–223.

Morgan, C. D., & Murray, H. A. (1935), A method for investigating fantasies. *Arch. Neurol. Psychiat.*, 34:289–306.

Morgan, D. G. (1992), *Aging and Longevity: A Seminar for Health Professionals*. Chicago: Author, University of Southern California, pp. 1–18.

Morgan, K. S., & Nerison, R. M. (1993), Homosexuality and psychopolitics: An historical overview. *Psychotherapy*, 30:133–140.

Mosak, H. H. (1989), Adlerian psychotherapy. In: *Current Psychotherapies*, 4th ed., ed. R. J. Corsini & D. Wedding. Itasca, IL: F. E. Peacock, pp. 65–116.

Murray, H. A. (1938), *Explorations in Personality*. New York: Oxford University Press.

——— (1943), *Manual: Thematic Apperception Test*. Cambridge, MA: Harvard University Press.

Nash, M. R., Hulsey, T. L., Sexton, M. C., Harralson, T. L., & Lambert, W. (1993), Long-term sequelae of childhood sexual abuse: Perceived family environment, psychopathology, and dissociation. *J. Consult. & Clin. Psychol.*, 61:276–283.

Nathan, P. E., & Harris, S. L. (1983), The diagnostic and statistical manual of mental disorders: History, comparative analysis, current status, and appraisal. In: *The Handbook of Clinical Psychology: Theory, Research, and Practice*, Vol. 1, ed. C. E. Walker. Homewood, IL: Dow Jones-Irwin, pp. 303–343.

Nichols, M. P., & Schwartz, R. C. (1991), *Family Therapy: Concepts and Methods*, 2nd ed. Boston: Allyn & Bacon.

Nietzel, M. T., Bernstein, D. A., & Milich, R. (1994), *Introduction to Clinical Psychology*, 4th ed. Englewood Cliffs, NJ: Prentice-Hall.

Norcross, J. C., Ed. (1987), *Casebook of Eclectic Psychotherapy*. New York: Brunner/Mazel.

——— Goldfried, M. R., Eds. (1992), *Handbook of Psychotherapy Integration*. New York: Basic Books.

——— Newman, C. F. (1992), Psychotherapy integration: Setting the context. In: *Handbook of Psychotherapy Integration*, ed. J. C. Norcross & M. R. Goldfried. New York: Basic Books.

——— Prochaska, J. O. (1982), A national survey of clinical psychologists: Views on training, career choice, and APA. *Clin. Psycholog.*, 35(4):1, 3–6.

——— ——— Gallagher, K. M. (1989), Clinical psychologists in the 1980s: II. Theory, research, and practice. *Clin. Psycholog.*, 42:45–53.

Offer, D., & Sabskin, M. (1974), *Normality: Theoretical and Clinical Concepts of Mental Health*. New York: Basic Books.

Ogdon, D. P. (1982), *Psychodiagnostics and Personality Assessment: A Handbook*, 2nd ed. Los Angeles: Western Psychological Services.

O'Leary, K. D., & Wilson, G. T. (1987), *Behavior Therapy: Application and Outcome*, 2nd ed. Englewood Cliffs, NJ: Prentice-Hall.

Ollendick, T. H., Weist, M. D., Borden, M. C., & Greene, R. W. (1992), Sociometric status and academic, behavioral, and psychological adjustment: A five-year longitudinal study. *J. Consult. & Clin. Psychol.*, 60:80–87.

Olmedo, E. L., & Barron, D. L. (1981), Mental health of minority women: Some special issues. *Prof. Psychology*, 12:103–111.

Olmsted, M. S. (1959), *The Small Group*. New York: Random House.

Orlinsky, D. E., & Howard, K. L. (1986), Process and outcome in psychotherapy. In: *Handbook of Psychotherapy and Behavior Change*, 3rd. ed., ed. S. L. Garfield & A. E. Bergin. New York: John Wiley.

Osipow, S. H., & Fitzgerald, L. E. (1993), Unemployment and mental health: A neglected relationship. *Appl. & Prevent. Psychol.*, 2:59–63.

Ownby, R. L. (1987), *Psychological Reports: A Guide to Report Writing in Professional Psychology*. Brandon, VT: Clinical Psychology Publishing.

Palmer, J. O. (1983), *The Psychological Assessment of Children*, 2nd ed. New York: John Wiley.

Paolo, A. M., & Ryan, J. J. (1993), WAIS-R abbreviated forms in the elderly: A comparison of the Satz-Mogel with a seven-subtest short form. *Psycholog. Assess.*, 5:425–429.

Parkinson, S. C. (1983), Family therapy. In: *The Handbook of Clinical Psychology: Theory, Research, and Practice*, Vol. 2, ed. C. E. Walker. Homewood, IL: Dow Jones-Irwin.

Paul, G. L. (1967), Outcome research in psychotherapy. *J. Consult. Psychol.*, 31:109–188.

——— Menditto, A. A. (1992), Effectiveness of inpatient treatment programs for mentally ill adults in public psychiatric facilities. *Appl. & Prevent. Psychol.*, 1:41–63.

Persons, J. B. (1991), Psychotherapy outcome studies do not accurately represent current models of psychotherapy: A proposed remedy. *Amer. Psycholog.*, 43:669–670.

Peterson, A. C., & Hamburg, B. A. (1986), Adolescence: A developmental approach to problems and psychopathology. *Behav. Ther.*, 17:480–499.

Phares, E. J. (1992), *Clinical Psychology: Concepts, Methods, and Profession*, 4th ed. Pacific Grove, CA: Brooks/Cole.

Phillips, E. L. (1988), Length of psychotherapy and outcome: Observations stimulated by Howard, Kopta, Krause, and Orlinsky. *Amer. Psycholog.*, 43:669–670.

Phillips, L., & Smith, J. G. (1953), *Rorschach Interpretation: Advanced Technique*. New York: Grune & Stratton.

Pichot, P. (1984), Centenary of the birth of Hermann Rorschach, tr. from the French by S. Rosenzweig & E. Schreiber. *J. Personal. Assess.*, 48:591–596.

Pinter, R. (1931), *Intelligence Testing.* New York: Holt.

Piotrowski, C., & Keller, J. W. (1984), Psychodiagnostic testing in APA-approved clinical psychology programs. *Prof. Psychology,* 15:450–456.

Plomin, R. (1989), Environment and genes: Determinants of behavior. *Amer. Psycholog.,* 44:105–111.

Polster, E., & Polster, M. (1973), *Gestalt Therapy Integrated: Contours of Theory and Practice.* New York: Brunner/Mazel.

Poppen, P. J., & Reisen, C. A. (1994), Heterosexual behaviors and risk of exposure to HIV: Current status and prospects for change. *Appl. & Prevent. Psychology,* 3:75–90.

Pritchard, D., & Rosenblatt, A. (1980), Racial bias in the MMPI: A methodological review. *J. Consult. & Clin. Psychol.,* 48:263–267.

Prochaska, J. O., & DiClemente, C. C. (1984), *The Transtheoretical Approach: Crossing the Traditional Boundaries of Therapy.* Homewood, IL: Dow Jones-Irvin.

——— Norcross, J. C. (1994), *Systems of Psychotherapy,* 3rd ed. Pacific Grove, CA: Brooks/Cole.

Prout, H. T. (1983), School psychologists and social-emotional assessment techniques: Patterns in training and use. *School Psychol. Rev.,* 12:377–383.

Putnam, S. H., Adams, K. M., & Schneider, A. M. (1992), One-day test-retest reliability of neuropsychological tests in a personal injury case. *Psycholog. Assess.,* 4:312–316.

Rabin, A. L. (1968), Projective methods: An historical introduction. In: *Projective Techniques in Personality Assessment,* ed. A. I. Rabin. New York: Springer, pp. 3–17.

Rapaport, D., Gill, M. M., & Schafer, R. (1968), *Diagnostic Psychological Testing.* New York: International Universities Press.

Raquepaw, J. M., & Miller, R. S. (1989), Psychotherapist burnout: A componential analysis. *Prof. Psychology,* 20:32–36.

Raskin, N. J., & Rogers, C. R. (1989), Person-centered therapy. In: *Current Psychotherapies,* 4th ed., ed. R. J. Corsini & D. Wedding. Itasca, IL: F. E. Peacock.

Reichalt, P. A. (1983), Location and utilization of available behavioral measurement instruments. *Prof. Psychology,* 14:341–356.

Reitan, R. M., & Davison, L. A. (1974), *Clinical Neuropsychology: Current Status and Applications.* New York: Hemisphere.

Reschly, D. J., Genshaft, J., & Binder, M. A. (1987), *The 1986 NASP survey: Comparison of practitioners, NASP leadership, and university faculty on key issues.* Washington, DC: National Association of School Psychologists.

Research Institute of America (1991), *Analysis of the Americans with Disabilities Act and Implementing EEOC Regulations.* New York: Research Institute of America.

Rickers-Ovsiankina, M. A. (1977), Synopsis of psychological premises underlying the Rorschach. In: *Rorschach Psychology,* ed. M. A. Rickers-Ovsiankina. Huntington, NY: Robert E. Kreiger, pp. 3–25.

Robertson, M. (1980), Neurotic cues. In: *Encyclopedia of Clinical Assessment*, Vol. 1, ed. R. H. Woody. San Francisco, CA: Jossey-Bass, pp. 128–147.

—————— (1995), *Psychotherapy Education and Training: An Integrative Perspective*. Madison, CT: International Universities Press.

Rogers, C. R. (1942), *Counseling and Psychotherapy*. Boston: Houghton Mifflin.

—————— (1961), *On Becoming a Person*. Boston: Houghton Mifflin.

Rose, S. D., Tolman, R., & Tallent, S. (1985), Group process in cognitive–behavioral therapy. *Behav. Therapist*, 8(4):71–75.

Rosenberg, R. P., & Beck, S. (1986), Preferred assessment methods and treatment modalities for hyperactive children among clinical child and school psychologists. *J. Clin. Child Psychol.*, 15:142–157.

Rosenhan, D. L. (1975), The contextual nature of psychiatric diagnosis. *J. Abnorm. Psychol.*, 84:462–474.

—————— Seligman, M. E. P. (1984), *Abnormal Psychology*. New York: W. W. Norton.

—————— —————— (1995), *Abnormal Psychology*, 3rd ed. New York: W. W. Norton, pp. 686–688.

Rosenzweig, S. (1954), A transvaluation of psychotherapy—A reply to Hans Eysenck. *J. Abnorm. Soc. Psychol.*, 49:298–304.

Roth, D. L., Hughes, C. W., Monkowski, P. G., & Crosson, B. (1984), Investigation of validity of the WAIS-R short forms of patients suspected to have brain impairment. *J. Consult. & Clin. Psychol.*, 52:722–723.

Rowe, D. C. (1980), Temperament. In: *Encyclopedia of Clinical Assessment*, Vol. 1, ed. R. H. Woody. San Francisco, CA: Jossey-Bass, pp. 400–409.

Rubenstein, A. (1985), Future projections of the psychotherapy marketplace. *Psychother. Bull.* 19(4):9.

Ryan, J. J., Larsen, J., & Prifitera, A. (1983), Validity of two- and four-subtest short forms of the WAIS-R in a psychiatric sample. *J. Consult. & Clin. Psychol.*, 51:460.

Salvia, J., & Ysseldyke, J. E. (1988), *Assessment in Special and Remedial Education*, 4th ed. Boston: Houghton Mifflin.

Sanderson, W. C. (1994), Introduction to series on empirically validated psychological treatments. *Clin. Psychologist*, 47:9.

Sattler, J. M. (1974), *Assessment of Children's Intelligence*, rev. ed. Philadelphia: W. B. Saunders.

Schacht, T. E., & Nathan, P. E. (1977), But is it good for psychologists? Appraisal and status of DSM-III. *Amer. Psycholog.*, 32:1017–1025.

Schafer, R. (1950), *The Clinical Application of Psychological Tests*. New York: International Universities Press.

Schauble, P. C. (1980), Facilitative conditions in communication. In: *The Encyclopedia of Clinical Assessment*, Vol., 2, ed. R. H. Woody. San Francisco, CA: Jossey-Bass, pp. 1035–1041.

Schwartz, F., & Lazar, Z. (1979), The scientific status of the Rorschach. *J. Personal. Assess.*, 43:3–11.

Schwarz, J. C. (1979), Childhood origins of psychopathology. *Amer. Psycholog.*, 34:879–885.

Seeman, J. (1989), Toward a model of positive health. *Amer. Psycholog.*, 44:1099–1109.

Shadish, W. R. (1989), Private-sector care for chronically mentally ill individuals. *Amer. Psycholog.*, 44:1142–1147.

———— Montgomery, L. M., Wilson, P., Wilson, M. R., Bright, I., & Okwumabua, T. (1993), Effects of family and marital psychotherapies: A meta-analysis. *J. Consult. & Clin. Psychol.*, 6:992–1002.

Shectman, F. (1973), On being misinformed by misleading arguments. *Bull. Menn. Clinic*, 37:523–525.

Shedler, J., & Block, J. (1990), Adolescent drug use and psychological health: A longitudinal inquiry. *Amer. Psycholog.*, 45:612 630.

Shevrin, H., & Shectman, F. (1973), The diagnostic process in psychiatric evaluations. *Bull. Menn. Clinic*, 37:451–494.

Silver, L. B., & Segal, J. (1984), Psychology and mental health. *Amer. Psycholog.*, 39:804–809.

Silverstein, A. B. (1982), Two- and four-subtest short forms of the Wechsler Adult Intelligence Scale—Revised. *J. Consult. & Clin. Psychol.*, 50:415–418.

Simons, L. S. (1989), Privatization and the mental health system. *Amer. Psycholog.*, 44:1138–1141.

Smith, D., & Dumont, F. (1995), A cautionary study: Unwarranted interpretations of the draw-a-person test. *Prof. Psychology*, 26:298–303.

Smith, G. B., Schwebel, A. I., Dunn, R. L., & McIver, S. D. (1993), The role of psychologists in the treatment, management, and prevention of chronic mental illness. *Amer. Psycholog.*, 48:966–971.

Smith, M. L., Glass, G. V., & Miller, T. J. (1980), *The Benefits of Psychotherapy*. Baltimore, MD: Johns Hopkins University Press.

Smyer, M. A., Balster, R. L., Egli, D., Johnson, D. L., Kilbey, M. M., Leith, N. J., & Puente, A. E. (1993), Summary of the report of the ad hoc task force on psychopharmacology of the American Psychological Association. *Prof. Psychology*, 24:394–403.

Sobel, S. B., & Russo, N. P. (1981), Sex roles, equality and mental health: An introduction. *Prof. Psychology*, 12:1–5.

Spearman, C. (1904), The proof and measurement of association between two things. *Amer. J. Psychol.*, 15:72–101.

Stagner, R. (1948), *Psychology of Personality*. New York: McGraw-Hill.

St. Clair, M. (1986), *Object Relations and Self Psychology: An Introduction*. Pacific Grove, CA: Brooks/Cole.

Steenbarger, B. N. (1994), Duration and outcome in psychotherapy: An integrative review. *Prof. Psychology*, 25:111–119.

Stern, S. (1993), Managed care, brief therapy, and therapeutic integrity. *Psychotherapy*, 30:162–175.

Stern, W. (1914), *The Psychological Methods of Testing Intelligence.* Baltimore, MD: Warwick & York.

Stiles, W. B., Shapiro, D. A., & Elliott, R. (1986), Are all psychotherapies equivalent? *Amer. Psycholog.*, 41:165–180.

Stoddard, G. D. (1943), *The Meaning of Intelligence.* New York: Macmillan.

Strider, F. D. (1980), Psychosis/schizophrenia: Cues. In: *The Encyclopedia of Clinical Assessment*, Vol. 1, ed. R. H. Woody. San Francisco, CA: Jossey-Bass.

Strole, L. (1972), Urbanization and mental health: Some reformulations. *Amer. Sci.*, 60:576–583.

Strupp, H. H. (1978), The therapist's theoretical orientation: An overrated variable. *Psychotherapy*, 15:314–317.

—— (1989), Psychotherapy: Can the practitioner learn from the researcher? *Amer. Psycholog.*, 44:717–724.

—— Binder, J. L. (1984), *Psychotherapy in a New Key: A Guide to Time-Limited Dynamic Psychotherapy.* New York: Basic Books.

Sue, D. W., & Sue, D. (1990), *Counseling the Culturally Different: Theory and Practice.* New York: John Wiley.

Sue, D., Sue, D., & Sue, S. (1994), *Understanding Abnormal Behavior*, 4th ed. Boston: Houghton Mifflin.

Sullivan, H. S. (1954), *The Psychiatric Interview.* New York: W. W. Norton.

Sullivan, M. J. (1995), Medicaid's quiet revolution: Merging the public and private sectors of care. *Prof. Psychology*, 26:229–234.

Sundberg, N. D. (1977), *Assessment of Persons.* Englewood Cliffs, NJ: Prentice-Hall.

Super, D. E. (1957), *The Psychology of Careers.* New York: Harper & Row.

Swenson, C. H., & Hartsough, D. M. (1983), Crisis intervention and brief psychotherapy. In: *Handbook of Clinical Psychology*, Vol. 2, ed. C. E. Walker. Homewood, IL: Dow Jones-Irwin.

Swenson, L. C. (1993), *Psychology and Law for the Helping Professions.* Pacific Grove, CA: Brooks/Cole.

Symonds, P. M. (1946), *The Dynamics of Human Adjustment.* New York: Appleton-Century-Crofts.

Takanishi, R. (1993), The opportunities of adolescence-research, intervention, and policy: Introduction to the special issue. *Amer. Psycholog.*, 48:85–88.

Tallent, N. (1993), *Psychological Report Writing*, 3rd ed. Englewood Cliffs, NJ: Prentice-Hall.

Teplin, L. A. (1984), Criminalizing mental disorder. *Amer. Psycholog.*, 39:794–803.

Terman, L. M., & Merrill, M. A. (1960), *Stanford-Binet Intelligence Scale: Manual for the Third Revision*, Form L-M. Boston: Houghton Mifflin.

Thomas, A., & Chess, S. (1977), *Temperament and Development.* New York: Brunner/Mazel.

Thoreson, R. W., Nathan, P. E., Skorina, J. K., & Kilburg, R. R. (1983), The alcoholic psychologist: Issues, problems, and implications for the profession. *Prof. Psychology*, 14:670–684.

Thorndike, R. L., Hagen, E. P., & Sattler, J. M. (1986), *The Stanford-Binet Intelligence Scale, Guide for Administering and Scoring*, 4th ed. Chicago, IL: Riverside Publishing.

Thorne, F. C. (1961), *Clinical Judgement: A Study of Clinical Error*. Brandon, VT: Journal of Clinical Psychology.

Tillitski, C. J. (1990), A meta-analysis of estimated effect sizes for group versus individual versus control treatments. *Internat. J. Group Psychother.*, 40:218–224.

Townes, B. D., Trupin, E. W., Martin, D. C., & Goldstein, D. (1980), Neuropsychological correlates of academic success among elementary school children. *J. Consult. & Clin. Psychol.*, 48:675–684.

Tremblay, R. E., Masse, B., Perron, D., Leblanc, M., Schwartzman, A. E., & Ledingham, J. E. (1992), Early disruptive behavior, poor school achievement, delinquent behavior, and delinquent personality: Longitudinal analysis. *J. Consult. & Clin. Psychol.*, 60:64–72.

Tuma, J. (1989), Mental health services for children. *Amer. Psycholog.*, 44:188–192.

VandenBos, G. R. (1986), Psychotherapy research: A special issue. *Amer. Psycholog.*, 41:111–112.

———— Deleon, P. H. (1988), The use of psychotherapy to improve physical health. *Psychotherapy*, 25:335–343.

Wachtel, P. L. (1977), *Psychoanalysis and Behavior Therapy: Toward an Integration*. New York: Basic Books.

Walsh, K. W. (1978), *Neuropsychology: A Clinical Approach*. New York: Churchill Livingstone.

Watkins, C. E., Campbell, V. L., Nieberding, R., & Hallmark, R. (1995), Contemporary practice of psychological assessment by clinical psychologists. *Prof. Psychology*, 26:54–60.

Wechsler, D. (1981), *Manual: Wechsler Adult Intelligence Scale-Revised*. New York: Psychological Corporation.

———— (1989), *Manual: Wechsler Preschool and Primary Scale of Intelligence-Revised*. San Antonio: The Psychological Corporation.

———— (1991), *Manual: Wechsler Intelligence Scale for Children*, 3rd ed. San Antonio: The Psychological Corporation. Harcourt Brace Jovanovich.

Welch, B. L. (1994), National grassroots call to action. *Practice Directorate Action Alert*. Washington, DC: American Psychological Association.

Wenar, C. (1994), *Developmental Psychopathology*, 3rd. ed. New York: McGraw-Hill.

Whiston, S. C., & Sexton, T. L. (1993), An overview of psychotherapy outcome research: Implications for practice. *Prof. Psychology*, 24:43–51.

272   References

White, R. W. (1969), Adult growth and emotional maturity. In: *The Healthy Personality*, ed. H. M. Chiang & A. H. Maslow. New York: Van Nostrand Reinhold.

Wierzbicki, M. (1993), *Issues in Clinical Psychology: Subjective Versus Objective Approaches*. Boston: Allyn & Bacon.

Wiggins, J. G., & Welch, B. L. (Guest Editors) (1988), Special issue: Psychotherapy and the new health care system. *Psychotherapy*, 25.

Wilson, G. I. (1989), Behavior therapy. In: *Current Psychotherapies*, 4th ed., ed. R. J. Corsini & D. Wedding. Itasca, IL: F. E. Peacock.

Wolber, G. J., & Carne, W. G. (1993), *Writing Psychological Reports: A Guide for Clinicians*. Sarasota, FL: Professional Resource Press.

Wolpe, J. (1990), *The Practice of Behavior Therapy*, 4th ed. Elmsford, NY: Pergamon.

Woody, R. H. (1966), Intra-judge reliability in clinical electroencephalography. *J. Clin. Psychol.*, 22:150–154.

––––––– (1968), Inter-judge reliability in clinical electroencephalography. *J. Clin. Psychol.*, 24:251–256.

––––––– (1969), *Behavioral Problem Children in the Schools: Recognition, Diagnosis, and Behavioral Modification*. New York: Appleton-Century-Crofts.

––––––– (1980a), Introduction: A conceptual framework for clinical assessment. In: *The Encyclopedia of Clinical Assessment*, Vol. 1., ed. R. H. Woody. San Francisco, CA: Jossey-Bass, pp. xxx–xli.

––––––– (1980b), *The Encyclopedia of Clinical Assessment*, Vol. 1. San Francisco, CA: Jossey-Bass.

––––––– (1980c), *The Encyclopedia of Clinical Assessment*, Vol. 2. San Francisco, CA: Jossey-Bass.

––––––– (1991), *Quality Care in Mental Health: Assuring the Best Clinical Services*. San Francisco: Jossey-Bass.

––––––– LaVoie, J. C., & Epps, S. (1992), *School Psychology: A Developmental and Social Systems Approach*. Boston: Allyn & Bacon.

––––––– Robertson, M. H. (1988), *Becoming a Clinical Psychologist*. Madison, CT: International Universities Press.

––––––– ––––––– (1996), *A Career in Clinical Psychology: From Training to Employment*. Madison, CT: International Universities Press.

World Health Organization (1992), *International Statistical Classification of Diseases and Related Health Problems* (ICD-10). Geneva: World Health Organization.

Ylvisaker, M., Ed. (1985), *Head Injury Rehabilitation: Children and Adolescents*. San Diego, CA: College-Hill Press.

Yontef, G. M., & Simkin, J. S. (1989), Gestalt therapy. In: *Current Psychotherapies*, 4th ed., ed. R. J. Corsini & D. Wedding. Itasca, IL: F. E. Peacock.

Zubin, J. (1977–1978), But is it good for science? *Clin. Psychol.*, 31(2):1, 5–7.

––––––– Spring, B. (1977), Vulnerability—A new view of schizophrenia. *J. Abnorm. Psychol.*, 86:103–126.

Name Index

Subject Index